THE SLOW FOOD GUIDE TO
NEW YORK CITY

D1509541

ABOUT SLOW FOOD

Slow Food is an international movement, founded in Italy in 1986. Today it has some 70,000 members and more than 600 convivia (or chapters) in 45 countries worldwide. Slow Food is dedicated to preserving regional cuisine and products from around the world. The goal of Slow Food is not to be a supper club but rather a movement that supports biodiversity in the food supply, taste education, and rediscovering the pleasures of sitting at the table with family and friends.

Participants in the Slow Food movement are committed to finding viable alternatives to the globalization and homogenization of the world's tastes. Through publications, events, and a Web site, Slow Food tries to provide the information members need to support our mission.

About Slow Food U.S.A.

Slow Food U.S.A. is a nonprofit educational organization dedicated to supporting and celebrating the food traditions of North America. From the spice of Cajun cooking to the purity of the organic farming movement; from animal breeds and heirloom varieties of fruits and vegetables to handcrafted wine and beer, farmhouse cheeses, and other artisanal products—these foods are all a part of our cultural identity. These foods, and the communities that produce and depend on them, are constantly at risk of succumbing to the effects of the fast life, which manifests itself through the industrialization and standardization of our food supply and degradation of our farmland. By reviving the pleasures of the table, and using our taste buds as our guides, Slow Food U.S.A. believes that our food heritage can be saved.

Slow Food U.S.A. oversees Slow Food activities in North America, including the support and promotion of the activities of more than 10,000 members in 100 chapters, each called a "convivium," that carry out the Slow Food mission on a local level. Each convivium advocates sustainability and biodiversity through educational events and public outreach that promote the appreciation and consumption of seasonal and local foods and the support of those who produce them.

About This Guide

The Slow Food Guide to New York City is the first in a series of guidebooks focusing on major cities or regions of North America and celebrating traditional, typical, or innovative foods, producers, restaurants, or other businesses that exemplify Slow Food principles.

We would welcome any corrections, suggestions, or nominations for future editions of this guide. To give us your input, please go to the comments section of the Slow Food U.S.A. Web site (www.slowfoodusa.org).

For more information about membership or the activities and programs of Slow Food U.S.A., go to the Web site, or contact us at the following address:

Slow Food U.S.A.
434 Broadway, 6th Floor
New York, NY 10013
(212) 965-5640

THE SLOW FOOD GUIDE TO
NEW YORK CITY
RESTAURANTS, MARKETS, BARS

PATRICK MARTINS AND BEN WATSON
WITH SLOW FOOD NYC

CONTRIBUTING EDITORS

Allen Katz
Bernadette Kramer
Erika Lesser
Zakary Pelaccio

Chelsea Green Publishing
WHITE RIVER JUNCTION, VERMONT

Book Design by Peter Holm, Sterling Hill Productions.

Printed in Canada on recycled paper.

First printing, May 2003.
07 06 05 04 03   1 2 3 4 5

Library of Congress Cataloging-in-Publication Data
Martins, Patrick.
The Slow Food guide to New York City : restaurants, markets, bars / Patrick
Martins and Ben Watson.
    p. cm. — (Slow Food guides)
Includes Index.
ISBN 1-931498-27-X (alk. paper)
1. Restaurants—New York (State)—New York—Guidebooks. 2. Grocery trade—
New York (State)—New York—Guidebooks. I. Watson, Ben, 1961– II. Slow Food
Movement. III. Title. IV. Series.
TX907.3.N72.N456 2003
647.95747'1—dc21

2003046205

Chelsea Green Publishing
P.O. Box 428
White River Junction, VT 05001
(800) 639-4099
www.chelseagreen.com

To Carlo Petrini and Alice Waters

THE SLOW FOOD GUIDE TO NEW YORK CITY

Patrick Martins and Ben Watson

Contributing Editors

Allen Katz   Erika Lesser
Bernadette Kramer   Zakary Pelaccio

Contributors

Yuri Asano   Stephanie Chayet
Dick Bessey   Gianluca di Liberto
Dalila Bothwell   Barbara Kafka
Serena di Liberto   Shawn Starbuck Kelly
Sara Firebaugh   Steve Kelly
Renee Gerson   Susie Kramer
Joshua Hakimi   Robert LaValva
Jim Hutchinson   Hanna Lee
Ana Jovancicevic   Zarela Martinez
Natalie Kalb   Cerise Mayo
Courtney Knapp   Megan Moore
Camille Labro   Saul Nadler
Howard Pfeffer   Norman Oder
Edwin Yowell   Linda Pelaccio
                                Michael Romano
Michael K. Anstendig   Marissa Sanchez
Mario Batali   Tristram Steinberg
Andy Birsh   Margo True
Kelly Caldwell   Tobias Tumarkin
Mary Caldwell

Slow Food NYC Contributors

Pina Belfiore   Lucy Norris
David Berman   Anne O'Connor
Rebecca Bowler   Nadia Pignatone &
Eric Eisner & Lizzie Scott   Fausto Pellegrini
Emma Johnson   Anne Stone
Sarah McElwain   Reynold Weidenaar

CONTENTS

THE SLOW FOOD INTERNATIONAL MANIFESTO
endorsed and approved in 1989 by delegates from 20 countries

Our century, which began and has developed under the insignia of industrial civilization, first invented the machine and then took it as its life model.

We are enslaved by speed and have all succumbed to the same insidious virus. Fast Life, which disrupts our habits, pervades the privacy of our homes, and forces us to eat Fast Foods.

To be worthy of the name, *Homo sapiens* should rid themselves of speed before it reduces them to a species in danger of extinction.

A firm defense of quiet material pleasure is the only way to oppose the universal folly of Fast Life.

May suitable doses of guaranteed sensual pleasure and slow, long-lasting enjoyment preserve us from the contagion of the multitude who mistake frenzy for efficiency.

Our defense should begin at the table with Slow Food. Let us rediscover the flavors and savors of regional cooking and banish the degrading effects of Fast Food.

In the name of productivity, Fast Life has changed our way of being and threatens our environment and our landscapes. So Slow Food is now the only truly progressive answer.

That is what real culture is all about: developing taste rather than demeaning it. And what better way to set about this than an international exchange of experiences, knowledge, products?

Slow Food guarantees a better future. Slow Food is an idea that needs plenty of qualified supporters who can help turn this (slow) motion into an international movement, with the little snail as its symbol.

PREFACE

Recently I saw a bumper sticker that said: "If I am what I eat, then I'm fast, cheap, and easy!" I didn't see it in New York, which makes sense if you consider that no other city is slower when it comes to food. I think one of the main reasons people perceive New York as fast is because of the overwhelming amount of choice that exists here. This guide is an attempt to pare down your food options so that it becomes easier to view this aspect of city life more slowly—of the more than 18,000 food establishments in the metropolitan area, only our favorite 600 or so appear in this guide. With a fork and this guidebook as your map, you can discover a lifetime of culinary delights from every culture imaginable!

In this book you will learn about the restaurants, bars, and markets that excel at serving foods that are in line with the Slow Food mission. Besides serving delicious food, all of the venues herein also possess one or more of the following virtues: artisanship, tradition, and conviviality. Many also possess what to us is the most important virtue: a commitment to serving sustainably grown and local ingredients. We have singled out the establishments that excel in this category for special recognition by using the Slow Food snail logo in their text descriptions.

Sustainable foods grown nearby simply taste better and likely come from independent family farms. They also represent a biodiversity in the food world that is at risk of disappearing in the flood of industrialized culture and big business. By supporting establishments that serve ecologically sound foods, you are supporting the vision of a landscape dotted with small, viable farms that today we are in danger of losing unless we understand that eating is a political act! As the Slow Food movement in America grows stronger, we hope to work with restaurants so that, in the second edition of this guide, you will find more "snail" ratings.

The publication of this book is only the latest effort in Slow Food's never-ending quest to save the myriad traditions and pleasures of the table. From the creation of our manifesto in 1989 (see page viii) to the formation in 2000 of a national office in the United States, where 10,000 members and 100 convivia (or chapters) now support our projects, such as opening gardens in grade schools and saving endangered foods like the Bourbon Red turkey and Iroquois white corn, Slow Food remains steadfastly committed to bringing the concept of eco-gastronomy to food lovers everywhere. While this guide does not claim to be perfect (please send us your comments so that our second edition will be even better!), it will no doubt be a helpful resource, whether you are looking for a good pastrami sandwich dripping with fat or a great French meal dripping with four stars.

I am a born-and-raised New Yorker, and I absolutely love this town. With this guidebook I hope to give back a little to this city that has given so much to me. I also hope that this book gives something back to our many members who have done so much to sustain our organization in the United States through their membership and through support of our projects and events. This guide promotes a tourism that nourishes both the vistor and deserving businesses. Slow Food is about doing good by eating well—what could be better?

Before I leave you to your reading, I would like to thank the many member volunteers who hit the fast streets of New York City to make the publication of this guide possible. Their hard work demonstrated what is most beautiful and most powerful about being a grassroots organization. It was only thanks to their enthusiasm, willing appetites, and expanding waistlines that we were able to write this first Slow Food USA guidebook!

Eat well and be slow,
Patrick Martins
Executive Director
Slow Food U.S.A.

SUSTAINABILITY AND THE CITY

One of the oldest of old jokes is the one about the man who tells his friend that he just bought an 800-pound gorilla. "Where does he sleep?" his friend asks him. "Anywhere he wants to," the man answers.

Great cities in general, and New York City especially, are a lot like that 800-pound gorilla. They make their own rules. They demand vast quantities of resources (global as well as regional) simply to exist from day to day. They even create their own local microclimates, with their miles of pavement, tall skyscrapers, and other aspects of the "built environment."

The first question we asked ourselves when we considered doing this book was the obvious one: "What is Slow about New York?" At first blush, the city appears to be a frenetic, voracious, one-way consumer of goods— the very epitome of fastness, unsustainability, and our throwaway society. Some social thinkers and rural philosophers have even gone so far as to suggest that the world doesn't need, and cannot support, a city the size of the Big Apple, with its roughly eight million inhabitants.

Their argument, of course, is purely academic. New York *does* exist, and it's not going anywhere. But dig a little deeper, beneath the surface *idea* of the city, and you'll find that there is much here to admire, and even emulate, from the standpoint of culture, efficiency, and quality of life.

New York has one of the greatest mass-transit systems in the world, both public (trains, buses, and ferries) and private (taxicabs). For such a large place, it's remarkably easy and affordable to get around without a personal car, an expensive luxury that is one of the biggest contributors to lousy air quality, congestion, and global warming.

Nearly everyone (except landlords) complains about the incredibly high rents in New York. Yet this very priciness ensures that space is used efficiently and not wasted, even by the wealthy. Compare this to less densely populated areas of the U.S., where suburban sprawl and the phenomenon of building "starter castles" are eating up far more productive land and natural resources than those used by the average New Yorker.

Food is surprisingly affordable in the city, because of fierce competition, market efficiencies, and other advantages of living in a global economic hub. There are four-star and celebrity restaurants, of course, but almost every neighborhood also has a host of inexpensive options, featuring almost every ethnic cuisine you can imagine.

Which brings us to cultural diversity. New York is without a doubt the most ethnically diverse and cosmopolitan city on Earth. Immigrants from every corner of the globe have passed through New York at some point in its history, and enough of them have remained here to turn the city's neighborhoods into a fascinating and ever-changing cultural patchwork. From expatriate Russians in Brooklyn's Brighton Beach section to the Puerto Ricans, Dominicans, and Mexicans in East Harlem, one of the greatest assets of the city is its diversity . . . of people and, for our purposes, of national and ethnic cuisines. One of the most exciting things about New York is the feeling that the whole world, or at least its various cultures, lies knowable, within your reach.

So then we return to the question: what makes New York a Slow Food kind of place? Well, for one thing, the number of artisanal food producers in the city is at once staggering and impressive. There are old-time shopkeepers who continue to make their own fresh mozzarella or handmade chocolates the same way their parents and grandparents did. There are pizzamakers who turn out the quintessential New York–style pie from coal-fired brick ovens. There's the neighborhood butcher shop, with its impeccable meats and personal service. The bakery that hand-fills your cannoli to order. The little dumpling place in Chinatown where you can buy a satisfying meal with the change you probably have under your sofa cushions. If you're adventurous and serious about good food, New York is definitely the place to be.

What we have attempted to do in this book is provide readers—native New Yorkers and visitors alike—with a broad and yet discriminating window on the city's incredibly rich "food landscape." Rather than limiting ourselves to restaurants and bars or to markets, specialty shops, and food producers alone, we've included a little of everything, from the street cart that sells goat tacos to the fanciest French restaurants. The one common denominator is that each of these places, in its own way, exemplifies one or more of the qualities that the international Slow Food movement celebrates and tries to defend, in the face of an increasingly homogenized, one-size-fits-all world.

We, the contributors to this guide, also reflect the diversity that is New York, and America. Chefs and food writers, professionals and grad students, we come to this task from all walks of life and from a wide range of cultural perspectives and tastes.

That diversity is captured in the entries that follow: our styles and voices may differ slightly, but the individual distinctions and idiosyncrasies are intentional, and they are intended to entertain readers as well as inform and educate.

Finally, it would be sheer folly to expect that such a large and moving target—the restaurants, food shops, and markets of New York—can ever be frozen in time. Businesses are born and die on a weekly basis, it seems. Many of the places listed here are old stalwarts, but there will inevitably be turnover, not to mention the rise of new Slow-worthy establishments. So we invite you, the readers and users of this guide, to contribute to future editions by sending your comments and critiques, updates and recommendations to us at the page dedicated to the Slow Food USA guidebooks series at our Web site: www.slowfoodusa.org.

Ben Watson

KEY TO SYMBOLS USED IN THIS BOOK

Prices

$ = average entrée or main course costs
less than $10

$$ = average entrée or main course costs
between $10 and $20

$$$ = average entrée or main course costs
between $20 and $30

$$$$ = average entrée or main course costs
more than $30

All price symbols are approximations made for comparison's sake only.

In this book we have designated with the symbol of the snail (the Slow Food mascot) those establishments that go above and beyond in their support of the concepts of sustainability and biodiversity through the producers they buy from and the foods that they prepare and sell.

We have included subway directions for establishments located in the outer boroughs and have also included any special information in the entries if something was different or unusual (for instance, "cash only" or "closed Monday").

Finally, we have added a "Notables" section of brief listings at the end of most sections. Think of these places as "honorable mentions"—definitely deserving but perhaps not yet slow enough or familiar enough to our reviewers to garner a full-fledged write-up.

THE **SLOW FOOD** GUIDE TO
NEW YORK CITY

PART ONE
CUISINES

AFRICAN

Africa Restaurant   *(Senegalese)*
Morningside Heights
247 West 116th Street, between Adam Clayton Powell Blvd.
  (Seventh Ave.) and Frederick Douglass Blvd. (Eighth Ave.)
(212) 666-9400
$ (Cash only)

Located in the "Little Africa" section of 116th Street in Upper Manhattan,
Africa Restaurant offers a good introduction to West African cuisine. The
daily specials, mostly meat based, are rich, satisfying, and uniformly good.
Lamb is always a good bet, whether it's *in mafé,* a Senegalese tomato-peanut
sauce, or cooked into *soupikandia,* a spicy stew thickened with okra, served
over white rice. The chicken *yassa,* cooked in a mustard sauce, is also worth
trying, as are the fish specials, including the typical *tiebou dienn* (bluefish in
a tomatoey sauce). To soothe and stimulate your palate, order a snappy,
sweet ginger drink or the bissap sorrel, made from hibiscus flowers.

Africa 2, the Midtown West location, attracts an upscale clientele,
including African diplomats and expatriates longing for the flavors and
atmosphere of home.

Other Location
Africa 2 Restaurant, 346 West 53rd Street, between Eighth and
  Ninth Aves.; (212) 399-6100

Al Baraka   *(Moroccan)*
Upper East Side
1613 Second Avenue, at 84th St.
(212) 396-9787
$$$

Al Baraka is best described as an intense explosion of colors and patterns.
Sumptuous smells envelop you as you make your way through the small
kitchen. The trance begins. Shortly after, a waiter dressed in the tradi-
tional *djellaba* and fez pulls back a dark curtain, and the threshold
between reality and dreams dissolves. The large dining room is filled with
small copper tables; the walls are covered with Moroccan tiles laid out in
complex patterns; and metal lamps, punctured by dozens of small holes,
project stars of light on the rich drapery that hangs from the ceiling.

The menu states that "good food comes to those who wait," but wait-
ing is half the fun, as a lively belly dancer drives you deeper into the
enchantment created by the restaurant's atmosphere. A spicy sauce that
accompanies small potato croquettes elevates your taste buds to the same
level as your other spellbound senses. The table is then adorned with
tagines, traditional ceramic plates used for both cooking and serving the

succulent food. The duck *tagine*, flavored with apricot, is nicely balanced with the delicateness of the accompanying couscous. The *pastillas*, the result of a long history of French colonial presence in Morocco, offer a very different texture, as the delicate phyllo pastry stuffed with myriad ingredients flakes in your mouth. Just as the trance reaches its apex, the spell is broken by a sip of the sprightly Moroccan mint tea, bringing you back to reality and sealing a truly enchanting night.

Keur N'Deye   *(Senegalese)*
Fort Greene, Brooklyn
737 Fulton Street, between So. Elliott Pl. and So. Portland St.
(718) 875-4937
Subway: C to Lafayette Ave.; G to Fulton St.
Closed Monday
$ (Cash only)

Along Fort Greene's principal street stands an unassuming entrance to a truly vibrant Senegalese experience. Open windows, from ceiling to floor, let in a warm breeze reminiscent of a West African savannah, while a Senegalese woman welcomes you with an equally warm smile. The rustic character of the culture is accentuated by woven basket lamps hanging from the ceiling, while bright yellow tablecloths echo the brightness of the Senegalese culture.

After just one bite of Senegal's national dish, *tiebou dienn* (succulent bluefish served with coarsely cut vegetables and white rice, all bathed in a rich tomato sauce), it becomes clear why this westernmost African nation has long been renowned for its cuisine. The country's second most popular dish, *yassa* (fish and brown rice immersed in a tangy lemon-mustard sauce), is also delectably prepared by the friendly staff.

Freshly made fruit drinks, including sweet guava, spicy ginger, and bissap sorrel, top off a truly authentic culinary experience. Keur N'Deye's home cooking will remind you of your Senegalese grandmother's cooking, even if you don't have a Senegalese grandmother.

Meskerem   *(Ethiopian)*
Theater District
468 West 47th Street, between Ninth and Tenth Aves.
(212) 664-0520
$$

Step inside Meskerem, and all at once your nostrils are greeted with the irresistable aroma of *berbere* (bear-BEAR-ee), the exotic mixture of spices (toasted cardamom, cumin, cloves, fenugreek, coriander, and cinnamon) and ground red pepper that gives many Ethiopian dishes their characteristic flavor and warmth.

One of the best things about Ethiopian cuisine is the tradition of sharing food communally: It's best to come with a group, and to be prepared to scoop up individual mouthfuls of dishes with pieces of *injera,* the spongy, round sourdough-like flatbread made from fermented teff (an ancient and nutritious type of grain). After a little practice, you'll wonder why anyone bothered inventing forks or chopsticks. The waiter brings a platter of *injera* to the table along with the entrées, which feature lamb, beef, and chicken, but also include vegetarian choices (the lentils and the ground chickpea dish—*shiro wat*—are particularly good).

For an appetizer, try the *sambosa,* a homemade flatbread pocket filled with spicy chopped beef or lentils mixed with peppers, onion, and garlic. You'll never buy those frozen "Hot Pockets" again. Entrées include *kitfo* and *gored gored,* both beef dishes prepared with *kibe* (or *kibbeh*)—the seasoned, clarified butter that is the Ethiopian equivalent of India's *ghee.* Depending on how hot and spicy you like your food, it's useful to know that an Ethiopian dish that has "wot" or "wat" in its name will be spicy, whereas "alecha" in the name indicates milder seasoning.

By the end of the meal you won't be left hungry or craving dessert. *Injera* has a way of expanding in your stomach, giving you a pleasantly full feeling as you linger over strong Ethiopian coffee and wrap up a laid-back, convivial repast.

Other Location
124 MacDougal Street, between Bleecker and West 3rd Sts.; (212) 777-8111

NOTABLE

African Grill   *(Ivorian)*
Morningside Heights
1496 Fifth Avenue at 120th St.
(212) 987-3836
$

The cuisine of the Ivory Coast is, not surprisingly, influenced by French colonial cooking, and at African Grill you will find bistrolike specials interspersed with national specialties such as *attieke* (cassava porridge topped with a fried fish and served with chile-onion relish).

Demu Café   *(Nigerian)*
Fort Greene, Brooklyn
773 Fulton Street, between South Portland St. and South Elliot Pl.
(718) 875-8484
Subway: C to Lafayette Ave.; G to Fulton St.
$$

The Demu family runs this large Nigerian café and bar located near the
Brooklyn Academy of Music. The café is known for hosting poetry read-
ings and house parties on the weekend with dancing to hip-hop, reggae,
and R&B. The cuisine is typical of West Africa, with hearty stews and
dishes such as *fufu* (mashed yucca or plantain) featured prominently. Try
a Nigerian beer or some palm wine with your meal.

Ghenet   *(Ethiopian)*
Chinatown/Little Italy
284 Mulberry Street, between Prince and Houston
(212) 343-1888
Closed Monday
$$

Yeworkwoha Ephrem opened Ghenet in Nolita back in 1998, and she has
quickly established it as one of the better Ethiopian restaurants in the city.
This is a good place to try *t'ej*, the typical Ethiopian honey wine, or to
sample *kategna*, an appetizer made of toasted *injera* coated with *kibe* and
garlicky hot sauce.

Kaloum   *(Guinean)*
Morningside Heights
120 West 116th Street, near Sixth Ave.
(212) 864-2845
$

One of the centers for Guinean culture in New York is the area that runs
along 116th Street, from Fifth Avenue to Manhattan Avenue. And Kaloum
is a neighborhood fixture, serving typical Guinean dishes such as *sauce de
feuilles*, beef stew thickened with puréed sweet potato leaves and served in
a bowl to accompany and flavor a plate of rice.

Madiba   *(South African)*
Fort Greene, Brooklyn
195 DeKalb Avenue, between Adelphi and Carlton Sts.
(718) 855-9190

Subway: C to Lafayette Ave.; G to Clinton-Washington Aves.
$$

Madiba serves South African comfort food that reflects the multicultural influences of that country, everything from *biltong* and *droewers* (Afrikaans-style jerkies) to vegetarian curries and Malay *bobotie,* a spicy meat pie. They also have entertainment and a shop that sells dry goods.

ELIZABETH LITTLES

Blue Hill
Greenwich Village

75 Washington Place, between Washington Sq. West and Sixth Ave.
(212) 539-1776
Open for dinner only; closed Sunday.
$$$

A true commitment to simplicity, to showcase the essence or character of a product, is an idea, and a nice idea at that. In fact, for many chefs in the upper strata this idea has become their mantra. There are few, however, who realize this idea as well as Chefs Dan Barber and Mike Anthony of Blue Hill. Shopping three to four times a week at the Greenmarket, and receiving most other products from small farmers in the Hudson Valley/ Catskill region, Dan and Mike select the best of what the seasons have to offer. One night they served *barramundi* braised in mussel broth, with incredibly fresh corn cooked in its own juice and mixed with poached shitake mushroom caps. The earthiness of the mushrooms played wonderfully off the sweetness of the corn and created a luscious setting for the briny and tender fish. This is thoughtful food that pushes the flavors of the products forward.

As for the simplicity, well, loving this food is simple. How could one not love salmon poached in duck fat and served over heirloom tomatoes in an heirloom tomato broth that is complemented by diced orange segments, drawing attention to the sweet-and-sour play in the juicy tomatoes? The meat dishes are just as elegant: A duck breast on the menu recently was poached in *beurre blanc* and served with glazed carrots in a carrot broth, finished with a crispy piece of duck confit and porcini mushrooms.

The dining room is sophisticated and warmly lit, but casual enough to walk in off the street and enjoy a meal at the limestone bar. A note of caution, though: Walking into such a seductive meal on a whim can quickly become addictive.

Craft and Craftbar
Gramercy Park/Flatiron District

43, 47 East 19th Street, between Broadway and Park Ave. South
(212) 780-0080
$$$$/$$

Tom Collichio and his restaurant Craft have created a whole new way to eat out. The concept behind the menu is to allow diners to build each meal according to their own whim. Side dishes are divided into categories: roasted (baby carrots, Jerusalem artichokes, turnips, or red peppers), braised (corn, escarole, or Romano beans), mushrooms (shiitakes, hen-of-the-woods, bluefoots, chanterelles, or lobster), or potatoes (potato risotto, boulangères, purée, gratin, gnocchi, or fingerlings). If you are bad at deciding, Craft is a dream come true. The first courses offer a varied selection of raw and cured fish, charcuterie, and salads. The main courses let you choose from among other items, such as dourade, quail, and veal cheeks. At Craft, you taste an array of elemental foods, sourced from the Greenmarket (of course), which are listed on the menu according to method of preparation. The essence of food is what you get here: The only problem is that the way the menu is designed it can be expensive; also, the atmosphere is a bit cold. However, the wine list, created by Matthew MacCartney, is excellent.

Craftbar is a newer, smaller adjunct to Craft, similar to the Cibreo in Florence, in that two separate restaurants work side by side with one chef running the whole ball game. Every day Craftbar serves just three main entrées: a meat, a fish, and a pasta, all priced at less than $20. Cold plates, appetizers, and sandwiches are also available. Because the menu changes daily, you will have to go many times to try everything. If you catch them, try the frisée with Gorgonzola and bacon, the tomato soup, or the assortment of salami. The roasted cod is a full, satisfying meal when you order it with a side of new potatoes.

The exposed kitchen in the rear feels very casual, and the restaurant is usually crowded with communal seating. The wine selections are well matched to the food (see Wine Bars, p. 217). Whether you eat at Craft or Craftbar, no one will go home hungry!

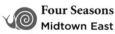

Four Seasons
Midtown East
99 East 52nd Street, between Lexington and Park Aves.
(212) 754-9494
Closed Sunday
$$$$

To say that the Four Seasons is a New York City landmark is an understatement: it has been a fixture of this city since before Kennedy was president. The Four Seasons was a concept of the original Restaurant Associates Group, and Joe Baum's vision and focus made it a reality. It remains as modern, elegant, and romantic today as it was forty years ago, as well as cool and comfortable. The Phillip Johnson interior is spacious and timeless. In the serene Pool Room, four enormous trees create shadows and light changes that are remarkable. The restaurant also houses an impressive art collection that includes four Lichtenstein lithographs, two Miro tapestries, a Jackson Pollock, and a Picasso among many other beautiful pieces.

The founding concept of the Four Seasons, as its name attests, was to change the menu according to each season of the year and highlight the wonders of change and growth that every season brings. This philosophy has endured for more than forty years. While always supporting and buying their products from local growers whenever possible, the Four Seasons has shone like a beacon since 1959 through the early 1970s, when so much about how we ate, where we ate, and how we cooked was evolving. And the restaurant continues to this day to serve as a blueprint for Slow Food, as it honors the integrity of the ripe tomato eaten at the right time!

You might want to try Long Island duck, *plateau de fruit de mer,* tender *ceviche,* and a Dover sole cooked to perfection. Bountiful vegetables and great salads are always available. You will also find meat and potatoes galore in the Grill Room, where longtime waiters remember the favorites of their regulars, extending to them and newcomers alike the unaffected hospitality that is the hallmark of the Four Seasons.

Fraunces Tavern
Financial District
54 Pearl Street at Broad St.
(212) 968-1776
Closed Sunday
$$-$$$

In 1762 Samuel Fraunces opened a tavern in this three-story brick mansion, originally known as the Queen's Head, from the sign depicting Queen Charlotte. And the rest, as they say, is history. Fraunces Tavern hosted meetings of the Sons of Liberty; it was where the New York Chamber of Commerce was formed in 1768; and (most famously) it was where General George Washington made his emotional farewell address to his officers on December 4, 1783, in the museum's Long Room.

Fraunces Tavern has recently been renovated, and is again serving everything from simple, untrendy fare (burgers, salads, and chicken pot pie) to more creative yet similarly uncomplicated dishes that emphasize fresh seafood and other seasonal ingredients. Save room for one of the desserts, which are particularly good and include such selections as Grand Marnier crème brûlée with blood orange coulis, or strawberry shortcake with sabayon, mint, and balsamic syrup.

You can choose to eat in the less formal Tavern itself, or in one of the fancier dining rooms, which are decorated with wood paneling, decorative moldings, and artwork—including one mural that depicts an eighteenth-century view of New York Harbor.

Gotham Bar & Grill
Greenwich Village

12 East 12th Street, between Fifth Ave. and University Pl.
(212) 620-4020
$$$$

It's been seventeen years since Chef Alfred Portale first stacked the majestic dishes at Gotham Bar & Grill that earned him a reputation as the inventor of "vertical food." Although most entrées no longer need to be knocked down before eating, the reviews are still towering: an unmatched four 3-star reviews in the *New York Times* and 1993 Best Chef in New York City award from the James Beard Foundation for Portale. Most recently, Gotham was named the 2002 S. Pellegrino Outstanding Restaurant, for being "the restaurant in the U.S. that serves as a national standard bearer of consistency of quality and excellence in food, atmosphere, and service." The award could not have been more apt. The restaurant is spacious and open, yet manages to feel intimate, with multitiered dining areas tucked behind gracefully curved stone walls. Soft, fabric-draped lighting and a glimpse of garden flowers through the tall back windows complement the peaceful, quiet environment, allowing you to concentrate on your dining companions—or on the food.

Anyone lucky enough to happen upon Gotham during tomato season will be well served: The heirloom tomato salad is a delectable botany lesson, the juicy fruits of many colors tossed with olives, slices of *ricotta salata,* and slender *haricots verts.* Nor will fall diners be disappointed in a hearty duck risotto, flavored with Niman Ranch bacon and caramelized butternut squash. If, like Ogden Nash, you like mustard even in custard, you'll find yourself eating the Dijon mustard–bone marrow custard without its New York steak accompaniment. Is the kitchen toying with us at dessert time? No matter, you'll enjoy the game. The milk chocolate caramel cake is the best Heath bar you've ever had, and the ethereal Mission fig tart is sided with a sugar-dusted "fig Newton."

Gramercy Tavern
Gramercy Park/Flatiron District

42 East 20th Street, between Sixth and Seventh Aves.
(212) 477-0777
$$$$ (prix fixe)

Gramercy Tavern is one of the principal jewels in restaurateur Danny Meyer's crown. For a grand occasion—or just a bite in the Tavern after the theater, you are likely to find just what you are searching for. You will be welcomed by a friendly, gracious host and served by a well-trained, courteous staff.

The interior indeed resembles a tavern, dusky and dimly lit. The ceiling is a work of art and the tables are well spaced so you have a comfortable, spacious feeling.

The menu is based on the freshest ingredients and changes by the seasons depending on what's available from the Greenmarket. Each menu section—Three-Course Market, Seasonal Tasting, and Prix Fixe—has a basic game plan that is constant, but specials are not decided upon until after purchases have been made that morning. On Greenmarket days, it is common to spot a kitchen porter wearing the Gramercy Tavern jacket making the rounds, searching for the freshest local produce of the day.

The food is layered and interesting but not intricate. A wonderful first course is the sweetbreads with bacon and sherry vinegar; rare on any menu, it boasts a lovely, balanced flavor that is the hallmark of this kitchen. The organic chicken is plain but perfect with nicely roasted vegetables. The hanger steak is superbly done, accompanied by a chutney-like side of wild mushrooms and slightly sweet salsify with a bit of bacon. The tasting menus are made for those who want it all, and the portions are satisfying. The same high standards apply to the Tavern menu served near the bar. The cheese board is great, showcasing artisanally made American cheeses such as the wonderful Humboldt Fog goat cheese from McKinleyville, California. The pork tenderloin sandwich is usually available, and the fava beans in the spring are not to be missed. The desserts here have always been homey and delightful.

The Grocery
Carroll Gardens, Brooklyn

288 Smith Street, between Sackett and Union Sts.
(718) 596-3335
Subway: F, G to Carroll St.
Closed Sunday
$$–$$$

If there is a silver lining to be found in the cloud of unaffordable Manhattan rents, it is the recent exodus of ambitious young chefs to the Outer Boroughs to open their dream restaurants—most notably in Brooklyn, and particularly on Smith Street in Carroll Gardens and Cobble Hill. On Smith Street, restaurants have cropped up like mushrooms in the rain, tempting the appetites of local residents as well as Manhattanites and farther-flung aficionados—in effect, a reversal of the "bridge-and-tunnel" syndrome. With the F train rumbling below (the mainline of western Brooklyn), Smith Street restaurants now offer diners

American, Italian, French, Middle Eastern, Vietnamese, Japanese, Spanish, and Argentine options—just to name a few.

Leading this pack are the Grocery's chef-owners Charles Kiely and Sharon Pachter, formerly of Savoy, who have brought an elegant touch and sophisticated palette of seasonal ingredients to an unassuming storefront and transformed it into a tiny and seductively low-key dining room, so intimate that you may feel like you've actually stumbled into someone's home. The menu is full of local and seasonal ingredients, many sourced from the Greenmarket, and many choices ride exclusively on the merits of perfectly fresh produce, from the "teenage greens" to roasted beets and butternut squash dumplings. Although *amuse-bouches* now seem to be a mandatory feature in many upscale New York restaurants, they still feel like a special surprise at the Grocery, especially if they are presented by the chef.

Daily specials fill out a carefully prepared selection of larger dishes, from grilled whole boneless trout to slow-rendered duck breast, and desserts such as Greenmarket fruit cobbler and homemade ice creams and sorbets compete with a charming selection of sweet wines to satisfy your sugar cravings. Everything at the Grocery seems quite simple, which is the trick—a well-executed menu full of fine ingredients, presented with polished service, and no hint of the complex efforts that went into it other than the smile that welcomes and bids you *adieu*.

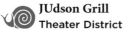

JUdson Grill
Theater District

152 West 52nd Street, between Sixth and Seventh Aves.
(212) 582-5252
Closed Sunday
$$$$

Chef Bill Telepan's commitment to sourcing local, seasonal foods would be justification enough for including JUdson Grill in a Slow Food guide. The fact that his food excels in flavor only enhances his restaurant's reputation. Telepan's contemporary American cuisine has reached local legendary status, from the gentle subtleties of seasonal organic greens and herbs to the rich and delicate house-made duck proscuitto. JUdson Grill's menu provides a veritable vocabulary for any Slow Food devotee—"organic," "pasture-fed," and "free-range" are commonplace terms on the menu. Situated in Midtown Manhattan, a neighborhood that's loaded with "hot spots" for power lunches, JUdson Grill is known more for its ethereal gastronomic lunch (or dinner, for that matter): a meal to be savored and appreciated not only for its culinary quality but, through conscientious choices, the restaurant's support of family farmers and producers.

March
East Side
405 East 58th Street, between First Ave. and Sutton Pl.
(212) 754-6272
Dinner only
$$$$ (prix fixe)

Tucked away in an elegant brownstone on Manhattan's East Side is March, one of the premier luxury restaurants in the city. The intimate comfort level of the dining room and enclosed garden offers the perfect ambience in which to relax and "put yourself in Wayne's hands," as the menu states. Wayne Nish, the executive chef and co-owner of March, has devised a menu of tastes: dishes to be enjoyed in whatever order the diner chooses, unless you let him choose for you. And one can't go wrong with such inspiring choices as simmered yellowtail with brown caper sauce, veal braised in tomato and veal jus with pine nuts and tarragon, or a fricassee of seasonal vegetables with black truffle.

One look at March's menu confirms that Nish cares about the food he serves: Millbrook venison, Niman Ranch pork, Four Story Hill Farm veal and chicken, specialty seafood. And the attention to vegetables bespeaks the same: Kermit eggplant, Ruby Crescent fingerling potatoes, Iranian barberries, and sweet Cambodian cucumber.

"Where and how food is grown truly makes a difference in the taste," according to Nish. "The resurgence of small farmers and the return to heirloom varieties have resulted in foods with more flavor, and when you cut out the middleman, you get the product faster and fresher, so it tastes better."

Wine director and co-owner Joseph Scalice has assembled an impressive wine list, which he helps the diner navigate and explains with an easy eloquence. If your budget allows, ask him to select a tasting of wines to match each course.

The menu changes with the season and the market, and it always includes a variety of Nish's trademark, "beggar's purse"—a delectable bite of a wonton pastry filled with the likes of lobster and black truffles or caviar and *crème fraîche*. And while the check may make *your* purse as light as a beggar's, too, March offers a unique dining experience, one meant to be savored slowly.

Savoy
Soho
70 Prince Street at Crosby St.
(212) 219-8570
$$$

Savoy's dining room—recently remodeled by chef-owner Peter Hoffman—has the inviting feel of a prairie grandmother's kitchen. The honey-colored floors and whitewashed, pressed-tin ceiling keep the room light, while a soapstone hearth lends warmth, even when dormant. And on each table there's a touch of whimsy: white porcelain salt shakers shaped like drooping gumdrops. Savoy also boasts a lovely bar downstairs, while the restaurant occupies the second floor.

Hoffman is the executive director of Chefs Collaborative, which promotes sustainable traditional foodways to chefs, and his restaurant's commitment to these ideals is evident in everything from the wine list to the desserts. No fewer than ten organic wines are highlighted, and two beers are locally brewed. Hoffman can be seen riding a recumbent bicycle with a massive basket to the Union Square Greenmarket on Mondays, Wednesdays, Fridays, and Saturdays: Whenever the Greenmarket is open, Peter is there.

Savoy's menu, which changes about five times a year, boasts Niman Ranch pork, local berries from the Greenmarket, and a house-cured pancetta. A server described heirloom tomatoes to one uninitiated diner as "tomatoes as they would have been a hundred years ago." Today, they're sparingly enhanced with coarse sea salt, coupled with curried onions and yellow lentils, and served in a salad that tastes like summer itself. The entrées include salmon served with spicy lentils, pulled duck with spinach and dried apricot salad, pistachios and duck cracklings, and an ideal warm-weather ravioli filled with creamy ricotta, cool mint, and fresh peas. For dessert, Savoy's cheesecake is among the best you'll ever eat, and it uses artisanally made Zingerman's cream cheese.

Greatly influenced by the philosophy of Alice Waters in California, Savoy is as close as you'll get to Chez Panisse in New York City.

The Tasting Room
East Village
72 East 1st Street at First Ave.
(212) 358-7831
$$$$

With only 735 square feet including the kitchen, dining room, bathroom, office, and wine storage room, where do you keep the plates? The first thing you ask yourself as you walk into this cozy East Village restaurant is how do they do it? This is a question you'll be asking yourself throughout dinner. Colin Alevras, the chef and co-owner with his wife Renée, rides his bike to New York's premier Greenmarket at Union Square several times a week, where he buys all the vegetables and fruits used in the Tasting Room's dishes. He scours the "circuit" of fish vendors in

Chinatown daily to find the freshest catch available, which ends up in dishes such as Poached Sea Bass with Lobster Mushrooms and Foie Gras. At one dinner, venison was featured in two dishes, a venison carpaccio and roasted loin of venison. When I asked Colin where he got the venison, he leaned over and confided in me, "A friend shot it yesterday." This is a man who loves his products; and he takes his job as procurer very seriously. The result is everything that ends up on the plate is super-fresh. In the intimate dining room, Renée showers the diners with genuinely good vibes and provides assistance in navigating the extensive all-American wine list that ranks among the best in the city. Almost everything on the menu can be ordered as a "taste" or a "share" portion—think appetizer size or entrée size. The robust flavors and well-considered riffs on classic combinations make it difficult to choose, so don't. Try a "taste" of everything on the menu.

Union Square Café
Gramercy Park/Flatiron District

21 East 16th Street, between Fifth Ave. and Union Sq. West
(212) 243-4020
$$$

Union Square Café opened in 1985, and it has consistently been rated the number one restaurant in New York City by the Zagat Survey. It is a lovely, airy, modern space with a spacious feel and a welcoming clublike atmosphere. The front of the house is friendly and will make you feel like you have not waited any time at all. The garlic potato chips and spicy nuts at the bar will keep you happy until your table is ready or just with a drink at the easy, friendly bar.

Chef and co-owner Michael Romano is an ardent supporter of the Greenmarket and committed to locally grown foods, serving them up with consistency and creativity. His "excellence reflex" is evident in every step of the process, from raw ingredient to finished dish.

A wonderful starter is the gazpacho risotto with its sweet tomato broth and creamy, satisfying texture. The grilled filet of tuna is a favorite of many and will be cooked the way you like it. Pastas are consistent and flavorful, with the sheep's-milk ravioli and spinach a meal in itself. The tuna club sandwich is delicious and the hamburger comes on a house-baked bun.

Desserts are sweetly satisfying: One very thoughtful thing the kitchen does, upon request for a special occasion, is to write a lovely chocolate message around the border of their delicious cookie plate.

Verbena
Gramercy Park/Flatiron District
54 Irving Place, between 17th and 18th Sts.
(212) 260-5454
Closed Monday
$$$

Compared to some New York restaurants, Verbena is a newcomer, but it is standing the test of time and making a mark. Run by Diane Forley and Michael Otsuka, these married chefs (with a new baby and a new book to their credit) treat this little wonder with great care and attention. Indoor seating is about 60, and the outdoors is almost 75. The bar is small and intimate with tables that seat about 12.

What's available at the Greenmarket largely determines what comes to the table on any given day, but there are some wonderful standbys as well. Seasonal menus mean quarterly changes that bring depth and interest to the food, giving it a sense of time and place. A salad with fresh tomatoes in the summer, and a very good *croque monsieur* are available à la carte, and the chefs offer an "oyster challenge" to try to help diners decide the best wine to pair with their bivalves. They also do interesting three-tiered tastings that match different varietals to all kinds of dishes. All tiers are recommended for two people, with each dish also available à la carte. The main dishes are varied and appealing. The halibut with ginger and scallions and the trout represent the best of the fish, and if you like a good pork chop, do not miss Verbena's version. You might come in just for the desserts: upside-down cake with plums and caramel, or pudding with chocolate cake and sauces and a coffee nougatine.

Washington Park
Greenwich Village
24 Fifth Avenue, between 9th and 10th Sts.
(212) 529-4400
Dinner only
$$$-$$$$

Jonathan Waxman is finally back in New York City after a ten-year absence, and he and his partners have created a beautiful restaurant in an attractive part of Greenwich Village. Located in a 1926 landmark building, the dining space is on the first floor with original moldings and big windows that offer a lovely view of the arch at nearby Washington Square.

The details and interior of the restaurant have been carefully designed;

nothing was left to chance. The bar is made of white onyx and is fashioned after Claridge's in London. The china is Ginori, the silver is Cristofle, and the linens are Frette. The same perfectionism and high standards guide the menu and the wine list.

Mr. Waxman is loyal to the philosophy of Alice Waters, who is the dedicated guardian angel of the organic food movement in this country. She remains a continuing influence on him, and he and his team show their respect with a market-driven menu; nothing comes through the door that is not in season. He has updated his classics from the eighties, and they are as modern and interesting as you might expect. The *fritto misto* "River Café" is light and fresh tasting, as is the Caesar salad. The foie gras preparation varies from day to day and is sometimes paired with white asparagus and brown butter or served with lamb's-quarter and sage. The JW chicken with fries is an old standby but it never disappoints, and the pork tenderloin with braised greens is flavorful and juicy. Perfectly cooked sweetbreads are crisp, tender, and delicious. Heather Miller is the pastry chef, and she also makes the most of seasonal Greenmarket produce: roasted apricots with *crème fraîche* ice cream, or rhubarb upside-down cake with buttermilk ice cream. (I only wish they used more chocolate!)

Patrick Bickford, formerly of Jean-Georges, is the sommelier and he oversees one of the most talked-about wine lists in the city. Partner Roy Welland has folded his enormous and impressive collection into the cellar, which offers more than 20,000 bottles from all over the world, including many selections by the glass. At the suggestion of Chef Mario Batali, the restaurant has created a cellar of 4,000 bottles around a cherry-wood table for private parties.

Washington Park is a gracious and elegant restaurant that somehow remains casual and unpretentious. When you walk out the door you will be plotting when you will next return. Welcome back, Chef!

NOTABLE

Aureole
East Side

34 East 61st Street, between Madison and Park Aves.
(212) 319-1660
Closed Sunday
$$$$ (prix fixe)

Charlie Palmer may have the Midas touch at this East Side townhouse, from the great garden views to the beautifully prepared and presented dishes that feature fresh vegetables, meats, and artisan cheeses.

Beacon
Clinton

25 West 56th Street, between Fifth and Sixth Aves.
(212) 332-0500
Closed Sunday
$$$

Excellent food is served in a beautiful atmosphere that features an open kitchen and a wood-burning oven. Chef Waldy Malouf excels with many dishes—but try the lamb chops or grilled swordfish steak. Save room for the chocolate and pecan-bourbon soufflés!

Diner
Williamsburg, Brooklyn
85 Broadway at Berry St.
(718) 486-3077
Subway: J, M, Z to Marcy Ave.
$$

Right under the Williamsburg Bridge, in a 1927 dining car beautifully restored with tile mosaics, wooden booths, and translucent lampshades, Diner offers classics such as burgers and mussels-and-fries, as well as surprisingly succulent daily specials. It also has an extensive list of cocktails and wines.

DuMont
Williamsburg, Brooklyn
432 Union Avenue, between Metropolitan Ave. and Devoe St.
(718) 486-7717
Subway: G to Metropolitan Ave.; L to Lorimer St.
$$

Fresh, comfortable American food served in a cozy storefront dining room with a lovely garden in back. Try the killer macaroni and cheese (four cheeses with bacon).

Etats-Unis
Upper East Side
242 East 81st Street, between Second and Third Aves.
(212) 517-8826
Open for dinner only; seatings at 6 P.M. and 8:30 P.M.
$$$

The unpretentious decor of this small restaurant won't distract you from the amazing alchemy that transforms fresh ingredients from the

Greenmarket into creative specials that change daily. Try the decadent chocolate soufflé, for which they are justly famous.

Also worth visiting is The Bar @ Etats-Unis, just across the street, where you can sample a large selection of wines from around world, and order from the restaurant menu (247 East 81st Street; 212-396-9928).

The Grange Hall
See Brunch, p. 174.

Jane
Greenwich Village
100 West Houston Street, between La Guardia Pl. and Thompson St.
(212) 254-7000
$$

Located on one of the open stretches of Houston Street, Jane has set out to be a neighborhood place where people can stop by for good, simple, honest fare. It has certainly accomplished this thanks to great cocktails, tasty appetizers (salmon and avocado tartare), fish (sautéed skate), and $12 Sundays where a selection of main courses costs just that. The international wine list is eclectic and inexpensive. The dining room and private room downstairs are beautifully designed by Tristam Steinberg.

Mercer Kitchen
Soho
The Mercer Hotel
99 Prince Street at Mercer St.
(212) 966-5454
$$$

Romantic and candlelit, the atmosphere is a nice complement to the excellent food coming out of the open-concept kitchen downstairs in this casual Soho hotel. Entrées are superb, or opt for pizza, risotto, or the raw bar. Have a drink in the upstairs bar, or unwind from a long day and choose from a wonderful tea selection. Be sure to try the caramel ice cream.

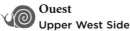 ## Ouest
Upper West Side
2315 Broadway, between 83rd and 84th Sts.
(212) 580-8700
Closed Monday
$$$

Ouest is a quiet little neighborhood place with serious diners and a loyal following. Chef Tom Valenti does interesting interpretations of comfort food standards. Valenti, along with co-owners Michael Lomanaco and Waldy Malouf, created the Windows of Hope Family Relief Fund, which provided aid to the families of the victims of the World Trade Center tragedy who worked in the food service industry throughout the entire complex.

Sparky's American Food
Williamsburg, Brooklyn
135A North 5th Street, between Bedford Ave. and Berry St.
(718) 302-5151
Subway: L to Bedford Ave.
$

Owner Brian Benavidez opened Sparky's in the fall of 2002 in a renovated warehouse. The food includes hot dogs, hamburgers, fries, milk shakes, and ice cream. All beef and pork are from Niman Ranch and most of the products on the menu are organic.

 ## Town
Clinton
The Chambers Hotel
13 West 56th Street, between Fifth and Sixth Aves.
(212) 582-4445
$$$

Upstairs in the Balcony, there's an edgy, happening bar with good drinks and a light menu of appetizers. Downstairs in the main restaurant, the servers are friendly and Chef Geoffrey Zakarian's food is splendid. Have a nice glass of red wine and the outstanding rack of lamb or just a fine burger. Town is also great for breakfast or brunch.

Union Pacific
See Fish and Seafood, p. 191.

KID-FRIENDLY RESTAURANTS

Dining in New York City with kids can sometimes feel very anti–Slow Food; finding a place where the whole family can enjoy a special-occasion dinner without causing raised eyebrows at nearby tables can be a struggle. In fact, many parents can't shake a nagging feeling that the city simply doesn't believe in children, as anyone who has attempted to navigate the subway system with a stroller will testify. For parents who love food, following the Slow mission of "developing taste rather than demeaning it" could have a battle cry: No more chicken fingers! Happily, there are many upscale restaurants that will welcome the smallest of your clan with open arms and vegetables from the non-potato families, letting you commune over fabulous food with those closest to you.

Restaurants already well known for great customer service are a good place to start. The hosts at **Union Square Café** and the **Tasting Room** will make you feel at home right away. But a salad bar of smiles won't make up for an inflexible menu. **Bright Food Shop** offers creative children's entrées served with colorful, homemade corn chips; **@SQC** boasts its own organic baby food, as well as dishes for kids past the teething stage. Even restaurants that aren't celebrated for macaroni and cheese (like **Bubby's**), peanut butter and jelly "sushi" (**Sushi Jones**), or fingerfood-friendly menus (**Ruby Foo's**) should be willing to whip up something special (read "plain") for your little one or serve a half-order of a regular menu item.

Until the food arrives, the entertainment value of the space is crucial. Not every restaurant employs a server whose hidden talent is making pinwheels and balloons from scraps of paper (**Herban Kitchen**), but the wall of diving statues at **Rosa Mexicano** is transfixing, and chess boards in the lobby at **Olives NY** will buy some time with older kids. If your table isn't ready at **Tabla**, trot over to the playground at neighboring Madison Square Park. The hosts there and at **Mary's Fish Camp** in the Village are happy to call your cellphone when they're ready to seat you.

As far as seating goes, in restaurants where it's not already crowded and noisy enough that no one notices a child crawling around on the floor, it's best if your family is not the entertainment for other tables. A call ahead to some restaurants can make sure that you can get a little private space to spread out: at **Union Pacific,** we were comfortable in our curtained space just feet from former mayor Ed Koch. Some restaurants, surprisingly, even have high chairs, or at least a spot to park the stroller.

What follows is obviously not a complete list of New York's child-friendly eateries. When scoping out a new spot, I usually call to get a feel for my family's likely reception. If the host responds to the words "four-year-old" with immediate and cheerful confidence and offers menu and seating suggestions, we give it a go.

@ SQC
(French)
270 Columbus Avenue, between 72nd and 73rd Sts.
(212) 579-0100
$$$

Á Table
(French)
Fort Greene, Brooklyn
171 Lafayette Street at Adelphi St.
(718) 935-9121
Closed Monday
$$

Blue Ribbon Bakery
(American)
33 Downing Street at Bedford St.
(212) 337-0404
Closed Monday
$$

Bright Food Shop
(Mexican/Asian fusion)
216 Eighth Avenue at 21st St.
(212) 243-4433
$$, (Cash only)

Bubby's
(American)
120 Hudson Street at North Moore St.
(212) 219-0666
$$

Herban Kitchen
(Vegetarian/organic)
290 Hudson Street at Spring St.
(212) 627-2257
Closed Sun.
$$

Lupa
(Italian)
170 Thompson Street, between Bleecker and Houston Sts.
(212) 982-5089
$$

Mary's Fish Camp
(Seafood)
64 Charles Street at West 4th St.
(646) 486-2185
Closed Sunday
$$

Mesa Grill
(Southwestern)
102 Fifth Avenue, between 15th and 16th Sts.
(212) 807-7400
$$$

Montrachet
(French)
239 West Broadway, between Walker and White Sts.
(212) 219-2777
Closed Sunday
$$$

Olives NY
(Mediterranean)
201 Park Avenue South at 17th St.
(212) 353-8345
$$$

Ouest
(American)
2315 Broadway, between 83rd and 84th Sts.
(212) 580-8700
$$$

Rosa Mexicano
(Mexican)
61 Columbus Avenue at 62nd St.
(212) 627-8273
$$$

Ruby Foo's
(Sushi, dim sum)
1626 Broadway at 49th St.
(212) 489-5600
$$

Sushi Jones
(Sushi, "sushi")
17 East 17th Street, between Fifth Ave. and Broadway
(646) 230-0033
Closed Sunday
$

Tabla
(Indian)
11 Madison Avenue at 25th St.
(212) 889-0667
$$$$

The Tasting Room
(American)
72 East 1st Street at First Ave.
(212) 358-7831
$$$

Tavern Room at Gramercy Tavern
(American)
42 East 20th Street, between Broadway and Park Ave. South
(212) 477-0777
$$$$

Union Pacific
(American)
111 East 22nd Street, between Park Ave. South and Lexington Ave.
(212) 995-8500
Closed Sunday
$$$$

Union Square Café
(American)
21 East 16th Street, between Fifth Ave. and Union Sq. West
(212) 243-4020
$$$

—Sara Firebaugh

BARBECUE

Blue Smoke
Gramercy Park/Flatiron District
116 East 27th Street, between Park Ave. South and Lexington Ave.
(212) 447-7733
$$

Blue Smoke opened its doors in 2002 to great fanfare, and while it has not yet achieved true greatness with its food, it surely has won distinction and respect with its dedication to sustainability and to serving ecologically sound foods such as Niman Ranch pork. With animals that are humanely treated; given no antibiotics, growth hormones, or animal proteins in their feed; and raised on land naturally suited to support their growth, Niman Ranch is the first company to be endorsed by the Animal Welfare Institute's Standards for the Humane Treatment of Animals. Blue Smoke is also a big supporter of New York City's Greenmarket, and Brooklyn Brewery brews a beer especially for the restaurant.

In an attempt to arrive at the same high standards with their food, Blue Smoke's owners enlisted the services of barbecue expert Mike Mills and also did much research in the Carolinas, Texas, and Tennessee working with the great pitmasters. Installing two Missouri-made wood-fired pit smokers that would be self-contained and meet Manhattan's stringent safty and environmental regulations was a major victory in and of itself. And Chef Kenny Callaghan has also helped point Blue Smoke in the right direction with his specialties, including Dry Rub Pork Ribs and Pulled Pork Shoulder. The ribs are good; the rest of the food needs to catch up. Expect things to only get better at Blue Smoke in years to come.

Pearson's Texas Barbecue
Jackson Heights, Queens
71-04 35th Avenue at 71st St.
(718) 779-7715
Subway: E, F, R, V, G to Jackson Hgts.–Roosevelt Ave.
Closed Monday–Tuesday
$$ (Cash only)

Devotees of real barbecue in New York used to make the pilgrimage to Pearson's when it was located in Long Island City, and for years before that former owner Robert Pearson ran it under the name Stick to Your Ribs in Manhattan. Now it's relocated once again to Jackson Heights, a few subway stops deeper into Queens, and longtime fans had every right to be nervous, since Pearson's new home is in the back of a sports bar, with only a few tables.

Never fear: The Texas-style barbecue is still outstanding, with brisket and links cooked "low and slow" at 180 degrees for at least five hours in an honest-to-goodness wood-fired barbecue pit. The meat comes out hickory smoked, tender yet chewy (not falling off the bone), and with just enough fat to keep it from drying out. In true Texas style, the sauce doesn't touch the meat until after it's cooked. You can order by the pound, or get a barbecue sandwich on a crusty Portuguese roll with the brisket, chicken, pulled pork shoulder, or sausage links. Pearson's sauce is nice and spicy, and there's a variety of good beers to wash it down, not just Lone Star and Shiner, which would be your two and only choices down in East Texas. The coleslaw, potato salad, and other sides are all made in-house, and the key lime pie is refreshing, assuming you have any room left over.

Jackson Heights may seem like a long way to go for barbecue, but it's a lot cheaper than a plane ticket to Austin and a drive out into the Hill Country. Am I implying that Pearson's is better than what you'd get in Lockhart or Luling or some other little town in Texas? Nope, and the atmosphere isn't much. But I've got to admit, the food itself is pretty darn close.

Virgil's Real BBQ
Theater District
152 West 44th Street, between Sixth Ave. and Broadway
(212) 921-9494
$$

Eric Asimov of the *New York Times* has rated Virgil's one of the "Best $25 and Under Restaurants in New York," but what really made me know it was good was when I heard real pitmasters talking it up at the Blue Ridge State BBQ Championship in Tryon, North Carolina. In a city that's not known for its barbecue, this down-home joint makes great Memphis Pork Ribs and Pulled Carolina Pork Shoulder covered with an in-house dry rub. If you can't decide, try the Pig Out, which includes ribs, chicken, brisket, pork, and Texas hot links. Virgil's uses two Southern Pride cookers, which cook the meat indirectly (only the smoke touches the meat) with hickory, oak, and fruit wood. This "low and slow" technique (low temperatures and long cooking time) is most evident in the brisket, which is cooked anywhere from twelve to sixteen hours.

As with all barbecue, beer is the drink of choice, and Virgil's has Brooklyn Brewery beers on tap and in the bottle. Desserts, biscuits, corn bread, and sauces (Memphis Mild or Hot, North Carolina Vinegar, and South Carolina Mustard) are all made on the premises. Located right in the heart of the Theater District, Virgil's is a nice place for a meal, as long as you don't mind seeing your show with a stain on your shirt.

A&A Bake Shop   (*Trinidadian*)
Bedford-Stuyvesant, Brooklyn
481 Nostrand Avenue, near Fulton St.
(718) 230-0753
Open until they sell out, usually by midafternoon/early evening
$ (Cash only)

The Trinidadians I know take their "doubles" very seriously. They must be well spiced and absolutely eaten fresh, and, if good, no one eats just one. The double is a lightly fried lentil-flour pancake on top of which a chickpea purée and spice mixture is placed, finished with a drizzle of tamarind syrup (chile paste can be added if you're in the mood). After the toppings are added, the pancake is doubled over on itself and promptly devoured. As far as discerning doubles fans are concerned, there is only one place in New York to enjoy this classic snack: A&A Bake Shop. Often, the queue extends into the street. While this is a good sign, it is by no means a magnificent feat, as A&A is no more than a stunted glass counter squeezed into a miniature storefront. The out-of-the-way location and small digs enable the folks at A&A to keep the prices very low. If you make the trip, be sure to try the "Bake" as well; an elliptical puff of fried bread that is cut open and filled with a choice of salt cod, smoked herring (my favorite), salmon, or shrimp and spices, and finished with a spicy-tangy pepper sauce. There are two preferred methods for getting these brightly flavored and surprisingly sophisticated treats in your mouth as quickly as possible. One is walk around the corner and find a stoop in front of one of the brownstones that line the side streets—the gems of Bed-Stuy, many of these old brownstones have been renovated to their former glory—pop a squat, and enjoy. The other method is slightly more dangerous, as stuffing your face in front of A&A will inspire jealousy in those desperate patrons at the rear of the queue.

NOTE: To try some authentic Trinidadian *roti*—large, thin, round bread wrapped around vegetable, fish, chicken, or goat curry, amongst a few of the choices—Ali's Roti Shop is just around the corner from A&A, about half a block down Fulton Street. And, approximately nine blocks south on Nostrand Avenue on the corner of Sterling is Gloria's, the favorite *roti* shop of many of those in the know.

The Feeding Tree   (*Jamaican*)
Concourse Village, Bronx
892 Gerard Avenue, between 161st and 162nd Sts.
(718) 293-5025
Subway: B, D, 4 to 161st St.–Yankee Stadium
$

Just a few short blocks from Yankee Stadium, the Feeding Tree offers an inexpensive alternative to overpriced ballpark fare. And, best of all, there's never an off-season for Jamaican food. The restaurant is divided between a dining room and a takeout counter with a few tables, where you can plunk down with your tray and tear into the tasty jerk chicken, among the best in the city. It's baked, not cooked over smoke (as is traditional), but all the flavor is there, and the gentle heat of allspice and chiles builds and radiates pleasantly on your tongue and throughout your mouth as you eat the rice and "peas" (beans), fried plantain, corn bread, and cooked vegetables that come with your order. Talk about value for your money!

If you're not in the mood for jerk chicken, try the oxtail stew, curried goat, or stewed or steamed kingfish. You can wash it all down with Ting, a grapefruit-flavored soda made down in Kingston, mon. And check out the baked goods and other products for sale behind the counter. You can take home some coco bread, fruit buns, or a bottle of genuine Root Tonic, which claims to give you the strength of four men. After a good meal and a little pick-me-up, who needs Viagra?

National Café   *(Cuban)*
East Village
210 First Avenue, between 12th and 13th Sts.
(212) 473-9354
Closed Sunday
$

Over the past two decades, National Café has developed a faithful following among the Cuban and Anglo community in this distinctly untrendy neighborhood near Beth Israel Medical Center. The Cuban dishes are classic and well prepared, from the tripe soup to the chicken fricassee and roast pork. Be sure to get a side of fried sweet plantain; it doesn't look like much, but it's particularly tasty here. The beverage of choice to accompany a hearty lunch or dinner, including the ubiquitous and healthy rice and beans, is Hatuey, a good beer made by Cuban exiles in Mayaguez, Puerto Rico. Try to save room for dessert, and get the delicious chocolate flan.

Scotch Bonnet   *(Jamaican)*
Garment District/Koreatown
32 West 31st Street, between Fifth Ave. and Broadway
(212) 594-7575
$$

"Scotch bonnet" is a colorful folk name for the habañero pepper, so called because of its resemblance to the Scotch version of the beret, the tam-o'shanter. The pepper is grown all over the Caribbean and used extensively in island cuisines.

The dining area at Scotch Bonnet is dimly lit and painted red, with Jamaican pop music playing softly in the background—a great place for a romantic dinner. Order a couple of Jamaica-politans from the bar (Cosmopolitans made with Appleton dark rum), and share some appetizers, such as the codfish fritters, triangular little nuggets that come with a fruity dipping sauce that tastes almost like spicy applesauce. The jerk chicken wings are superb, with a beautiful brown glaze.

Most of the entrées are familiar Jamaican home cooking, with stewed or grilled chicken in a variety of sauces figuring prominently. Curried goat with a side of collard greens is flavorful, if a bit salty. You can even get ackee and codfish here, which is the Jamaican national dish. (The ackee tree is named *Blighia sapida,* after Captain Bligh, of H.M.S. *Bounty* fame, who brought it to Jamaica from Guinea in 1793.)

A good accompaniment to the spicy dishes is "sorrel," a nonalcoholic drink that bears no relation to the lemony garden herb. This sorrel drink is as vividly red as the decor at Scotch Bonnet, and made from the flower sepals of a hibiscus species native to the Caribbean. The flavor is sweet, somewhat clovelike, and quite refreshing.

Sucelt Coffee Shop   *(Dominican/Pan-Caribbean)*
Chelsea
200 West 14th Street, between Seventh and Eighth Aves.
(212) 242-0593
Closed Sunday
$ (Cash only)

There's nothing fancy about Sucelt—just two parallel counters with stools and a central aisle between. But the food is terrific: tasty, plentiful, and inexpensive. You'll hear a smattering of English from neighborhood office workers picking up takeout, but most conversations are conducted *en Español*, something that is usually a good indicator of the authenticity of the cooking. Cuban, Puerto Rican, and Dominican dishes are all covered on the menu, which includes oxtail and chicken stews, served as *platos* with yellow rice and your choice of beans—red, white, or black, plus vegetables. Specials for every day of the week are posted high on the back wall of the restaurant. Make no mistake: This is comfort food that fills the belly and satisfies the soul.

In the front window there's a case with *empanadas,* crisp pastry pockets surrounding a variety of delicious fillings. The beef ones are very good—tender, juicy, and flavorful, with just the right amount of spice.

You'll have to arrive early in the day to have a chance at the more unusual *empanadas,* including the octopus and shrimp.

Sucelt makes good *batidos*—refreshing, fruity milk shakes made with papaya, mango, and guayabana (soursop). My favorite, for poetic reasons alone, is *morir sonando,* which means "to die dreaming." It's a citrusy shake that's said to have originated in Santo Domingo in the Dominican Republic. At Sucelt, they've got its preparation down to a science.

Victor's Café 52 *(Cuban)*
Theater District
236 West 52nd Street, between Broadway and Eighth Ave.
(212) 586-7714
$$$

Ropa vieja literally means "old clothes," but it's also the name of one of the most representative Cuban dishes: steak braised with onions, tomatoes, and peppers. And Victor's not only produces a splendid version, but it's served in a fried plantain "basket" that makes for a sophisticated and appetizing presentation. Most Caribbean restaurants offer good home cooking in a fast-paced, indifferent setting. Victor's Café is a nice exception, an upscale, sit-down restaurant where traditional dishes meet food art.

Victor del Corral opened his first restaurant forty years ago on the Upper West Side and moved to this location, right in the heart of the Theater District, about twenty years later. The dining space at Victor's is attractive, with a colorful mural and a skylight giving the sometimes noisy room an airy, open feel. The entrées, everything from *vaca frita* to lobster in Creole sauce, are carefully prepared. And the waiters are dignified old-school types, attentive without being annoying, and glad to answer questions or make intelligent suggestions about the menu or the wine list.

As someone who normally passes on dessert, I would make an exception here. Both the Cuban bread pudding and the semisweet cheese with guava slices are standouts and well worth sharing or taking home for a late-night snack.

NOTABLE

El Economico *(Puerto Rican)*
Kingsbridge, Bronx
5589 Broadway, between West 231st and 232nd Sts.
(718) 796-4851
$

This Puerto Rican restaurant serves delicious food that is also (as advertised) "economical." The oxtail stew is a must, but also try the roast chicken, *arroz moro* (black beans and white rice), and the hot sandwiches.

Isla   (*Cuban*)
West Village
39 Downing Street, between Bedford St. and Seventh Ave. South
(212) 352-2822
Closed Sunday–Monday
$$$

With one of the most stylish counter bars in town, reminiscent of 1950s Havana, Isla is a perfect spot to meet for a cocktail and a bite. Try the tangy Luna Roja Margarita (rimmed with cayenne pepper) or the flawless *mojito,* along with a Cuban-inspired appetizer such as the *Trés Empañaditas* or the *ensalata de calamares* (squid tossed with bananas and grilled almonds).

Krik Krak   (*Haitian*)
Upper West Side
844 Amsterdam Avenue at 102nd St.
(212) 222-3100
$

Haitian cuisine is a mix of French and Creole traditions, and Krik Krak represents it well with dishes such as *griot limbe,* diced pork shoulder that is marinated, boiled, then fried, and typically served with a fiery hot sauce. Krik Krak is a small takeout place with few tables; main dishes are typically served with all the accoutrements of Caribbean cooking including rice and beans *(riz et pois colles)* and plantain *(bananes pesées).*

La Fonda Boricua   (*Puerto Rican*)
East Harlem
169 East 106th Street, between Lexington and Third Ave.
(212) 410-7292
$$

This restaurant expanded a couple years ago from its original cramped takeout space and is now an attractive place to sample terrific Puerto Rican dishes, with an emphasis on meats—roasted, marinated, baked, stewed, and fried.

Strictly Roots
See Vegetarian, p. 153.

Bahar Shishkebab House *(Afghani)*
Midwood, Brooklyn
984 Coney Island Avenue
(718) 434-8088
Subway: Q to Ave. H
$

The fact that Bahar uses real charcoal to grill their kebabs isn't the only reason why many argue it's the best Afghan restaurant in New York, but it's a good one. These days, it's hard to find anything other than gas grills, and gas just doesn't impart the same flavor to meat, fish, and vegetables that charcoal does. Some of the other reasons Manhattanites trek out to Bahar are the *ashi lobya* (homemade noodles with beans and yogurt) and the outrageously good *boulanee* (pumpkin turnovers). All the food is filling and fit to be served after playing a long game of *buzkashi,* Afghanistan's national sport, where players ride around on horses and battle each other for possession of a headless calf or goat. The rinsed, soaked, boiled, drained, and then baked rice served with a variety of ingredients is a fantastic way to load up on carbs. The best way to end the meal, if there's any room left, is with *firni,* a pudding topped with rose water and crushed pistachios. As you saddle up to leave, don't forget your headless calf; it'd be a shame to leave it behind.

Chio Pio *(Uzbeki)*
Brighton Beach, Brooklyn
3087 Brighton 4th Street at Brighton Beach Ave.
(718) 615-9221
Subway: Q to Brighton Beach
$ (Cash only)

The neighborhood of Brighton Beach is predominantly Russian. Layer cakes, cherry preserves, pickles of all sorts, sprats, and many other small fish packed in oil fill the windows of the local stores. It's helpful to know how to speak even the most basic Russian when dining in Brighton or shopping in the markets. It's no surprise that several Uzbeki restaurants are also in the area, as Uzbekistan was once a satellite of the former Soviet Union. Chio Pio is a small restaurant that is big on flavor. *Samsa* is like an Uzbeki calzone, a dough commonly stuffed with meat and onions, folded over on itself, sealed, and fried. The protein of choice in Uzbekistan is mutton, but beef and horse meat are also very popular. In the States, lamb is often substituted for mutton, and such is the case at Chio Pio. Try a lamb kebab and order a side of *katyk,* or yogurt. The light, sour yogurt is the perfect foil for the salty gaminess of the charcoal-grilled lamb. Do not miss the specialty of the house, Tashkent Salad. It is a cold beef salad served with eggs, radish, dill, parsley, and coriander and is expertly prepared by the chef, who hails from the capital of Uzbekistan, for which the dish is named. After your meal, be sure to order a pot of green tea, and, like me, think about what you'll order the next time you come back—that is, if you are not able to catch a second wind and go in for Round Two.

Salut   (Uzbeki)
Rego Park, Queens
63-42 108th Street
(718) 275-6860
Subway: E, F, V, G, R to Forest Hills–71st Ave.
$

Uzbekistan is a young nation, gaining its independence after the dissolution of the Soviet Union in 1991, but it is an ancient culture. Within its borders are massive mountain ranges, deserts, and fertile valleys, all of which have played a part in the development of the cuisine. Salut offers a little bit of insight into the vast culinary chronicles of this land that sits on the Silk Road.

The *lagman* is a soup of lamb, seasonal vegetables, lamb broth, chile oil, and homemade noodles. It is reminiscent of the Tibetan *thukpa* soup, eaten in the colder months when there is little refuge from the cold winds. The chicken (with bones), lamb, lamb ribs, and ground meat kebabs are tender, well seasoned, and delicious dipped into the *tkemali* sauce (a tomato-based sauce with lamb stock, chile, and dill). The *babaganoush* (roasted eggplant spread) is something of a surprise at Salut, a kosher restaurant. The look and texture is so creamy, and yet it is light and wonderfully fresh tasting. Served with the warm, round homemade bread, this is a treat for which it is worth returning again and again. *Palov* is probably the closest thing to a national dish one will find in Uzbekistan, and it is served here under the title "Asian Pilaf" (rice cooked in lamb broth and served with lamb meat, coriander, parsley, carrots, and onions). Do not be deterred by the drab interior and the two droning television sets constantly tuned to the Russian channel; the food is authentic and the prices cannot be beat.

Tibetan Yak   (Tibetan)
Jackson Heights, Queens
72-20 Roosevelt Avenue
(718) 779-1119
Subway: E, F, G, R to Jackson Hgts.–Roosevelt Ave.
$

When you walk into the simple dining room at Tibetan Yak, it feels as if you could be walking into a restaurant in Lhasa. Sparse decorations, a few *tangka* wall hangings, a picture of the Dalai Lama, and a television that is often playing Indian musicals are no different than what you'd see in that impoverished, Chinese-occupied Buddhist region that sits on top of the world. When the salty butter tea *(bocha)* is placed before you, all that is missing is a woman in the corner churning the fresh *nak* (the term for a female yak) butter.

The simple decor echoes the uncomplicated dishes served here. Try *momo* (dumplings, similar to Chinese), either steamed or fried, or the richly flavored lamb broth with homemade short noodles. The *shamdey* is a Northern Indian–style curry; the lamb version is particularly good, as is the tongue, very simply sautéed and served with onions and chile. The beef cooked with jalapeños, ginger, and garlic is a perfect balance of spice, earthy richness, and sweet aromas.

As you become immersed in the dining experience, the only reminder that you're in New York and not about to head off trekking in the Himalayas is the rumbling of the elevated 7 train that runs along Roosevelt Avenue. The best thing to do is fantasize that it's an avalanche rolling down the mountain above, flag down a waiter, and order another cup of butter tea to keep you warm on the long journey home.

NOTABLE

Afghan Kebab House #4 *(Afghani)*
Jackson Heights, Queens
74-16 37th Avenue, between 74th and 75th Sts.
(718) 565-0471
Subway: E, F, G, R to Jackson Hgts.–Roosevelt Ave.
$$

Great rice cooked in meat broth with caramelized onions and turnovers with spinach, potatoes, and scallions.

Other Locations
764 Ninth Avenue, between 51st and 52nd Sts.; (212) 307-1612
1345 Second Avenue, between 71st and 72nd Sts.; (212) 517-2776
155 West 46th Street, between Sixth and Seventh Aves.; (212) 768-3875
2680 Broadway at 102nd St.; (212) 280-3500

Tibet Shambala   *(Tibetan)*
Upper West Side
488 Amsterdam Avenue, between 83rd and 84th Sts.
(212) 721-1270
$

Just like Tibetan Yak, the *bocha* (butter tea) is offered when you sit down. Equally solid are the curries and fried *momo,* or *kothey,* as they call them here.

Uzbekistan Community Center   *(Uzbeki)*
Kew Gardens, Queens
120-35 83rd Avenue, between Grenfell St. and Beverly Rd.
(718) 850-3426
Subway: E to Union Turnpike
$

Fresh *lepeshka,* Uzbeki bread, and delicious *samsas.*

DUMPLINGS

My dear father-in-law used to say that "every culture has a *kreplach*," and there is no better evidence of this than here in New York City. Every neighborhood in every borough teems with foods that were brought to this country from all over the world: Dumplings are everywhere. Delicious doughs wrapped around fillings, usually boiled or fried; universally loved and quickly devoured. Russian *varenike* and knishes, as well as Uzbeki *samsa*, all contain meat, potatoes, and onions, though not necessarily combined. Polish *pierogi* have meat, farmer's cheese, potatoes, sauerkraut, or mushrooms. Japanese *gyoza* are seasoned with soy sauce and have pork, chives, and scallions inside, and Korean *mandoo* combine meat and tofu with pickled cabbage. Chinese *wonton* from every province are made with a paste of pork, shrimp, and vegetables and can be served in broth, pan-fried like potstickers, or deep-fried like plump chips. *Kreplach* have only meat or cheese, and, when served with a light chicken broth, they become Jewish penicillin!

Italian calzone are pockets of dough enfolding meat, ricotta cheese, and spices, while Greek *spanakopita* triangles contain feta cheese and spinach; both of these are traditionally baked and browned. Argentinian *empanadas* have various combinations of potatoes, tomatoes, meat, raisins, almonds, cheese, and onions and are baked but not browned. Tibetan *momos* are similar to wonton and filled with beef, mutton, or even horse meat. The Mexican *gordita* has beans, cheese, and chorizo with a *crema* topping, while the Salvadoran *pupusa* has beans and cheese and is topped with pickled cabbage. Flat-pocket Ethiopian *sambosas* have lentils, beef, onions, and garlic spiced with cardamom, cloves, coriander, and cinnamon. But not all dumplings have both a wrapping *and* a filling.

Some are just the wrapping. Good old American chicken and dumplings is made with round, feather-light biscuits and vegetables simmered in a rich, thick broth similar to a stew. Potato and flour combine to make traditional Italian *gnocchi*, which are gently formed with a fork, while Austrian *spaetzle* are grated over boiling salted water. They are simply served with butter or sauce, but there are countless variations. *Matzoh* balls are made with *matzoh* meal, a pinch of salt, rendered chicken fat, and a little soda water, then gently simmered in a broth made with caramelized onions.

Some are just the filling. French *quenelles* are made from a paste of meat, fish, or vegetables and are light and airy. The Lyonnaise speciality uses pike with a paste of milk, butter, egg, and flour, while Alsatian calf's liver dumplings use semolina flour and have the smoky flavor of bacon. Little Vietnamese beef balls are made with beef shank, potato starch, sugar, garlic, and sesame oil and are steamed or boiled in *pho,* the wonderful Vietnamese noodle soup. *Albondigas* from northern Mexico are small but substantial. They combine ground beef with cilantro, onions, garlic, and *masa harina* and are cooked in a clear broth with a squeeze of lime.

The dumpling-maker in the family holds an honored position; for a special touch is required to make these delicate treats, and this technique is passed from parent to child to grandchild. There is a communal aspect to this process where everyone gathers around the table to talk and laugh, fill and fold. Telling stories and sharing family secrets; making certain that the past of the family becomes the future of the family wherever they are living. This is the real treasure to be found in the kitchen and at the table.

—*Bernadette Kramer*

ELIZABETH LITTLES

CHINESE

Congee Village
Lower East Side
100 Allen Street, between Broome and Delancey Sts.
(212) 941-1818
$

The definition of comfort food has been run through the mill so many times that some of us might begin believing that three-star Michelin chefs are serving comfort food in their flagship establishments. If I had to think of a classic Chinese comfort food, though, it would have to be *congee:* yesterday's rice mixed with a little bit of water and salt, and slowly cooked into a porridge of broken grains to which an endless variety of ingredients are added, no doubt originally determined by whatever was in the larder. After eating at Congee Village, I no longer yearn for mashed potatoes on a rainy day, but for warm *congee* with ginger, tender squid, cilantro, scallions, and a little squirt of hot sauce. The name is a clear indication that this restaurant's mission is to produce great *congee*. I suggest trying several types: chicken, frogs' legs, salted fish—the list is long, and one will surely suit your fancy.

Congee is not the only dish done well here: There are a number of hardy casseroles as well. Top on my list is a rolled rice noodle and pork rib in black bean sauce casserole. Another specialty of the house is the slightly more dramatic rice steamed in (and served in) a bamboo log, which comes accompanied by a variety of toppings.

East Corner Wonton
Chinatown
70 East Broadway at Division St.
(212) 343-9896
$ (Cash only)

In Asia, soup is quite possibly the most popular breakfast dish: noodle soup, *congee* (rice porridge), chicken soup, fish soup, fish ball soup—the list goes on and on. Living in Manhattan, it's not always easy to find soup for breakfast, and good soup is even harder to find. On one of my extended dog walks a few years ago, I noticed an incessant stream of customers piling into a nondescript Chinese restaurant on a forgotten corner near the Manhattan Bridge. Curious, I tied the dogs to a parking meter and headed in. Once inside, I could barely see the street through the steam rising from two vigorously boiling kettles into which two cooks were dropping noodles of all shapes, sizes, and colors. I pointed to something in a bowl the women next to me had just ordered, and what I received was a delicate chicken broth with wheat-flour noodles and moist chunks of soy sauce chicken. I devoured this and then ordered a small bowl of *congee* with scallions and salt fish and a deep-fried savory cruller, the accompaniment of choice for all *congee* eaters. Full and completely content after my 7:30 A.M. snack, I returned to my dogs, who were jealously drooling on the sidewalk from the smells of another specialty of East Corner Wonton, roasted duck. Go, sit there one morning or afternoon, have a soup of pork and preserved vegetables or fish balls and squid, and watch as people parade in and out, conspicuously holding up their prized duck.

Fried Dumpling
Lower East Side
99 Allen Street, between Broome and Delancey Sts.
(212) 941-9975
$ (Cash only)

When I used to live on Grand Street just off of Forsyth in the heart of Chinatown, I would frequent the Dragon Market. Wedged between Forsyth and Chrystie Streets on a little sliver of pavement, the Dragon Market held anywhere from ten to fifteen vendors on any given day. There were cobblers, phone card salesmen, fake jade Buddhas, and the food stalls. Even after dinner, sometimes before, and often as a whole dinner, I'd go to the stall that sold the best fried pork dumplings I'd ever tasted, and sesame pancake. Five dumplings cost $1. A buck!

One day walking home from work, exhausted and longing for dumplings and beer, I reached the strip of pavement between Chrystie and Forsyth only to find the pavement and the rats—no food stalls. The market had been cleared out for violating multiple city codes. And with the market went the dumplings. Apparently, though, there were enough devotees that the dumpling entrepreneurs decided to open a legitimate store—or barely legitimate, with three tables and a tiny counter behind which an incessant rotation of freshly made pork dumplings are fried in a large wok all day long. They also make fried pork buns. The buns resemble squat, doughier dumplings. They are made with a yeast-based dough that rises slightly and has a somewhat chewy texture. New York City has no better deal than five dumplings and four pork buns for $2. You just can't beat it. There are a few other items served at Fried Dumpling, but the only other one I would recommend is the sesame pancake; ask the counter person to stuff it with beef—a lovely snack, if he can understand your English.

NOTE: Also serving dumplings: Fried Dumpling on Mosco Street, and Dumpling House on Eldridge Street, between Grand and Broome Sts.

Funky Broome
Chinatown/Little Italy
176 Mott Street at Broome St.
(212) 941-8628
$

As hipsters began penetrating Chinatown and the Lower East Side, new restaurants with slick interiors started opening. In turn, Chinese restaurateurs have begun to place more emphasis on the design, or overdesign, of many new places in the neighborhood. Funky Broome, name and all, is an awkward attempt to assimilate with the movement of cool and casual eating places. Neon lights, brash colors, and fish tanks line the walls, making the diners feel like they are in the aquarium as passersby look in. Once you open the menu, however, and begin to peruse the more than 200 selections, all your attention will be focused on which few dishes you will order. Try any one of the mini-wok selections, which are served in a small wok brought to the table, heated by a Sterno. The razor clams in black bean sauce are fresh and salty-sweet, and the casserole of tofu, shiitake mushrooms, and ground pork is a rich, earthy delight. The seafood selections, such as crab with chile sauce, drunken shrimp, and steamed fish done in a variety of ways, are always fresh and delicious, but what else would you expect when dining in an aquarium?

Grand Sichuan International Midtown
Clinton
745 Ninth Avenue, between 50th and 51st Sts.
(212) 582-2288
$$

Midtown does not have anywhere near the same per block density of Chinese restaurants as Chinatown. Perhaps, due to this lack of density, the owners of Grand Sichuan International decided to put together a 25- to 30-page book that they refer to as a menu. The book covers cuisines of a variety of regions in China, but, as indicated by the name of the restaurant, it is wise to stick to the Sichuan dishes. One dish, in particular, has something of a cult following. This is the Kung Pao chicken. Made with freshly killed chickens bought from a live poultry distributor in Chinatown, this is a dish I never order in other Chinese restaurants. Here, though, it is stellar. There are, however, many other dishes to choose from, and half the fun is reading through the menu book and trying to find the most elaborately named dish: "Green Parrot with Red Mouth" is sautéed spinach; "White Feathered Egrets Flying Over Broad Water Fields" is sautéed shrimp. There's even a section of the menu book devoted to Chairman Mao's childhood favorites, which, the menu explains, is in no way a political statement. Other favorites at this Midtown oasis are the Spicy Ground Beef over Noodles, and the Tea-Smoked Duck with Red Cooked Chestnuts and Fatty Pork. If you're in the mood for seafood, an abundance of fresh fish is served steamed, braised, or fried in a variety of styles. Variety is one thing Grand Sichuan definitely has in ample supply; the customer's task is to discover the outstanding dishes that do exist amidst the seemingly endless choices.

Harmony Palace
Chinatown/Little Italy
98 Mott Street, between Canal and Hester Sts.
(212) 226-6603
$

Not as impressive in size or operational efficiency as the dim sum temple Jing Fong, Harmony Palace does excel in one all-important area: food quality. The *lo man gai* (sticky rice mixed with scallion and Chinese sausage, then wrapped in a bamboo leaf and steamed) is dense and savory, perhaps the best in town. For newcomers to dim sum, this is definitely the place to expand your horizons and go beyond what you normally order in a Chinese restaurant. Women rule the carts that are pushed through the crowded dining room, and though they rarely charm, don't refuse their offer of the braised chicken feet as they wheel by. And be sure to stop one of these hard-working cart matrons as the slow-cooked tripe with ginger goes past. These may not sound like the most appetizing delicacies you've ever had, but then again, you may be surprised. More palatable for the uninitiated or those unwilling to experiment are the short, wormlike rice noodles with pork and vegetables. The texture of these noodles is a marvel. The fried crullers wrapped in rice-flour crêpes are another highly successful textural play. Please do not forget the succulent pork rib bits in black bean sauce. The luxury of dim sum is that all the food passes before your eyes, and you get to choose whatever tickles your fancy. At only $2 to $3 per dish, that's a lot of tickling.

Jing Fong
Chinatown/Little Italy
20 Elizabeth Street, between Bayard and Canal Sts.
(212) 964-5256
Dim sum served daily 9:00 A.M.–2:30 P.M.
$$

Imagine the biggest restaurant you've ever eaten in. Not cafeteria, restaurant. Now double it, fill it with Chinese patrons and maybe you'll come close to envisioning Jing Fong. This is a true Cantonese dim sum hall. Jing Fong serves a massive array of dim sum to throngs of Chinatown residents and a few folks from other neighborhoods around New York who know enough to make the trip. It's noisy, crowded, you sit with other people (some of whom spit the bones of the chicken feet they're eating directly on the table), but it's also very authentic and often quite delicious.

It's also simply fascinating to watch the place run. A friend once compared the operation to a casino. The floor manager greets you downstairs, gives you a number, and lets you know when you are allowed to ride the long escalator upstairs to the dining room. You are then greeted by his assistant just outside the main dining room, where you stare through the glass doors greedily as diners devour little plates of shrimp dumplings, longevity noodles, sticky rice, fried shrimp, crab claws, black bean clams, snails, dumplings of all different colors, and, yes, chicken feet. Just then (to extend the casino metaphor), one of the "pit bosses" signals to you and you go sit in his area. You place an order for tea, soda, or any other beverage with the "dealer," who then makes way for the waitresses (invariably all are women), who in turn bring you small plates of delicacies on carts. Before leaving, a man in a red or black coat adds up your bill, but don't worry—at an average of $10 to $12 per person you'll never go bust here.

Joe's Shanghai
Chinatown/Little Italy
9 Pell Street, between Bowery and Mott St.
(212) 233-8888
$$ (Cash only)

If you're looking for the best steamed buns west of the Yangtze River, Joe's Shanghai should be on your short list. Constantly busy from lunch straight through to dinner, Joe's draws New Yorkers from all over with its consistent Shanghai-style fare and its famed Shanghai soup dumplings. Joe's soup dumplings are composed of a rice-flour dumpling wrapper filled with pork, or a pork and crab mixture, and pork broth. The dumpling is then steamed on top of lettuce leaves in a bamboo steamer. A word of caution: Be careful when you bite into one; it takes many dumplings and an expert touch to get all the broth into one's mouth as opposed to onto one's lap. Other specialties of the house include fried rice cakes (round rice noodles sautéed with meat and vegetables), Shanghai noodles (long, thick noodles that are chewy and delicious), and salt-and-pepper duck (crispy fried duck that is tender and succulent, served with a mixture of salt and cracked Sichuan peppercorns). Joe's Shanghai is an institution that attracts all types, who come and sit at the large round tables to eat and dine with other ravenous strangers. Within one week, in three visits, I sat with a Chinese family from Beijing, an old Jewish couple from the Upper East Side, and Mario Batali, the famous Italian-American chef.

Other Locations
24 West 56th Street, between Fifth and Sixth Aves.; (212) 333-3868

82-74 Broadway, between Whitney and 45th Aves., Elmhurst, Queens; (718) 639-6888

136-21 37th Avenue, between Main and Union Sts. Flushing, Queens; (718) 539-3838

Natural Restaurant
Lower East Side
88 Allen Street, between Broome and Grand Sts.
(212) 966-1321
$ (Cash only)

Walk down Allen Street and stop into any Asian restaurant, and odds are it will be a good one: There are at least three other Allen Street restaurants listed in this guide alone. Yet if the attraction of restaurant owners to the area is anything other than cheap rental space, it's a mystery to me. One look at Natural Restaurant and you're sure cheap is what they were going for. As a customer, you're immediately grateful for the choice of location, since it is reflected in the restaurant's prices.

As anyone who has eaten here knows, you can put the regular printed menu down as soon as you sit down and order off of the handwritten menu of authentic Hong Kong–style Cantonese dishes. Start with the oysters in a garlic purée or the large bowl of Westlake Beef soup, topped with a pile of fresh coriander leaves. In an interesting twist, ostrich is offered, cooked in several different preparations; all are worthwhile, and the meat is surprisingly flavorful. I could nibble all day long on the beef ribs with a jalapeño-and-black-pepper sauce, spicy and highly addictive. If you're not appalled by the idea, you can even select a fresh fish from one of the tanks along the wall and watch as the kitchen staff steams it alive. At least you know it's fresh—an absolute must for Chinese seafood aficionados. There are also other very suitable alternatives for the customer who doesn't eat meat and prefers not to watch his dinner flip its final flop.

Ping's Seafood
Chinatown/Little Italy
22 Mott Street, between Mosco and Pell Sts.

(212) 602-9988

$$

When the leaders of Slow Food Italy come to New York for an important event, where do you take them to eat? For the leaders of the New York convivium, the answer was simple: Ping's. A delicate hand with seafood reigns at Ping's, unlike the heavy, sweet fare with which many run-of-the-mill-Chinese-food-eating Americans are familiar. This is the place you go to indulge in the truly refined art that is Chinese cooking. Chinese cooking differs greatly from region to region, and at Ping's the influence is almost exclusively the Cantonese cuisine of Hong Kong, the *alta cucina* of China.

I can think of no better example than to list some of the dishes presented to the Italian Slow Food representatives. We began with a mixed plate of lightly fried whiting with chile; delicate shrimp dumplings; cold sliced jellyfish drizzled with sesame oil; and peppery fried squid. And this was only the warm-up for diced squab with vegetables served in lettuce leaves; stir-fried squid, salted fish, chives, and Chinese celery; wilted pea shoots in a light chicken broth with minced pork; dried shrimp and eggs three ways; fried and then braised lobster served on top of buttered noodles; steamed fish with ginger and soy; and fried rice with salted fish, raisins, and XO sauce (a spicy mix of chile, oil, dried scallops, and other ingredients particular to each chef). At the end of this splendid feast, one of the Italians leaned over to me. "This," as he gestured to the room, "this is not New York. This is China!"

Other Location

83-02 Queens Boulevard at Goldsmith St., Elmhurst, Queens; (718) 396-1238

NOTE: One and a half blocks north from Ping's, between Bayard and Canal Streets on the east side of Mott Street, is a small stall run by a man who makes the most fantastic turnip cakes, filled with ham and scallions at the absurd price of three for $1.50.

Sweet-n-Tart Restaurant
Chinatown/Little Italy

20 Mott Street, between Park Row and Pell St.

(212) 964-0380

$

Bubble teas filled with sticky tapioca balls, fresh blended fruit drinks, egg custards, and vibrantly colored candies. Such were the offerings that made Sweet-n-Tart Café feel like a shrine to the colorful pop culture of

China, and made its popularity soar. It became so popular, in fact, that the owners decided to outdo themselves and open a three-level restaurant combining the signature sweets, shakes, and teas with a full menu of Cantonese-style savory dishes such as braised tofu and minced meat and a mushroom casserole with fresh peas. Sweet-n-Tart Restaurant executes the sweet snacks with skill and quite a bit of playfulness. The playfulness starts with the design of the restaurant itself. Oddly shaped walls, fun lighting, and Day-Glo colors are everywhere; the connoisseur can slurp up delicious noodle dishes and roast meats, all the while wrapped up inside this bright candy package.

NOTE: If you go for lunch, check out the stall on Mosco Street (which runs perpendicular into Mott Street right near the restaurant) run by a woman who makes Hong Kong pancakes. These little, sweet, eggy pancakes make the perfect snack while walking around Chinatown.

Yummy Noodles
Chinatown/Little Italy
48A Bowery at Canal St.
(212) 374-1327
$ (Cash only)

Have you ever suffered from an incredible jonesing for Hong Kong street food? I have. And every time I feel it creeping, I head to Yummy Noodles. Yummy Noodles has been open for several years, but somehow it has managed to fly below the radar of most food reviewers. This is fine with me because it's already busy enough, with the hordes of Chinese who crowd the small dining room until 3 A.M. Roast meats, noodle soups, and rice casseroles dominate here. Soy sauce chicken, scallion baked chicken, roast pig, *charsieuw,* and duck are all sold individually, and, if you like, over rice; you can also get everything to go. Two sure signs of a Chinese restaurant where flavor is paramount are when the hanging roasted meats are dripping on the cooked cuttlefish below, and when the butcher is constantly cleaning his block of meat juices and spilling them into a bubbling Master Stock that sits on a burner behind his station. One of the premier treats at this tiny flavor palace is the rice casserole. Choose from minced pork and salted fish, preserved duck and Chinese sausage, frogs' legs, and several other very Chinese combinations, and the waiter will bring you a clay pot filled with rice and your topping of choice. Cooked on the grill, the outside layer of rice is crispy and nicely browned, and inside the rice is moist and chewy. Mixed with any of the toppings, this is a satisfying, well-balanced snack, and only $5 too.

NOTABLE

David's Taiwanese Gourmet
Elmhurst, Queens
84-02 Broadway, between St. James and Corona Aves.
(718) 429-4818
$$

Wonderful Taiwanese cooking. Light, steamed seafood dishes and a refreshing use of spices. We'll be hearing more about this place in years to come!

Dumpling House
Chinatown/Little Italy
118A Eldridge Street, between Grand and Broome Sts.
(212) 625-8008
$ (Cash only)

Excellent fried dumplings, sesame pancake with beef filling, and chive and egg pancake.

New York Noodle Town
Chinatown/Little Italy
28½ Bowery at Bayard St.
(212) 349-0923
$ (Cash only)

There are many who swear by the suckling pig, pan-fried noodles, noodles, soups, and *congee* at this Chinatown dive. It can be excellent, but it's also rather inconsistent.

No. 1 People and Place's
Flushing, Queens
38-06 Prince Street, between 37th and 38th Aves.
(718) 460-8686
Subway: 7 to Flushing-Main St.
$

Chinese Corn on the Cob. For this alone it is worth the trip to Flushing. But don't run home too quickly, because there are a number of tempting dishes and fresh grilled meat and fish.

Ocean Palace
Sunset Park, Brooklyn
5421-5423 Eighth Avenue, between 54th and 55th Sts.

(718) 871-8080
$$

This is the place to go for the best dim sum experience in Brooklyn.

Other Location
1414-1418 Avenue U, between East 14th and 15th Sts.,
  Homecrest/Madison, Brooklyn; (718) 376-3838

Saint Alp's Tea House
Chinatown/Little Italy
20 Elizabeth Street, between Canal and Bayard Sts.
(212) 227-2880
$

A branch of the well-known Hong Kong bubble tea chain. The real deal, the tea here is brewed and not the sweet, sticky, powdered substitute.

Other Location
39 Third Avenue, between 9th and 10th Sts., 212-598-1890

Win Sing
Sheepshead Bay Brooklyn
1321 Avenue U, between East 13th and East 14th Sts.
(718) 998-0360
Subway: Q local to Ave U
$

Cantonese fare with excellent fresh seafood, including drunken shrimp!

Wong's Rice and Noodle
Chinatown/Little Italy
86 Mulberry Street, between Canal and Bayard Sts.
(212) 233-2288
$ (Cash only)

Competitor of New York Noodle Town, Wong's offers similar fare, often at lower prices.

XO Kitchen
Chinatown/Little Italy
148 Hester Street, between Bowery and Elizabeth Sts.
(212) 965-8645
$ (Cash only)

Named after the classic Cantonese spicy condiment, XO offers dishes from many regions in China as well as other Asian countries.

EASTERN EUROPEAN

NOTE: In two of the following entries the word "Yugoslavian" is used as a descriptive term for the cuisine. While the entire world recognizes that Serbia and Montenegro, Croatia, and Bosnia-Herzegovina have fought to maintain independent identities, it's a fact that these nations are still inextricably linked by many cultural and culinary ties. Additionally, knowing firsthand the ferocity with which the different nationalities argue, we are reluctant to cause a dispute over the origins of particular dishes.

Cevabdzinica Sarajevo *(Yugoslavian)*
Astoria, Queens
37-18 34th Avenue, between 37th and 38th Sts.
(718) 752-9528
Subway: R, G, V to Steinway St.
$

Cevapcici, more often called *cevap* or *cevape* (small, succulent sausages traditionally made from a mix of ground lamb, beef, and pork) is the central focus at Cevabdzinica Sarajevo. This little sausage is revered throughout the former Yugoslavia, and is most often purchased uncooked at the butcher shop or in small stores specializing in *cevape.*

Like any great ethnic restaurant, English is the second language spoken here, and it's a distant second at that. The menu, too, has only vague English translations of the actual Yugoslavian dishes, but the choices are few, and the clear specialty are the *cevape:* after a few bites of these, you may never eat another hot dog again. Order the *cevape* in quantities of five or ten, and as accompaniments you will receive homemade bread, made with plenty of salt and oil, and chopped white onions. To do this right, be sure to order *kajmak* with your *cevape. Kajmak* is a soft, creamy spread made by repeatedly skimming the layer of fat that rises to the top of boiling, unpasteurized milk. The layers are placed in a container on top of each other and salted individually, until the desired quantity has been amassed. A liberal spreading of *kajmak* on a tear of homemade bread, a sprinkling of onions, and a salty, fatty *cevape* . . . oh, to luxuriate in simple peasant food. *This* is the real thing.

House of Pizza *(Yugoslavian)*
Astoria, Queens
42-20 30th Avenue at 43rd St.
(718) 545-9455
Subway: R, G, V to 46th St.
$$ (Cash only)

I grew up with *burek.* From my early childhood in Belgrade to summers in the mountains of Serbia, *burek* was eaten, usually for breakfast or as a snack, and served with a homemade, drinkable plain yogurt to soothe the heaviness of the flavor-packed slice of pie. In fact, *burek* is so good and satisfying that it is perfect for lunch or dinner as well. It really is a simple dish, but simple dishes are always the hardest to execute, as there is little or no room for error. Layers of handmade phyllo dough surround fillings of meat (usually a mix of lamb, pork, and beef), feta, or a spinach and feta mix. These large pies are then slowly fried on large griddles. The end product should be a golden, crisp outer layer shielding moist inner layers of dough and warm, savory fillings.

House of Pizza produces the most well-executed *burek* in New York. One wouldn't know this just by walking by, or even by going inside, since from the street House of Pizza looks like your average pizza joint (the only exception is the neon *Burek* sign in the window). When you step inside, you'll see the place is filled with Yugoslavians and Albanians (everyone gets along here—it's New York!), who are smoking, drinking Yugoslavian coffees, and eating. In addition to *burek*, you can order *pasulj* (a bean soup flavored with smoky pork), *cevape* (little sausages), and other home-cooked Yugoslavian specialties. Next time you're planning a big party, call House of Pizza in advance and they'll slow-cook a lamb or kid for you on the rotisserie that sits behind the pizza counter. It's comforting to know that, no matter what your ethnic background, in New York you can always find someplace that reminds you of home.

NOTE: Half a block down the street from House of Pizza is the Black Bull Market, a Yugoslavian market. Inside you'll find smoked meats, raw *cevape,* *kajmak,* pickled chiles, *ajvar,* and other assorted Yugoslavian specialty foods.

Pod Wierchami   *(Polish)*
Greenpoint, Brooklyn
119 Nassau Avenue at Eckford St.
(718) 383-0670
Subway: G to Nassau Ave.
$ (Cash only)

In what is easily one of the largest Polish neighborhoods in North America, Pod Wierchami stands out as one of the most consistent and rewarding Polish dining experiences available. Greenpoint, Brooklyn, is situated in the northernmost tip of Brooklyn, just south of Queens and just east of the East River. Along the streets in this clean and somewhat isolated neighborhood, Polish signs dominate and storefront windows are stocked with kielbasa, rye bread, Welka chocolate, and sundry other products from Poland. Passing the butchers, smelling the smoked pork loins, ribs, and bacon, fills one with the longing for a hearty, satisfying meal cooked by the Polish grandmother you wish you had.

And so the stage is set for Pod Wierchami, a simple, cafeteria-style restaurant where you might see through the pick-up window that Polish grandmother pan-frying a veal cutlet or boiling freshly made, over-stuffed pierogies. Walk up to the counter and, unless you speak Polish, ask the woman who is busily heaping potatoes, beets, pickles, carrots and peas, sauerkraut, pork ribs, veal meatballs—and a variety of other dishes fit for a lumberjack in wintertime—what she has under the lids of her steam tables. Or ask for a plate-sized, made-to-order chicken or veal cut-let, or the best pierogies outside of Warsaw. Pierogies come either boiled or fried and are filled with potato and cheese, sauerkraut and mush-rooms, or meat. With your meal comes a free fruit-syrup-based drink called Kompot, but you're also welcome to bring your own beers, or, if you prefer, vodka.

Sammy's Roumanian Steakhouse _(Romanian)_
Lower East Side
157 Chrystie Street at Delancey St.
(212) 673-5526; 673-0330
$$$

There are precious few restaurants in which you find yourself presented with a small pamphlet to take home called "The Dictionary of Basic Yiddish." Nor are there many restaurants where the waiters and wait-resses take intermittent breaks from service to play caricatured live Yiddish music for all the diners. These are just a couple of the idiosyn-crasies that make Sammy's Roumanian a legendary New York restaurant. There are Roumanian specialties, such as sliced brains, unborn eggs, and overly sweet stuffed cabbage, but they play second fiddle to the anachro-nistic seltzer spritz bottles delivered to your table and the bottles of vodka served in blocks of ice. The entire restaurant seems to be a thing of the past, untouched: pictures on top of pictures, business cards on top of business cards pasted to the walls, and _New York Times_ food reviews from more than a decade ago hanging in the entryway. As you marvel at the _chatchkes,_ be sure to watch for the chopped chicken liver, mixed tableside with cooked and raw onions, _gribbenez_ (chicken cracklings), and a liberal pour of the _schmaltz_ (rendered chicken fat) that sits in the center of your table in a diner-style maple syrup bottle. If you can still breathe, sit back, enjoy the entertainment, and wait for your 28-ounce rib steak, so big it arrives half off the plate. And, just so you don't forget you're in another time and another place, you can finish off your meal with a "build your own egg cream"—don't worry when you don't see any eggs or any cream.

Uncle Vanya Café   *(Russian)*
Clinton
315 West 54th Street, between Eighth and Ninth Aves.
(212) 262-0542
$$

With the recent demise of the gaudy, glitzy Russian Tea Room, and Kalinka on the Upper East Side, there are precious few Slow choices remaining among the city's Russian restaurants. The food at the hokey disco-era throwback cafés of Brooklyn's Brighton Beach is inconsistent at best, so the best choice for Russian comfort food at a reasonable price is Uncle Vanya Café. Even better, it's conveniently located close to the Theater District.

The *zakuska*, or appetizers, are a good start to your meal, from the beet salad with currants and dill to the *varenike*, potato dumplings with caramelized onions served with sour cream. Entrées include the house specialty, Chicken Vanya, which is the café's version of the Russian standard, chicken *tabaka* (a partly boned whole chicken that's flattened, coated with garlic, and deep-fried). The beef Stroganoff is rich and good, as you'd expect, but the *golubtsy* (cabbage stuffed with meat and rice) is truly exceptional.

NOTABLE

Cornel's Garden Restaurant   *(Romanian)*
Sunnyside, Queens
46-04 Skillman Avenue
(718) 786-7894
Subway: 7 to 46th St.
Closed Monday
$ (Cash only)

One of the few Romanian restaurants in the city. Try the polenta topped with grated feta and sour cream or the grilled beef sausages.

Mocca Hungarian   *(Hungarian)*
Upper East Side
1588 Second Avenue, between 82nd and 83rd Sts.
(212) 734-6470
$$ (Cash only)

Goulash, and chicken or veal paprikash are inexpensive, very filling, and go well with a glass or two of a nice Hungarian wine.

Polska   *(Polish)*
Greenpoint, Brooklyn
136 Greenpoint Avenue at Manhattan Ave.
(718) 389-8368
Subway: G to Greenpoint Ave.
$ (Cash only)

Pierogies, blintzes, stuffed cabbage, cutlets—you'll need to bring a hearty appetite along when you visit Polska. Don't be deterred by the decor, which leaves much to be desired.

Primorski Restaurant   *(Russian)*
Brighton Beach, Brooklyn
282 Brighton Beach Avenue
(718) 891-3111
Subway: Q to Brighton Beach
$$$

Rude service and standard Russian fare are not necessarily indicators of a great restaurant. In fact, Primorski is not great, but what it does offer is an excellent representation of the quintessential Brighton Beach Russian-restaurant-cum-nightclub dining experience. All of the big Russian restaurants in the Brighton community have nightly entertainment to help you digest the leaden *kreplach* sitting in the bottom of your belly.

Rasputin (2670 Coney Island Ave.; 718-332-8111) is another Russian large-scale operation, notable for its very elaborate cabaret and festive weddinglike atmosphere.

ELIZABETH LITTLES

FRENCH

BISTROS & BRASSERIES

Balthazar
Soho

80 Spring Street, between Broadway and Crosby St.
(212) 965-1414
$$$

Balthazar is the perfect place for all occasions. Keith McNally has created a masterpiece. The massive space is filled with typical bistro tables, red leather banquettes, and waiters dressed in black running to and fro to feed hundreds of well-dressed diners. Balthazar boasts a massive bar area that includes tables (no reservations required) as well as a raw bar, which turns out a wide variety of delicious oysters, including a three-tiered splendor of chilled oysters, clams, crab legs, and shrimp. But if the cooks at Balthazar have mastered one thing, it's the simple foods, such as steak frites, grilled chicken salad, and macaroni and cheese. Balthazar also serves one of the best breakfasts in the city, and you can often find New Yorkers weaving their way in and out for a tasty bread plate and delicious coffee. But we like to think that the genius of Balthazar is not in its bistro menu, antique mirrors, or beautiful diners, but rather in service that is based on the concept of "civil inattention," a kind of laissez-faire attitude that allows your meal to be about you and not the quirks or games that people are often forced to play in the theater of fine dining. The service is seamless, invisible, and yet completely capable of responding to any need or desire. If you are hungry for both a meal and an experience, come to Balthazar—it is a happy place!

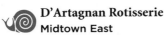

D'Artagnan Rotisserie
Midtown East

152 East 46th Street, between Lexington and Third Aves.
(212) 687-0300
$$–$$$

D'Artagnan got its start when a farmer brought a fresh foie gras to Ariane Daguin while she worked for a pâté producer in New York. It was clear to her that distributing such a delicacy would be a great business opportunity, and so D'Artagnan was born. Since its beginnings in 1985, Ariane Daguin and George Faison have made D'Artganan, Inc., into the leading purveyor of foie gras, pâtés, sausages, smoked delicacies, and organic game and poultry in the nation.

D'Artagnan was established on the principles of procuring the freshest, cleanest, and most natural products available. Ariane says, "We have three absolute requirements for our producers: no hormones, no antibiotics, and no animal byproducts in the diet. Whenever possible, free-range products are purchased. We look for the 'best of the best' in all of our product lines." D'Artagnan's broad product line and strict standards make the company a leader in organic foods. With more than 300 different items, D'Artagnan sells both at retail and wholesale.

D'Artagnan's flagship product line, its foie gras, comes from both America and France. The subtle differences in flavor come from differences in diet: French ducks are fed only corn, while Hudson Valley ducks get a little soy added to their diet. The French foie gras shines in terrines and cold preparations, while the Hudson Valley foie gras is best in a seared or sautéed preparation.

In addition to providing meat and charcuterie products to the world, D'Artagnan has opened a restaurant, D'Artagnan Rotisserie, that serves both as a Gascon outpost and as a showcase for the company's products. Located in the heart of Midtown, you feel as if you're walking into a medieval castle, with suits of armor, family crests hanging on the walls, and medieval-style cutlery on the tables. Specials on the menu are basically anything with more than 2,000 calories, for example, pasta dishes served with a topping of foie gras. It's frankly high-octane comfort food, so be forewarned, but prepare to be very, very happy.

La Luncheonette
Chelsea
130 Tenth Avenue at 18th St.
(212) 675-0342
$$

Take a walk on the once-wild east side of Tenth Avenue, and at the corner of 18th Street you will find this cozy and romantic bistro. Once inside (the entrance is actually on 18th Street), the warmth and energy draw you in. The rich, rouge walls that envelop you and the snug seating combine to create a wonderful balance that feels intimate, not intrusive, and lively without being bustling.

The daily menu is brought to your table on a chalkboard, one of the endearing and authentic touches at La Luncheonette that replace those all-too-prevalent "bistro" trappings, such as piles of Pernod bottles and assorted faux-discolored mirrors. Although for me the ambience is what sets La Luncheonette apart, of course the food is what keeps people coming back, and the artichoke vinaigrette, sautéed foie gras, cassoulet, lamb sausage and roast rack of lamb are all wonderful.

Directly across Tenth Avenue is the infamous Roxy Night Club, and although the lines for La Luncheonette will thankfully never compare, trying to get a seating without a reservation may leave you staring across the street at the theatrical throngs also awaiting admittance.

Les Halles
Gramercy Park/Flatiron District
411 Park Avenue South, between 28th and 29th Sts.
(212) 679-4111
$$

Despite all the notoriety gained with the publication of *Kitchen Confidential,* a revealing and thoroughly irreverent look at the restaurant business by Executive Chef Anthony Bourdain—a part-time novelist, part-time *enfant terrible* of the food world—Les Halles remains a terrific place to get straight-ahead brasserie food. If you're counting your cholesterol, though, be advised: It is nearly impossible to order a "heart-healthy" meal here.

Appetizers range from a tasty salad made with frisée and lardons to the dreaded *tartiflette,* a concoction of potatoes, bacon, and massive amounts of Reblochon cheese. It is sufficient as a meal for one, even if you are fairly hungry.

Main courses are typical fare—a hanger steak deftly prepared, *boudin noir* (blood sausage) for the adventurous, roast chicken, or mussels, all accompanied by excellent steak frites. A delightful steak tartare can be had as well, and if you are lucky enough to be at Les Halles when the hordes are not, you can get all kinds of specials in your steak tartare upon request.

And you can't get in or out of Les Halles without passing the French-style butcher shop in the front. "If you like what you ate, take some more home and cook it yourself" seems to be the message here, and it's not a bad idea.

Other Location
15 John Street, between Broadway and Nassau St.; (212) 285-8585

RESTAURANTS

Alain Ducasse
Clinton
The Essex House
155 West 58th Street, between Sixth and Seventh Aves.
(212) 265-7300

Open for lunch Thursday–Friday, for dinner Monday–Saturday;
   closed Sunday
$$$$ (prix fixe)

In June 2000, Alain Ducasse, the internationally renowned chef of two Michelin-starred restaurants in Paris and Monte Carlo, opened his first American fine-dining restaurant at the Essex House. His American out-post has not missed a step compared to its older brothers: the *New York Times* gave it four stars, and *Bon Appetit* rated Ducasse "Chef of the Year" in 2001. The goal of the visually ornate restaurant is to use only the finest local produce: more than 95 percent of the ingredients on the menu are sourced in this way. The dining room seats 65 (with a staff of 55!), but the restaurant also boasts a lounge, a private dining room, and a chef's table. There is only one serving per evening, at which diners can feast on unbelievable Mediterranean-influenced and contemporary classic cuisine ranging from three- to six-course prix fixe tasting menus. Lunch is a relative bargain for $65. Because of Ducasse's dedication to the best produce, the salad, which is mixed in front of you, might be worth the price of lunch in and of itself! I wish I could say I ate there more than once because it is so spectacular (which I would expect for what I paid), but what I tasted I can recommend: the chicken served with Louisiana crawfish and morels and the halibut with roasted figs. The cheese, which comes on one of many carts, boasts a dizzying selection. The desserts transport you to another place. It's expensive, but as the French themselves say, *c'est la vie!*

Chanterelle
Tribeca

2 Harrison Street at Hudson St.
(212) 966-6960
Closed Sunday
$$$$ (prix fixe)

One of the last independent haute cuisine restaurants in the city, Chanterelle is the grand dame of New York City restaurants. Opened in 1979 by David and Karen Waltuck, Chanterelle has continued to shine for twenty-three years by settling for nothing but the best. Located just blocks from Ground Zero at the former World Trade Center site, the restaurant has weathered the events of September 11, 2001, like most New Yorkers: with class, dedication, defiance, and a stiff upper lip.

Combining classic French cuisine with modern accessibility of ingredi-ents, David Waltuck has created a truly special selection of entrées to delight his patrons. The menu changes often and never fails to astound the palate. Past works of genius include a ravioli and *brandade* with saffron-braised leeks, tomato, and parsley; sweetbreads with sherry vinegar and fresh chanterelle mushrooms; Provençal *pistou* with grilled white tuna; and a Valrhona chocolate soufflé with black mint ice cream. The simplicity of the menu and the presentation of the food shows where this kitchen's priorities lie. The use of exceptional local produce and the fine sauce preparation are where Chanterelle stands head and shoulders above the crowd.

Service is impeccable at Chanterelle—it rained on our last visit there, and the hostess offered us an umbrella for our walk home. A tome of a wine list is also available for perusal, though an expert sommelier will gladly help you choose the perfect wines to complement your meal. Overall, Chanterelle provides its patrons with a gustatory experience to match the best France has to offer.

Daniel
East Side
60 East 65th Street, between Madison and Park Aves.
(212) 288-0033
Closed Sunday
$$$$ (prix fixe)

The flagship of Daniel Boulud's empire of fine cuisine, Restaurant Daniel is a world-class dining experience. From the moment you enter the grand lobby, Daniel transports you to a world where culinary masterpieces and sumptuousness are the standard, and nothing less is possible.

The 18-foot ceilings and bronze-studded mahogany doors are just part of the feast for the eye you'll encounter here. Daniel's Renaissance-era decor is truly exquisite. But even the impeccable surroundings nearly pale in comparison to the food. Chef Boulud's seasonally driven creations are always flawless. Nothing warms you in winter like roast squab stuffed with fois gras and black truffles, winter vegetables, and chestnuts. In the heat of the summer, a chilled Cavaillon melon velouté with Gulf shrimp, lemongrass, kaffir lime leaves, and purple basil soothes the palate and cools the soul. The combinations are both classical and experimental, and they all hit right on the mark.

Perhaps the secret to Boulud's success is that he himself is a friendly, approachable man. He's most often on hand at the restaurant, ensuring that the service and food are to his exacting specifications.

Combine this luxury with fine European service and a first-class wine list, and it is no surprise that Daniel is one of New York's, America's, and the world's top dining experiences.

Jean Georges
West Side
Trump International Hotel
One Central Park West, between 60th and 61st Sts.
(212) 299-3900
Closed Sunday
$$$$

We have been to this restaurant three times, and each time we've left breathless. Jean Georges has two dining areas: a formal one with only six to eight tables and a less formal one called Nougatine, which includes a lovely bar. It is possible to order the prix fixe menu of the formal dining room at Nougatine as long as the whole table participates and as long as someone at the table is rich! Jean Georges is obviously French, but it does not serve "stuffy classical" food—it is very imaginative and very fresh, worth every nickel. When you call for a reservation, the hostess will often ask if you are dining there for a special occasion. We went there for our anniversary and, when dessert came out, a candle was in our cake with the words "Happy Anniversary" written on it. A small, simple detail, perhaps, but still a nice gesture.

Needless to say, the service is superb: If your eyes ever rise above the horizontal, a waiter materializes to get you whatever you need. Try the filet mignon and anything with foie gras in it. And then, when you get home, open the dictionary and look under the word *sin*—we'll bet you will find a picture of your foie gras!

La Caravelle
Clinton
33 West 55th Street, between Fifth and Sixth Aves.
(212) 586-4252
Closed Sunday
$$$$ (prix fixe)

New York is a city teeming with hot restaurants where people trot out their finery to be seen and the food contains an array of the trendiest international ingredients. Often they are noisy playgrounds for the young and with-it. They have no sense of history.

There are, of course, exceptions. There are elegant French restaurants of great price with starry chefs, Italian restaurants of tradition, restaurants based on one specialty—seafood or steak—and an increasing number of good eateries of every ethnicity known to man.

After a series of such meals, I crave a grown-up experience with excellent food that is served with charm but also with professional reticence. In such a mood, I often turn to La Caravelle, which taught me about fine restaurant dining. The year was 1960, the year they opened. I was twenty-seven. I had been to good restaurants with my parents; but this was my first splurge on my own. I must have appeared impossibly young and naive among the Kennedys and their ilk, who were the clientele. I was greeted with courtesy and charm by those two graduates of Henri Soule, the owners along with Chef Roger Fessaguet, Robert Meyzen, and Fred Decre.

The food was classically French: *quenelles de brochet,* chicken with a mushroom and Champagne sauce, and a serving wagon with the dish of the day, usually a roast with various puréed vegetables. It was heaven.

Today, the owners since 1984, Rita and Andre Jammet, and their new chef, Troy Dupuy, still serve *quenelles.* Alas, in our more timid times they are a main course, not a starter. These excellent professionals have added some updated and lighter dishes—often fish. There are more modestly priced wines than there were in the old days. The enchanting murals of Paris by Jean Pages survive, although the velour of the banquettes has been subtly toned from restaurant red to coral to go with the murals.

If some famous New Yorker of yore like the artist and writer Ludwig Bemelmans were to walk through the door and sit down to enjoy a meal at La Caravelle, it would probably not even raise an eyebrow. Go, and treat yourself to a splendid evening of civilization.

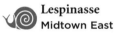

Lespinasse
Midtown East

St. Regis Hotel
2 East 55th Street, between Fifth and Madison Aves.
(212) 339-6719
$$$$

Since 1991, Lespinasse has occupied an odd position in New York: a relatively young restaurant bedecked in the fine robes of an old-school French restaurant—folded in turn into the regalia of the St. Regis Hotel.

Named after Mademoiselle de Lespinasse, the hostess of a famous Parisian salon during the reign of Louis XV, the tradition of nobles and diplomats dining on precious delicacies, including foie gras, caviar, and truffles, lives on. Appropriately enough, with Chef Christian Delouvrier's signature menu of *terroir* cooking redolent of southwestern France, diners have come to depend upon a very high standard of service, elegant ambience, and luxurious ingredients. Many dishes perform as prodigal paradigms of French haute cuisine, from a ragout of seasonal baby vegetables to a decadent risotto inundated with a blizzard of black truffle shavings. Four stars don't come easily in New York, but Delouvrier earned them from the *New York Times* and hasn't looked back since.

NOTABLE

BISTROS & BRASSERIES

Artisanal
Murray Hill
2 Park Avenue at 32nd Street
(212) 725-8585
$$$

One of the best cheese selections in the city, constantly changing and evolving. Friendly atmosphere with excellent bistro fare, fondues, and an extensive selection of wines available by the glass. See also Dairy, p. 251

Bistrot Margot
Chinatown/Little Italy
26 Prince Street, between Elizabeth and Mott Sts.
(212) 274-1027
$$

Bistrot Margot is easy to miss, with just a small window and door on the street. This place is bigger than it appears, but the linked small rooms preserve a sense of intimacy. The wine list is a model for this kind of restaurant, with no fewer than seven wines available by the glass. Main dishes include poached salmon with lentils dressed with *pistou; boudin blanc* with mashed potatoes and caramelized onions; and pork with gratinéed potatoes and ratatouille.

JoJo
East Side
160 East 64th Street, between Lexington and Third Aves.
(212) 223-5656
$$$

Jean-Georges Vongerichten's first restaurant recently underwent a million-dollar makeover, and has added a sexy decor to its fantastic menu. His creative associations of ingredients give a unique twist to classic French bistro fare, such as the seared venison or the buttery lobster.

L'Absinthe
Lenox Hill
227 East 67th Street, between Second and Third Aves.

(212) 794-4950
$$$

This expensive brasserie serves a "chef invention" every day, but also such standards as beef tartare, rabbit, pork, and lamb. Many of the ingredients are organic and the wine list is extensive. The dessert soufflé changes daily.

L'Acajou
Chelsea
53 West 19th Street, between Fifth and Sixth Aves.
(212) 645-1706
Closed Sunday
$$$

Co-owned by the same owner as Raoul's, L'Acajou changes the menu seven times a year—four times for the seasons and three times for special festival menus, in which Chef Bernie Pitt features products from the Loire Valley, Rhône Valley, and Alsace.

Le Jardin Bistro
Chinatown/Little Italy
25 Cleveland Place at Spring St.
(212) 343-9599
$$

This restaurant's beautiful garden, adorned with thick vines, exudes the atmosphere of a summer Provence haven. The food is fresh and full of simple pleasures, such as a perfectly seasoned steak tartare or a *bavette l'échalotte* (hanger steak with caramelized shallots), and the wine list is remarkable.

Le Tableau
East Village
511 East 5th Street, between Aves. A and B
(212) 260-1333
Dinner only
$$

The small dining room seats about three dozen persons. Main dishes are solid bistro fare—veal shank in enriched demi-glace sauce, served with cheese-flavored potatoes; bouillabaisse; whole boneless striped bass stuffed with crab; rack of lamb. Prix fixe tasting menus are also available at a very fair cost.

Provence
Soho
38 MacDougal Street at Prince St.
(212) 475-7500
$$

At its cute corner location in the West Village, Provence features a quaint garden and serves up consistent southern French fare.

Prune
See Brunch, p. 176.

Quatorze Bis
Lenox Hill
323 East 79th Street, between First and Second Aves.
(212) 535-1414
$$$

You'll find a quality *choucroute* plate and good steak and bearnaise sauce at this nice but expensive neighborhood bistro.

Raoul's
Soho
180 Prince Street, between Sullivan and Thompson Sts.
(212) 966-3518
Dinner only; open to 2:00 A.M.
$$$

An old Soho standby with a romantic setting and patio seating, Raoul's is known for its good steak au poivre. Being there late at night makes you feel like you're in a Woody Allen film.

26 Seats
East Village
168 Avenue B, between 10th and 11th Sts.
(212) 677-4787
Dinner only; closed Monday
$$

Both the seating and the menu are somewhat limited, but 26 Seats offers a comfortable dining experience with an unapologetic and very un-PC policy on smoking (they're for it).

RESTAURANTS

Bouley
Tribeca

120 West Broadway at Duane St.
(212) 964-2525
$$$$

The good news is that David Bouley is back in the kitchen; the bad news is the bakery he used to operate at this location has closed. Bouley's energy is now focused exclusively on the kitchen and on refining the French classics we love. His support of the Greenmarket and insistence on freshness and quality ingredients have become the restaurant's trademark. The steamed organic chicken with black truffle is a standout dish, both rich and light at the same time.

Le Bernardin
See Fish and Seafood, p. 187.

Le Cirque 2000
Midtown East

New York Palace Hotel
455 Madison Avenue, between 50th and 51st Sts.
(212) 303-7788
Dinner only
$$$$

The First Family of New York City restaurants are the Maccionis; Sirio and his sons Mauro, Marco, and Mario extend their warm and gracious hospitality at this elegant and refined, yet easy and un-self-conscious restaurant. The food is uniformly well prepared and classic more than overtly creative; but the quality of service and overall experience are the real reasons to dine here.

Le Refuge Inn
City Island, Bronx

620 City Island Avenue at Sutherland St.
(718) 885-2478
6 train to Pelham Bay Park, then Bx29 bus to Sutherland St.
Dinner only; closed Monday–Tuesday
$$$$ (prix fixe)

Exquisite northern French food in a restored nineteenth-century sea captain's house owned by flutist-chef Pierre Saint-Denis. The nine-room inn makes for a nice getaway that seems far from downtown; overnight guests get an especially good deal at dinner, which otherwise runs around $45 per person, excluding wine. The inn also hosts chamber music and serves tea from 12:30 to 1:30 P.M. on Sunday for $15 per person.

Other Location

Le Refuge, 166 East 82nd Street, between Lexington and Third
    Aves.; (212) 861-4505

Picholine
West Side

35 West 64th Street, between Broadway and Central Park West
(212) 724-8585
$$$$

Picholine's chef-owner Terrence Brennan has set a new standard for the cheese course in New York. The crowd here is elegant—it's a perfect place to visit before a night at Lincoln Center or Carnegie Hall.

THE FUTURE STARS OF FRENCH CUISINE

The French Culinary Institute is New York City's pre-eminent training ground for beginning chefs, pastry cooks, and artisanal bread bakers, and it also runs L'École, a popular, spacious, and reasonably priced French restaurant on its premises at the edge of Soho.

L'École cooks are, in fact, the FCI's advanced students, who learn from FCI's master chefs (Jacques Pepin, Alain Sailhac, Andre Soltner, and Jacques Torres). They have learned the techniques of the professional French kitchen (knife skills, cooking methods, the basic sauces, etc.) in the early stages of their schooling, and now, under their chef-instructors' strict direction, they cook for the public.

The restaurant serves weekday lunches and prix-fixe multicourse dinners Monday through Saturday. It's always wise to call ahead, not only because L'École is usually well filled, but also because it closes at regular intervals to accommodate FCI's final cooking examinations, which are judged by panels of culinary luminaries who taste in the dining room while the students give their individual all to produce a variety of classical and currently fashionable French dishes that will be rated for presentation (40 percent of the grade) and degustation (60 percent of the grade).

This demanding examination system works to the advantage of L'École's customers because the test includes consommés, savory pastry dishes, seafood and meat sautés, roasts, braises, and the elegant hot and cold desserts—the same dishes the students have made to order for lunch or dinner service. So their future can hinge on how well they cook for you.

Also worth noting: The dining room is professionally staffed (the students just cook); the kitchen uses only top-quality ingredients; and the wine list is more extensive and free of pitfalls than lists in many pricier places.

—*Andy Birsh*

L'École
Soho
462 Broadway at Grand Street
(212) 219-3300
Closed Sunday
$$$ (prix fixe)

Danube *(Austrian)*
Tribeca
30 Hudson Street at Duane St.
(212) 791-3771
$$$$

Nowhere else in New York is Austrian food enjoyed in such unapologetic opulence. At Danube, the walls bear paintings that pay homage to Gustav Klimt and the ceiling is crowned with a delicately wrought web of gold-leafed vines; the banquettes are deep and expansive, and tasseled lamps cast creamy light on all the gold and jewel-like colors.

The staff is young and elegant, in both clothing and accents, and the service is attentive yet unobtrusive. While David Bouley is notorious for being a stubborn and egotistical perfectionist, his talent, taste, and sense of style have produced an unimpeachable fine-dining experience at Danube—and, in case you're still feeling ambivalent, the numerous complementary dishes and *amuse-bouches* that are always presented will win you over.

Perhaps Danube's only weakness is that there are not more traditional Austrian dishes to choose from on the menu; but without calling undue attention to itself, each traditionally styled option, whether it is *Wiener schnitzel* or braised beef cheeks, is accompanied by authentic and well-executed touches, including tiny *spaetzle* (German pasta), potato salad, and cucumbers in cream. An oxtail consommé holds tiny aromatic dumplings and a medallion of creamy marrow in its absurdly rich broth; delicate ravioli filled with "high-altitude Austrian cheese" are bathed in a foam of foie gras and a tumble of wild mushrooms.

A thoughtful and extensive wine list includes numerous Austrian, Hungarian, and Balkan choices, and while the dessert menu is not noticeably Austrian, it will tempt even those who normally eschew sweets.

Hallo Berlin *(German)*
Clinton
402 West 51st Street at Ninth Ave.
(212) 541-6248
$

Billed on the menu as "New York's Wurst Restaurant," Hallo Berlin is actually sure to please (as long as you don't have a heart condition). Owner Rolf Babiel arrived in the U. S. from Germany in 1980 and opened a push cart serving German sausages (as well as a selection of other items) on the corner of 54th Street and Fifth Avenue. He chose that corner because of its close proximity to the offices of Lufthansa Airlines, which was filled with employees desperate for a taste of their homeland. The café opened in

1995 and features a full array of German tradition. The biggest draws include the Berliner-Currywurst (a standard midnight snack in Berlin made of beef), Bratwurst (pork), Bauemwurst (beef and pork), and Bavarianwurst (veal), with a choice of toppings that include sauerkraut, red cabbage, onions, and mustard. Rolf will tell you that it is best to eat the sausage separate from the bread, but even he realizes that in this era, where frenzy is often mistaken for efficiency, this is not always possible.

Whether it is the tiny café on West 51st, the "beer hall" on Tenth Avenue, or a dog on the run from the push cart, make it a point to drop by and say "Hallo."

Other Locations
626 Tenth Avenue at 44th St.; (212) 977-1944
Hallo Berlin push cart, corner 54th Street and Fifth Avenue

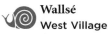 **Wallsé** *(Austrian)*
West Village
344 West 11th Street at Washington St.
(212) 352-2300
$$$

Pickled ramps with coriander and mustard seed greeted me at the bar of this jewel of a restaurant in the heart of the West Village. After finishing my glass of Gewürztraminer, which was recommended by a very knowledge-able bartender, I made my way to the stylish but relaxed backroom, which looks out to West 11th Street. The *spaetzle* (handmade German pasta) with duck was a light and delicious lead-in to the hearty *Wiener schnitzel* served with cucumber salad and lingonberries on the side. I also managed to sneak a taste of the *Palatschinken* (crêpes) with smoked trout, apples, red onions, and horseradish, and the Viennese *Rostbraten,* which is produced in upstate New York. Both were delicious. The Austrian wine selection is just as rich. The strudel missed something, but on the whole Wallsé is def-initely worth a visit. If you don't feel like walking so far west, some New Yorkers will tell you that the chef's Upper East Side establishment, Café Sabarsky, located in the Neue Gallerie, is even more worthy of a visit.

Other Location
Café Sabarsky, 1048 Fifth Avenue; (212) 628-6200. Closed Tuesday

Zum Schneider *(German)*
East Village
107-109 Avenue C at 7th St.
(212) 598-1098
$$ (Cash only)

All food is under $20 at this East Village hangout. The all-German beer selection is excellent, including a dozen on draft and many more in bottle, each one served in appropriate glasses. A very cool place to be, the tables are set up family-style with benches for seating. With music playing in the background, you will rub shoulders with a young and hip crowd at Zum. Boasting one of the best *Wiener schnitzel* in town (served with potato salad and cucumber salad), you will also find numerous delicious sausages as well as seasonal specials on the menu, such as salads in summer and roasts in winter. Zum also organizes special events for important rites of passage such as Octoberfest, Carnival, and the World Cup (although it might be better to go visit our Brazilian picks for the soccer finals). For founding this fun German restaurant, we all say to owner Sylvester Schneider, *"Danke schön."*

Zum Stammtisch   *(German)*
Glendale, Queens
69-46 Myrtle Avenue at Cooper Ave.
(718) 386-3014
Subway: L to Myrtle Ave.; M to Wyckoff Ave.
$$

Walking into Zum Stammtisch, there is an air of bonhomie and affability that only increases as the night wears on. *Stammtisch* means "family table," and it's easy to see that many of the guests are regulars; the restaurant has been serving traditional German food for the past thirty years: Founded in 1972 by John Lehner, the restaurant is now run by his sons Hans and Werner. The decor is German chalet-style—all dark wood, with boar and moose heads hanging from the walls. Waitresses bustle to and fro with enormous plates of food. The beer-barrel tables and German folk music help set the tone for the evening.

The bar has a nice selection of beers, but the focus of the evening has to be the food. Everything on the menu looks delicious, but our server made us comfortable with some suggestions. The goulash soup is spicy with paprika and is an excellent start to the meal. The herring in cream sauce is surprisingly fresh compared to the herring available in delis all over the city. The smoked trout with horseradish sauce is moist and delicate, just as the menu promises.

When my platter of *sauerbraten* was set in front of me, I was astounded by the size of my portion. *Sauerbraten* is one of Germany's most famous dishes, and this one is very good, with a sweet-and-sour sauce. The potato dumplings are a homey touch. Zum Stammtisch is well known for its *jaegerschnitzel,* a very generous veal cutlet breaded and served with a mushroom sauce.

The main reason to go to Zum Stammtisch, though, is the apple strudel, made with real strudel dough instead of phyllo. According to tradition, the dough is stretched by hand until it is thin enough to read a newspaper through. The strudel is stuffed with mounds of caramelized apple scented with cinnamon.

NOTABLE

Café Steinhof   (Austrian)
Park Slope, Brooklyn
422 Seventh Avenue at 14th St.
(718) 369-7776
Subway: F to 15th St.–Prospect Park
$

A recent addition to the Park Slope restaurant scene, Café Steinhof features hearty, inexpensive Austrian food in a relaxed, publike atmosphere.

Heidelberg   (German)
Upper East Side
1648 Second Avenue, between 85th and 86th Sts.
(212) 628-2332
$$

This Old World Yorkville restaurant has been serving hearty German fare for half a century. Here you will find a great long bar where you can drink big cold mugs of dark German beer and sample excellent wursts, many made by neighborhood butcher Schaller & Weber.

Killmeyer's Old Bavaria Inn   (German)
Staten Island
4254 Arthur Kill Road at Sharrotts Rd.
(718) 984-1202
Staten Island Ferry, then S74 bus to Sharrotts Rd.
$$$

Killmeyer's is located in a beautiful old beer hall that's nearly 150 years old. Here you will find great traditional German cuisine such as *Wiener schnitzel* and *sweinerbraten*. Ingredients such as sauerkraut, bread dumplings, potato dumplings, and sweet German mustard are imported from Germany. Red cabbage is made from scratch. The inn serves more than 100 different beers, two-thirds of which are German.

The Silver Swan   *(German)*
Gramercy Park/Flatiron District
41 East 20th Street, between Broadway and Park Ave. South
(212) 254-3611
$$$

Founded in December of 1991, the Swan specializes in *Wiener schnitzel,* *sauerbraten,* wild boar, and venison. Goose is served during the holidays and is so fresh it almost flies out of the restaurant. The atmosphere is as homey as an English (or should we say German) drawing room. Many people patronize the bar in front, which serves some 70 types of beer, including wheat beers and *rauchbier* (brewed with smoked malt).

ELIZABETH LITTLES

GREEK

Metsovo
West Side
65 West 70th Street at Columbus Ave.
(212) 873-2300
Dinner only
$$

Although quite unassuming from the outside, Metsovo's romantic charm will transport you to a time when life was a bit simpler. This rustic Greek tavern just off 70th Street on the West Side offers a welcome respite from the heavily trodden Columbus Avenue. The staff at Metsovo takes great care to ensure that your dining experience is truly fit for the gods. The service is attentive and every dish is prepared with divine precision. Zeus himself would be envious of the meticulous attention paid to creating an exceptionally enjoyable atmosphere with dim candlelight and soft Greek music. Dionysus, the god of wine, could not have created a more balanced wine list, offering premium wines from Greece and elsewhere, including the distinct Retsina, a Greek white with bold oak undertones. The *mezedes,* a selection of hot or cold hors d'oeuvres served on a two-level stand, are especially recommended for those who want to experience the widest variety of flavors. Main courses include traditional Greek selections such as shepherd's pie and myriad lamb and feta cheese–based dishes. Poseidon, the god of the seas, could not be left out and would easily be appeased by Metsovo's large selection of fresh fish, lightly grilled with olive oil and lemon. The celestial feast cannot end until you have one of the several desserts accompanied by a cup of Greek coffee.

Molyvos
Clinton
871 Seventh Avenue near 55th St.
(212) 582-7500
$$$

Around the corner from Carnegie Hall sits Molyvos, a temple to Greek cuisine and cooking both modern and traditional. Based on the home-style cooking of Greece, the menu reflects the freshest ingredients of the season. Day-boat fish; grilled baby octopus with olives, fennel, lemon, and oregano; as well as house-made *trahana,* phyllo, and spoon sweets highlight an overwhelming number of exciting and intriguing dishes. In addition to award-winning fare, Molyvos, which is the name of the owner's hometown, has an extensive collection of Greek wines from Macedonia to the Peleponnese and the Aegean islands, as well as a comprehensive selection of ouzos. Wines from other regions around the world are also featured on the wine list. *Mezedes,* smaller tastings, are available and are best enjoyed in the café, which provides a comfortable and refreshing atmosphere looking out onto Seventh Avenue.

Snack
Soho
105 Thompson Street, between Prince and Spring Sts.
(212) 925-1040
$ (Cash only)

In the frenzy of fashionable restaurants that Soho has become, who would have expected such a modest—and marvelous—authentic ethnic eatery? With only five tables, ten chairs, and a tiny kitchen, Snack relies heavily on slow-braised peasant dishes that actually improve in flavor in the time spent resting on the steam table. The restaurant turns out soups, *mezedes,* sandwiches, pita, *boureki,* and other Greek specialties with the intense, unique flavors of the Adriatic.

Favorite dishes include *avgolemono* (chicken soup with lemon and orzo), salt cod cakes, vegetable and "soaked bread" salad, and *melitzano salata* (eggplant purée).

If the place is busy, as it frequently is, order your food to go and take it to the small park and playground nearby on Thompson Street, which has plenty of picnic tables and no lines.

Trata
Lenox Hill
1331 Second Avenue, between 70th and 71st Sts.
(212) 535-3800
$$

Gregory Zapatis, the executive chef and co-owner of Trata, uses some of his mother's and grandmother's recipes, taken from a cookbook that his great-grandmother wrote back in 1891. Zapatis's father was a fisherman back in Kefalonia, so it's no surprise that there are pictures of Greek fishing villages in the restaurant, and a big counter with the catch of the day iced down for customers to inspect on the way in.

Trata (the name refers to the Greek fishing boats) feels a bit like your formal dining room at home—that is, if your home were open to the noisy comings and goings of Second Avenue street life. Customers get bowls of marinated olives and grilled bread to accompany the *mezedes,* or appetizers. Diners ordering wisely could make a light and satisfying meal from these alone. The *spanakopita* is excellent, perhaps the best we've ever had, with a fresh herby taste. The char-grilled octopus sprinkled with lemon juice is typical of many Greek restaurants; here it's done master-fully. And the *saganaki,* or fried kasseri cheese, is a wonderfully complex taste sensation with a crispy, cheesy consistency. (Our teenage dining companion compared the taste to Cheese Puffs; if so, they'd be the best damn Cheese Puffs on Earth.)

For entrées you can't go wrong with one of the seasonal char-grilled fish such as loup de mer, snapper, Arctic char, halibut, or rascasse (scor-pion fish). *Kakavia* is a centuries-old Greek dish, a sort of bouillabaisse traditionally made from the leftovers of the day's catch that couldn't be sold at market; these are cooked with tomatoes, onions, garlic, and herbs. That's the hallmark of most native cuisines—the ability to transform odds and ends almost magically into something absolutely delicious.

NOTABLE

Christos Hasapo-Taverna
See Steak Houses, p. 214.

Estiatorio Milos
Theater District
125 West 55th Street, between Sixth and Seventh Aves.
(212) 245-7400
$$$$

Milos is the New York sibling of chef-owner Costas Spiliadis's restaurant in Montreal. The fish is incredibly fresh and well prepared here, but perfect quality and presentation doesn't come cheap; prices run more than $30 per pound for fish, and most fish are large enough that you'll want to share.

Milos is definitely the most extravagant Greek dining experience you can have in New York. Is it that much better than the many other fine Greek places that char-grill their seafood? We doubt it, but it's worth a try to make up your own mind.

Ithaka
West Village
48 Barrow Street, between Bedford and Bleecker Sts.
(212) 727-8886
$$

Ithaka is located in a brownstone on a quiet street in the West Village. For thirty years, Chef Harris Hadjiparaskeves has been doing traditional Greek home cooking, along with his business partner, Sam Sirimouzes, who owns the Ninth Avenue International Grocery and Meat Market (see p. 280), a shop that specializes in Mediterranean products.

Periyali
Gramercy Park/Flatiron District
35 West 20th Street, between Fifth and Sixth Aves.
(212) 463-7890
Closed Sunday
$$$

In Greek *periyali* translates, somewhat more poetically, to "seashore" or "strand." Yet Periyali reflects a wide range of Greek country cooking, not just seafood. Appetizers include *glikadakia,* sautéed sweetbreads served in a sauce over warm "giant beans" *(gigandes).* For entrées, there's a naturally farmed roast chicken, as well as *kouneli stefado,* rabbit stewed in tomato with red wine and pearl onions.

Telly's Taverna
Astoria, Queens
28-13 23rd Avenue, between 28th and 29th Sts.
(718) 728-9056
Subway: N, W to Astoria-Ditmars Blvd.
$$ (Cash only)

Astoria is home to a large Greek community, and Telly's is one of the most popular spots in the neighborhood for Greeks and non-Greeks alike who value no-nonsense, well-prepared grilled meats, fish, and seafood.

INDIAN & PAKISTANI

Bukhara _(Pakistani)_
Midwood, Brooklyn
788 Coney Island Avenue at Foster Ave.
(718) 462-6922
Subway: Q local to Ave. H
Open 24 hours
$

The block Bukhara calls home is nicknamed "Little Pakistan" after the immigrants who first started to move into the Midwood neighborhood of Brooklyn in the 1980s. Bukhara takes its position in the middle of the block seriously—it is as much neighborhood center as restaurant. A sumptuous banquet hall provides a place for residents to share community concerns, as they did at a meeting with government officials to discuss fears about anti-Pakistan sentiments in the wake of September 11th. The rest of this popular restaurant's business is mostly takeout, though there are a few tables where you can settle in to watch Pakistani soap operas with your meal.

Bukhara has developed a reputation for achingly sweet carrot _halwa_ and other desserts, scooped from a large tray and sold by the pound. But the main courses go beyond the requisite kebabs (which are nonetheless assertively flavored with large flakes of red pepper and can be served sandwich-style with peppery white dressing or atop rice with cumin seeds). The servers are a bit reticent, so you may have to employ the guess-and-point method, but it's worth the effort to discover chicken _achari,_ a hot-and-sour specialty, and fish curry.

Chola _(Indian)_
East Side
232 East 58th Street, between Second and Third Aves.
(212) 688-4619
$$

On a Midtown block chock-full of Indian restaurants, with the celebrity sparkle of Dawat just a _samosa's_ throw away, it's no wonder if Chola sometimes seems to be trying too hard. The plush carpeting and advertisement of an "executive lunch buffet" set a certain mood, and the servers need only the slightest excuse to go the extra mile, explaining this dish or bringing a sample of that one. But best of all, it's clear that Chef Narayan Swami is trying hard in the kitchen, drawing a diverse group of eaters that includes not only the previously mentioned executives but the stroller set, too. Even dishes common to the city's Indian restaurant are raised a notch by their bright, fresh flavors and texture variations. _Sag paneer_ is a gift to spinach-lovers, a big contrast to the unappetizing sludge with decidedly un-cheeselike white chunks that dish frequently connotes. Other vegetable specialties, such as pumpkin *kootu* in a yogurt and coconut sauce, are equally worthy of attention, as are Chola meat favorites, including *vindaloos* that come with heat warnings and chicken sauced with mango chutney. Given Chola's huge menu, which rambles across the subcontinent (many items specify their origin), an especially rewarding way to gorge is at the weekend brunch, an extension of the weekday lunch buffet that boasts an ever-changing selection of dishes and condiments, including a stuffed *poori* bar and a sour, hot, and biting pickled lemon chutney with whole cloves of garlic.

Dawat   *(Indian)*
East Side
210 East 58th Street, between Second and Third Aves.
(212) 355-7555
$$$

Dawat means "invitation to a feast," and the tuxedoed servers are determined to bring you one, whether you thought you wanted to completely cover the tablecloth with gold dishes or not. After selecting a main course, be prepared for prompting: Would you like the special rice, with nuts and raisins? A side dish of "dry" gingery cauliflower? *Naan* topped with garlic or stuffed with caramelized onions? The correct response is yes, please, and some minced lamb *samosas,* too. The multitalented Madhur Jaffrey, prolific author of Indian and vegetarian cookbooks and children's books, and film actress, consulted on Dawat's menu; many menu items are attributed to her own recipes. Jaffrey's knack for adapting traditional recipes to utilize available ingredients, along with a true appreciation for vegetables shines through in *farasvi bhaji,* green beans and split peas cooked with coconut, cumin, coriander, and other flavorings. Seafood, whether steamed, sauced, or right out of the *tandoor* oven, is another highlight on the menu. "Fish is our national dish," one server said proudly as he placed a bowl of tilefish in fragrant mustard oil sauce on the table. Overwhelmed by the too many, too good choices? Ann Marie, the on-site tarot card reader, might be able to help. Our prediction: You'll be back again soon.

Grameen   *(Bangladeshi)*
Jackson Heights, Queens
75-18 37th Avenue
(718) 505-4083
Subway: E, F, R, V, G to Jackson Heights–Roosevelt Ave.; 7 to
    74th St.–Broadway
$

A riot of ripe-to-bursting mangoes, melons, bananas, and other fruits crowds the window of Grameen, a peaceful Bangladeshi eatery that seems out of place amid the Indian buffets that line the blocks. The tantalizing juice bar, ice cream freezer, and dessert case are just inside the entrance, and Grameen will package your meal for takeout, but the gentle atmosphere and solicitous servers deserve to be appreciated at a slower pace. The tables seem to be arranged in a bright village square, between nearby thatched roofs. Colorful woven panels decorate one wall, the curtains of imaginary windows another, and intricately embroidered fabrics are draped across the ceiling.

The food, too, has a homey feel: Fish *biryani* is a house specialty, with fish *kofta* (fried nuggets of ground fish, aromatics, and spice) and shrimp hidden like small treasures in a plate of basmati rice. Chunky mashed eggplant *bhorta* provides a complementary bitter heat. A whole-wheat *porata* is filled with ground beef for another traditional side dish or appetizer. After your meal, lean back, sip a yogurt smoothie, and fortify yourself for the inevitable moment when you must leave Grameen's calming environs for the busy avenue outside.

Mirchi   *(Indian)*
West Village
29 Seventh Avenue South, between Morton and Bedford Sts.
(212) 414-0931
$$

Those who like their beer cold and their Indian hot aim for Mirchi, where the menu comes with a warning to diners accustomed to milder fare, and where martinis like the "Sassy Lassi" keep the joint hoppin'. Main dishes hail from all corners of India, but Mirchi's popularity has been built upon its creative appetizer list. *Chats* are described as "street vendor snacks," though it's doubtful that many of them could be consumed without a chair, fork, and firmly tucked napkin. The *samosa chat* is an elaborate, heaping concoction: a traditional *samosa* buried under chickpeas, onions, tomatoes, and streaks of tamarind chutney, mint and coriander sauce, and yogurt. Other first courses are prepared on the *tawa*, a wok-type pan that doubles as a steel drum when the metal spatulas start flying (how the onomatopoeic dish "tak-a-tak" got its name). The molded cakes of rice served with the entrées and a side of *raita* will help counter the fiery spices, but those who order the 30-chile *jaipuri lal maas* will just have to tough it out.

New Asha   *(Sri Lankan)*
Staten Island
322 Victory Boulevard
(718) 420-0649
Staten Island Ferry to St. George terminal, then MTA bus S61,
    S62, S66, S67, S91 to Cebra Ave.
$

Only a few short months ago, New Asha's customers were drawn mostly from among the Sri Lankan residents of Staten Island's north shore. But then Robert Sietsema placed New Asha at the tippy-top of the *Village Voice*'s "100 Best and Cheapest Asian Restaurants" list for New York City, and, well, the crowd's a little different now. "The first few weeks after the article, we didn't even know how to handle all the people," laughed Viji, whose family owns New Asha, New Pakland Groceries next door, and a Sri Lankan video rental business a few storefronts down the block. It's impossible to hyperbolize the freshness and quality of what Viji's brother Subhas calls "home-cooking." In Sri Lanka this means hot, hot, hot, but New Asha never sacrifices taste for heat. The innocent-looking *masala vada,* a fried yellow lentil patty, contains "all the spices," while another snacking favorite, the vegetable *roti,* is both mouth- and eye-watering. On the steam table, the dishes filled with dangerous-looking twigs are "black curries," named for their toasted spice blends. While the meaty versions are superb, there are choices for vegetarians as well: Yellow lentils cooked with coconut milk and curry leaves could well become the new comfort food.

 ## Tabla Bread Bar   *(Indian)*
Gramercy Park/Flatiron District
11 Madison Avenue at 25th St.
(212) 889-0667
$$

Bread Bar is as different from its upstairs counterpart, Tabla, as two sibs can be. Tabla is elegant and reserved, Bread Bar casual and raucous. Executive Chef Floyd Cardoz oversees both menus, but while Tabla's dinners are more accurately described as "Indian-inspired," Bread Bar offers fare that is somewhat less expensive and somewhat more traditional. Diners select from a variety of small and large dishes, supplementing them with street snacks, breads, *raitas,* and chutneys. Everything is served family-style, though families with tables this small might not attempt to serve quite so many baskets and bowls at the same time. No matter; it shouldn't take long to consume mussels and calamari seasoned with chiles, tamarind, and coconut, or to divide a crock of organic chicken *biryani.* Many of the menu's dishes utilize organic ingredients: the yogurt in the *raita* and desserts, the tomatoes in a "fried green tomato" special. More fruits and veggies are gathered from the city's Greenmarket, so there's no need to miss out on seasonal American favorites such as buttered corn on the cob (with a squeeze of lime juice and a dusting of cumin powder). And finally, sweet relief for those who don't usually frequent Indian restaurants for their desserts: Tahitian vanilla bean *kulfi,* a sort of Indian ice cream, and steaming, orange-scented doughnut holes are house favorites.

NOTABLE

Dosa Hutt   *(Indian)*
Flushing, Queens
45-63 Bowne Street, between 45th and Holly Aves.
(718) 961-6228
Subway: 7 to Flushing–Main St., then MTA bus Q17 to 45th Ave.
$

Could "South Indian fast food" be worth a trek to the end of the 7 line? Yes! *Medhu vada* is a kind of lentil doughnut that begs to be dunked in coconut chutney, while *masala vada* is a crunchy fried lentil patty that packs enough punch on its own. And then there are the excellent *dosas,* with many fragrant and delicious choices for fillings.

NY Dosas   *(Indian)*
Greenwich Village
Corner of West 4th Street and Sullivan Street
(917) 710-2092
$ (Cash only)

Those looking for something a little spicier than a hot dog in Washington Square Park are placing an order with Thiru Kumar, a former chef at Dosa Hutt, who will pack your *dosa* for traveling or park-bench eating.

Pakistan Tea House   *(Pakistani)*
Tribeca
176 Church Street, between Duane and Reade Sts.
(212) 240-9800
$

A friendly conversation with a cab driver led me to Pakistan Tea House, where combo meals priced well below $10 allow your pick of the big-spice dishes on the steam table. There's also a large selection of sweets and homemade *kulfi.*

Qasim   *(Indian)*
Chelsea
339 Ninth Avenue, between 29th and 30th Sts.
(212) 695-6556
Open 24 hours
$ (Cash only)

A unique selection of fresh and astonishingly tasty dishes that rarely appear in standard Indian restaurants. Try the excellent *tandoori* and *sag* special, a spicy purée of mustard greens and spinach.

Raga   *(Indian)*
East Village
433 East 6th Street, between First Ave. and Ave. A
(212) 388-0957
$$–$$$

Daily specials such as filet mignon with spicy blueberry sauce allow Chef Vijayan Francis to showcase seasonal ingredients in his Indian-accented cuisine.

Tamarind   *(Indian)*
Gramercy Park/Flatiron District
41-43 East 22nd Street, between Broadway and Park Ave. South
(212) 674-7400
$$$

So what if the spiced apple *samosas* with caramel sauce and ginger ice cream in this sleek, noisy Flatiron restaurant aren't *exactly* authentic? Fried spinach leaves have the delicacy of butterfly wings, and house-made *paneer* (curd cheese) is a chewy delight in any dish it touches.

ITALIAN

Al Di La Trattoria
Park Slope, Brooklyn
248 Fifth Avenue at Carroll St.
(718) 783-4565
Subway: M, N, R to Union St.
Dinner only; closed Tuesday
$$

Venetian Emiliano Coppa founded Al Di La in 1998 with his wife, Anna Klinger, a born-and-raised New Yorker. In a reversal of roles Anna is the one you will find working in the kitchen when you visit Al Di La; Emiliano works the front of the house. This Park Slope trattoria serves mostly Venetian food, but features other Northern Italian styles as well. When you go, be prepared to wait awhile, for Al Di La does not take reservations and only has room for 50 people. To make life easier on patrons, Emiliano encourages guests to have a drink at one of the many local watering holes, where he will call you when the table is ready. Plans are also underway to expand to include a bar at the restaurant. Specialties of the house include *fegato alla Veneziana* (a traditional Venetian recipe with liver and caramelized onions), rabbit with black olives and polenta, and *baccala* (codfish cooked in the Venetian style). For dessert try the *gianduiotto*, a chocolate and hazelnut ice cream served in a tall glass with whipped cream. *Wine Spectator* has awarded the Al Di La wine list its Award of Excellence. Remember to dedicate time to visit more than just the restaurant when you are there, for Park Slope is one of Brooklyn's more enjoyable neighborhoods to walk around and window-shop.

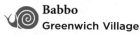 Babbo
Greenwich Village
110 Waverly Place, between MacDougal St. and Sixth Ave.
(212) 777-0303
Dinner only
$$$$

In the building that once housed New York's legendary Coach House, restaurateur/winemaker Joe Bastianich and chef/television personality Mario Batali founded Babbo in 1998. Batali is one of the nicest and most down-to-earth chefs you will ever meet, and he can often be found talking with patrons in the front of the house, or at the bar after his night is over, having a drink.

The goal of Babbo is not to replicate the Italian dining experience in Italy, but rather to replicate the spirit of it, emphasizing the use of local produce while keeping as close to the Earth as possible. Local New York State farmers, food producers, and the patrons who get to eat their fresh foods couldn't be happier! As Joe explains, "Babbo is our take on a contemporary Italian restaurant in New York City."

When you go, rest assured that everything will be delicious, but consider trying the beef cheek ravioli and the Calamari Sicilian Lifeguard Style ("If a Sicilian lifeguard cooked calamari, this is most likely how he would do it . . .")—it includes currants, capers, pignoli nuts, and olives. And for an antipasto, try the homemade *testa* (head cheese) with waxy potatoes and the selection of house-cured meats. Babbo features one of the best Italian wine lists in New York, overseen by wine director David Lynch. And Pastry Chef Gina DiPalma also sources the best local produce for her exquisite *dolci*.

Barbetta
Theater District
321 West 46th Street, between Eighth and Ninth Aves.
(212) 246-9171
Closed Sunday–Monday
$$$

Opened in 1906 by Sebastiano Maioglio, and now run by his daughter Laura, Barbetta is the oldest restaurant in New York that is still owned by its founding family. Specializing in Piedmontese food, Barbetta introduced many products to New York for the very first time, including Porcini mushrooms, risotto, and a Piedmontese classic, *bagna cauda*.

When you enter Barbetta, you feel like you are walking into an elegant home and being received by friends, who walk you to a dining room decorated with eighteenth-century-style furnishings and dominated by a massive crystal chandelier. A beautiful garden boasts smells of magnolia, wisteria, oleander, jasmine, and gardenia, as well as a lovely fountain, making you feel as if you are indeed in eighteenth-century Turin. One can also dine in the Mirrors Gallery, which overlooks the garden.

Married to Dr. Gunther Blobel, winner of the Nobel prize for medicine, Laura plays an active role in assuring that the food at Barbetta maintains a high standard that reflects the true taste of Piedmontese cuisine. Under the watchful eye of Chef Alberto Leandri and Sommelier Leopoldo Frokic, you are sure to receive the kind of attentive service seldom seen today. The *agnolotti* and roast fresh peppers are delicious. The *fegato alla Veneziana* is one of the best in New York. *Fonduta, carne cruda, bollito,* and *tajarin* round out Barbetta's stellar tribute to Piedmont.

Beppe
Gramercy Park/Flatiron District
45 East 22nd Street, between Broadway and Park Ave. South
(212) 982-8422
Closed Sunday
$$$

A little piece of Tuscany lives in New York City! Chef Césare Casella, whose grandfather Beppe owned one of the most famous *osteria* in Italy, opened his restaurant two years ago to the acclaim of everyone who loves Tuscan, or perhaps we should say American, food. A big supporter of New York City's Greenmarket, Casella has also begun raising his own Chianina cattle in upstate New York—a Tuscan breed of cow worshiped by meat lovers the world over. But perhaps Beppe is most associated with the bean (featured in soups and salads), a number of varieties of which Casella has introduced to farmers in the U.S. Specialties of the house include Tuscan-style ribs, fried green tomatoes, and herb-drenched French fries—at times you wonder if you are eating food from Italy or from the Deep South. But when Césare comes by, with herbs sticking out of his breast pocket, you know you're much closer to the Tuscan countryside than the bayou.

The warm atmosphere, genuine products, professional service, and dedication to old traditions and to starting new ones makes Beppe a place worthy a visit, or two.

Da Silvano
Greenwich Village
260 Sixth Avenue, between Bleecker and Houston Sts.
(212) 982-2343
$$$

Before you even walk into this Greenwich Village mainstay, you might hear the raspy voice of its owner, Silvano Marchetto, bellowing a story about his native Tuscany or one of the specials of the day. Founded in 1975, Da Silvano has stood the test of time. Of utmost importance to its success is its consistent food, which provides guests with a true taste of Tuscany. The pastas are excellent, including the *spaghettini puttanesca, tagliatelle con pesto e fiori di zucca,* and homemade gnocchi with lobster. Main courses are also delicious, including the *ossobuco* and the tripe. Specials abound at Da Silvano and often feature surprises such as fried blowfish with tartare sauce. Another reason why Da Silvano is fun to visit is that stargazing is often part of the scene, even when you sit indoors and not at one of its sidewalk tables, one of the few places in the city where sitting outside is pleasant.

Felidia
East Side
243 East 58th Street, between Second and Third Aves.
(212) 758-1479
Closed Sunday
$$$$

In the early 1970s, Lidia Bastianich was a pioneer in introducing regional Italian cuisine using regional Italian ingredients to the New York public. Today's chefs have the luxury of concentrating on using local products to craft their Italian dishes (see Babbo) or growing Italian foods on American soil (see Beppe), but none of this would have been possible without getting quality Italian products such as balsamic vinegar, Arborio rice, and great olive oils here in the first place, and for that Lidia has been a great influence. Lidia went on to found Felidia in 1980, and it continues to be one of the leading Italian restaurants in New York, featuring some of its best pastas and most extensive wine lists.

As Lidia has gone on to become an author and television host, Chef Fortunato Nicotra, a.k.a. Bobo, continues to carry on the legacy of great cuisine, respecting its traditions but keeping it contemporary. At Felidia, you will find all Italian regions represented on the menu, with special emphasis of the region of Friuli/Istria, where Lidia was born.

Le Zie
Chelsea
172 Seventh Avenue, between 20th and 21st Sts.
(212) 206-8686
$$

Located in the heart of Chelsea, this small and cozy trattoria boasts some of the best Italian dishes in New York: In fact, as an Italian, this is the only place I will eat at once a week. Under the adept hand of Chef Roberto Passon, owner Francesco Antonucci, and manager Claudio Bonotto, Le Zie specializes in pastas and fish. Of particular importance is the *chiccheti* (an assortment of typical Venetian appetizers), *dentice* (a red snapper baked in sea salt), and a blackened squid risotto. Le Zie also makes the best spaghetti and meatballs in New York. But at a place that seems to have more specials than menu items, we also recommend trying different dishes. Le Zie recently expanded to include a bar and backroom (for smokers) and an outdoor garden with only one table for four. If you are in the neighborhood, and don't feel like spending a lot to eat generous portions of great food, you will love Le Zie.

Le Zoccole
East Village
95 Avenue A at East 6th St.
(212) 260-6660
$$

Chef Roberto Passon of Chelsea's Le Zie ("the aunts") is lending his talents to this new East Village restaurant. Le Zoccole is Francesco Antonucci's third restaurant, which is managed by Tony Perez. With a playful wink to its name, Le Zoccole ("the whores") features fast and easy fare—such as Italian panini and and fresh oysters—in its casual downstairs lounge. Patrons in need of something more substantial will be seated in the (only slightly) more formal upstairs dining room. Highlights include Passon's most requested offerings from Le Zie—including his signature "Maccheroni and Cheese" with freshly grated truffles; a salad of mixed greens with *ricotta salata,* bacon, and shiitakes; and his expertly grilled *Branzino* (sea bass).

For those who prefer sidewalk service, Le Zoccole offers its wares outdoors with table seating for 30 during the warmer months.

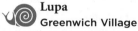

Lupa
Greenwich Village
170 Thompson Street, between Bleecker and Houston Sts.
(212) 982-5089
$$

Founded in 1999, Lupa was designed to be the classic Roman *trattoria,* not unlike some place you would find in the Trastevere, one of the most popular and historic neighborhoods in Rome. Some of the characteristics that make the cuisine live up to this billing is its use of tertiary cuts and innards, as well as an incredible array of perfectly cooked vegetables. Owned by the country's hottest chef, Mario Batali (Food Channel's *Molto Mario Show*), Joe Bastianich (author/restaurateur), and Jason Denton, Lupa skillfully brings rustic food to a casual environment, with a menu based on ingredients from the farmers' market. It's a place that all Italian lovers must visit.

Special antipasti include an array of house-cured meats such as *coppa, mortadella,* and *soppressata* (cured meats are one of Batali's passions, thanks chiefly to the work of his father in Seattle). The pastas are delicious as well, especially the *bavette cacio e pepe, bucatini all'Amatriciana,* and *spaghetti alla carbonara.* The Violet Hill chicken, raised on seaweed, is excellent. And for the brave among you, try the *coda alla vaccinara* (oxtail braised in "the butcher's style").

Rao's
East Harlem
455 East 114th Street at Pleasant Ave.
(212) 722-6709
Dinner by reservation only
$$$ (Cash only)

Growing up in East Harlem in the fifties and sixties was very much a culinary treat. Supermarkets were not so prominent, and small, family-run shops were more the rule. My family's food shopping consisted of visits to my uncle's butcher shop, the bread bakers who were friends of the family, the fishmonger, the cheese shop (I still recall with delight the fresh, glistening mozzarella balls displayed on the counter), the fruit and vegetable stands, and so on. Each proprietor was a specialist in his field and could give advice on what to buy and how to prepare it.

One of the very few reminders of that time gone by is Rao's restaurant. Tucked away in a quiet corner on the east side of Manhattan, bordered by a park with views of the East River and its bridges, Rao's has been serving honest and simple Neapolitan fare since 1896, and its popularity shows no sign of waning.

Just as food shopping was more engaging in those days, so is a visit to Rao's more than just eating at a restaurant. Frank Pellegrino, the proprietor (who is also an accomplished singer and actor), welcomes you with open arms and tremendous pride in his family's establishment. There are no menus or wine lists at Rao's. All the information you need is handled in a most personable and friendly manner, with Frank sitting at your table and discussing what's for dinner. Nick "the Vest," so-named for the colorful and whimsical waistcoats he invariably sports, is your bartender and your wine list.

The food and service are wonderful at Rao's, but it is the totality of the experience—a party every night—with the jukebox jumping, or *a cappella* street singers wandering in, that make this place the quintessential neighborhood joint. As I heard the great Arrigo Cipriani exclaim one evening at Rao's, "This is what a restaurant should be!"

Remi
Theater District
145 West 53rd Street, between Sixth and Seventh Aves.
(212) 581-4242
$$$

At Remi, where a massive Venetian mural dominates a room that seats 200 people, you will have the opportunity to taste excellent and unpretentious food that, for an Italian, is like a taste from home. Since 1987, chef-owner Francesco Antonucci has been filling up this one-block-long restaurant with theater-goers and New Yorkers looking for honest food in Midtown. Antonucci is a trendsetter, and many restaurateurs have imitated his elegant style in the running of their businesses. He is also the author of many books, including one with *New York Times* food writer Florence Fabricant.

All food, cooked in a Venetian style, is worthy of a taste, including the pastas, meats, and fish. You might want to try the *chiccheti* (like Venetian *tapas*), *risotti*, and an amazing array of desserts. The wine list is extensive and the service is deft. And in Slow fashion, one of the newest additions to the menu is the locally grown organic tomatoes (in season) with aged balsamic vinegar. Remi, designed by architect Adam Tihany, also boasts one of the nicest covered outdoor spaces in the city, seating 100 and featuring films of Toto, Anna Magnani, and Charlie Chaplin. Remi is also available for parties, with a gorgeous backroom and chef's table off the kitchen.

San Domenico
Clinton
240 Central Park South, between Seventh and Eighth Aves.
(212) 265-5959
$$$

San Domenico was founded in 1988 by Tony May, who was born in Torre del Greco near Naples, in the region of Campania. May is committed to promoting the regional specialties of Italy through his menu and also through events, such as special dinners that celebrate the products of particular regions, such as Friuli Venezia Giulia (you will find San Daniele prosciutto on the menu as well as a gorgeous Berkel meat slicer on the restaurant floor). San Domenico is also the New York representative at the annual world truffle auction, an Italian television event where bidders sitting in restaurants around the world call in to try to win massive samples of this treasured food. Thus San Domenico promotes Italian culture to New York and is the lens through which many Italians understand the culture of their expatriates. May also encouraged cultural exchanges at his second restaurant, Gemelli, which was destroyed during the September 11th attacks, and is very active in supporting local charities throughout the city. All bread, focaccia, ice cream, and desserts are made in-house.

NOTABLE

Bamonte's
Williamsburg, Brooklyn
32 Withers Street, between Lorimer St. and Union Ave.
(718) 384-8831
Subway: L to Bedford Ave.
Closed Tuesday
$$

This Williamsburg Italian is truly old school. It's more than one hundred years old, and for the life of the restaurant it has served great eggplant *parmigiana* and other red sauce regulars. Note of caution: Keep your eyes on your food and not on the clientele, because there are some diners who would rather remain anonymous!

Bar Pitti
Greenwich Village
268 Sixth Avenue, between Bleecker and Houston Sts.
(212) 982-3300
$$ (Cash only)

Fresh daily specials are brought to you on a chalkboard. Large photos of Florence decorate this restaurant, which boasts great outdoor seating. The food is simple but fresh.

Convivium Osteria
Park Slope, Brooklyn
68 Fifth Avenue, between Bergen St. and St. Mark's Pl.
(718) 857-1833
Subway: Q to Seventh Ave.; 1, 2 to Bergen St.

This is a place where regional dishes from Italy, Spain, and Portugal live together in a peaceful atmosphere. Friendly people, a well-conceived wine list, and unique food make this a restaurant that people want to keep a secret, especially in the summer when the outdoor garden is open.

Crispo
West Village
240 West 14th Street, between Seventh and Eighth Aves.
(212) 229-1818
Closed Sunday
$$

Newly opened, the word about Crispo's great pizza is spreading, and the other entrées are well worth trying.

Ecco
Tribeca
124 Chambers Street, between Church St. and West Broadway
(212) 227-7074
$$$$

It's way downtown, but many people think Ecco is worth the trip because of its atmosphere, its elegant barroom, and its good old-school Italian cooking.

Elio's
Upper East Side
1621 Second Avenue, between 84th and 85th Sts.
(212) 772-2242
$$$

Northern Italian cooking blossoms in Elio's elegant and welcoming setting, which is known for its celebrity clientele and classic Italian fine dining menu, including veal Milanese, risotto, *osso buco,* and linguine with white clam sauce.

Frank
East Village
88 Second Avenue, between 5th and 6th Sts.
(212) 420-0202
$ (Cash only)

The first of a slew of popular East Village Italian restaurants, Frank boasts a great flame-filled open kitchen. It has become so popular that they have annexed the adjacent storefront to create lovely wine bar.

Gennaro
Upper West Side
665 Amsterdam Avenue, between 92nd and 93rd Sts.
(212) 665-5348
Dinner only
$$ (Cash only)

If the rapport between quality and price is important to you, then you would be hard-pressed to find a better deal in New York than Gennaro—but be prepared to wait for a table. Chef Genarro Picone makes great *orechiette* with broccoli and garlic, and also *bucatini* with cacio cheese and black pepper. He is also considered a master at cooking duck.

Il Buco
Noho
47 Bond Street, between Bowery and Lafayette St.
(212) 533-1932
$$$

Il Buco, located on a quiet cobblestone street in Noho, was once an antiques store by day and a restaurant at night, and the decor still bears the marks of its former life. From the Mediterranean *tapas*-like appetizers, to the wonderful fresh pastas, house-cured salamis, and Umbrian oils and wines, it's no wonder Il Buco remains popular. The downstairs cantina, it's said, gave Edgar Allen Poe the inspiration for his famous short story, "A Cask of Amontillado."

Locanda Vini & Olii
Clinton Hill, Brooklyn
129 Gates Avenue at Cambridge Pl.
(718) 622-9202
Subway: A, C to Clinton-Washington Aves.
Dinner only; closed Monday
$$ (Cash only)

This Tuscan-themed restaurant is owned by Milanese François Louy (formerly manager of the Cipriani restaurants) and Florentine Catherine de Zagon Louy (formerly manager of Balthazar). The owners wait the tables and are knowledgeable and enthusiastic about what they serve. Before opening in January of 2001, Locanda had been an active pharmacy for more than 130 years, and many of its features remain intact. But don't worry: The food does not taste like medicine.

Malatesta
West Village
649 Washington Street at Christopher St.
(212) 741-1207
Dinner only
$$ (Cash only)

This warm West Village trattoria built its reputation on simple home cooking. Try the baby artichoke and shaved Parmesan salad, the fluffy arugula *piadina*, or the beautiful lamb chops. The staff is as laid back as the prices.

Peasant
Chinatown/Little Italy
194 Elizabeth Street, between Prince and Spring Sts.
(212) 965-9511
Dinner only; closed Monday
$$$

Chef-owner Frank de Carlo has installed a brick wood-burning oven in which he roasts fish, shellfish, and meats that will delight your senses.

Pó
West Village
31 Cornelia Street, between Bleecker and West 4th Sts.
(212) 645-2189
Closed Monday
$$

Long before Mario Batali became a national figure, he opened Po. The prices are good, and the food has remained fresh and delicious even after all these years and even though Batali is no longer involved.

RINALDO FRATTOLILLO

JAPANESE

Donguri
Upper East Side
309 East 83rd Street, between First and Second Aves.
(212) 737-5656
Dinner only; closed Monday
$$$

Simply stated, Donguri (Japanese for "acorn") is the next best thing to dining in Japan, especially for homesick Japanese residents of New York City. Do not expect sushi, since it is not on the menu. This quaint Japanese restaurant is located in an Upper East Side brownstone that exudes a feeling of comfort. Although very small, with fewer than 30 seats, Donguri offers many delicately crafted traditional Japanese dishes such as *buri* (yellowtail) with daikon braised in *bonito* (fish) broth, broiled seasonal fish, sashimi, *shiso gohan* (rice with a fresh aromatic Japanese herb, like a minty, grassy basil) and much more. Needless to say, the quality and the variety of items on the menu surpass home cooking . . . along with the check, which may not be so "homey."

 ## Honmura An
Soho
170 Mercer Street, between Houston and Prince Sts.
(212) 334-5253
Closed Monday
$$$

From the second you pull open the door to Honmura An (the New York branch of a restaurant founded seventy years ago in Tokyo) and take your first breath of cool air, scented with fresh sweet fish and seaweed and soy sauce, peace begins to steal into your crazed urban soul. By the time you've ascended the stairs in front of you to the luminous, open restaurant at the top and taken in the elegance of the floral arrangements—more like fragments of a Japanese garden, combining black stone, sprays of grasses, dried pods from exotic and unidentifiable plants—you'll be in Slow mode. This feeling lets you fully savor good food, which is always better when it's been made without pretension and with respect for tradition. Graceful service enhances your dining experience, and the waiters at Honmura An have perfected the art of being reassuringly calm, knowledgeable, and fast. And so you open the menu. Apart from one or two sushi and sashimi offerings (including chilled sea urchin so fresh it gives you the tingling sensation of standing in the ocean), you will find mostly *soba* (buckwheat) noodles. They are served either hot, in rich duck or chicken broth, or cold, arrayed on a lacquer tray, with dipping sauce on the side. Toppings can range from simple radishes to marinated wild greens or mammoth sweet crunchy prawns, shipped from Tokyo's famed Tsukiji fish market. The noodles are a true Slow food: Against the back wall of the restaurant, in view of anyone who wants to watch, the noodle-makers grind organically grown buckwheat groats in a large mill, mix the soft buckwheat flour into a dough, swiftly cut the dough into pale brown noodles, and coil them in lacquer boxes. The soba are cooked to order, and have an unparalleled purity of flavor and resilience. A scoop of intensely flavored green tea ice cream, made with pulverized macha tea and served in a perfect porcelain bowl, ends what is always, for us, the most serene dining experience in New York City.

Jewel Bako
East Village
239 East 5th Street, between Second and Third Aves.
(212) 979-1012
Dinner only; closed Monday
$$–$$$$ (prix fixe)

Nestled among crumbling, prewar apartment buildings in the East Village, this tiny sushi bar's name is Japanese slang for "jewel box," but while the ethereal and intimate setting fits the description, more precious than the box are the jewels themselves—the slivers of raw fish that make up the menu. The best place to sit at most sushi restaurants is the bar, and Jewel Bako is no exception. Here, the chef will most likely prepare all your sushi and also engage you in conversation without losing his focus or momentum. The *omakase,* or chef's menu, is the best way to go (and requires that you sit at the bar so that he can serve it to you directly), and you can opt to keep it in the ballpark by capping it at a certain price (it starts at $50 per person)—or not, if you prefer to experience the full spectrum of that day's freshest finds. The menu, encompassing both tradition and modernity (but not fusion) changes frequently, based on what is fresh and in season, and dishes are often accented with fresh herbs and wild vegetables unique to Japanese cuisine. Many of the more precious cuts of fish, such as *toro, chutoro* (two grades of fatty tuna), and *uni* (sea urchin) are of impeccable quality, as are less-common varieties flown in daily from Japan that are otherwise unknown in New York. The husband-and-wife owners, Jack and Grace Lamb, provide elegantly choreographed service and dramatic yet intimate presentation, drawing each diner into a nightly performance with all the dramatic elements of desire, gluttony, generosity, surprise, and denouement. Jewel Bako may cost you a few carats, but the experience of a slow and sensual meal is worth it.

Nobu
Tribeca
105 Hudson Street at Franklin St.
(212) 219-0500
$$$$

Nobu Next Door
105 Hudson Street at Franklin St.
(212) 334-4445
$$$$

When Nobu Matsuhisa opened Nobu in Tribeca in 1994 with the backing of restaurateur Drew Nieporent and actor Robert De Niro, it was a marriage of two different worlds: show business and restaurants. Yet these two worlds seemed to meld seamlessly at Nobu, for over the ensuing decade, Nobu Matsuhisa has become the most famous Japanese chef in America, opening elegant outposts in Beverly Hills and Las Vegas, not to mention Milan, Miami Beach, London, and Tokyo; while the restaurant itself continues to attract the most glittering of New York and international bold-type names, appearing itself regularly in the gossip columns alongside those names.

Fortunately, for those looking for a fine meal first and a celeb sighting as an afterthought, the hype is not in vain: Nobu was ahead of its time in breaking out of the traditional sushi restaurant mold in favor of bold flavor combinations and unusual ingredients, and the menu still lives up to the standards that set new precedents nearly ten years ago. Signature dishes such as black cod marinated in miso, monkfish liver pâté, and squid "pasta" are complemented by Peruvian-accented dishes (Matsuhisa lived in Peru for several years) including ceviche, sashimi with jalapeño, and spicy "anti-cucho" chicken. Of course the sushi and sashimi are always very, very fresh, and the *omakase* menu (chef's choice) is a pricey but worthwhile option, starting at $70.

The Asian-accented decor, with a cherry-blossom-stenciled floor and wall of live bamboo, is courtesy of restaurant designer David Rockwell.

Nearly the same signature menu can also be found next door at sister restaurant Nobu Next Door, which solves the notorious difficulty of getting a reservation at Nobu by not taking any—hence the lines. (Come early and be patient.)

Omen
Soho
113 Thompson Street, between Prince and Spring Sts.
(212) 925-8923

Dinner only
$$ (à la carte) to $$$$ (prix fixe)

It's no coincidence that the most popular item on the menu at Omen is also its namesake. The Omen *udon* noodles arrive in a deconstructed state, inviting you to combine different flavors, textures, and accents: a terra-cotta plate of freshly cooked hot noodles, a bowl of steaming broth, a large square plate with a colorful assortment of raw, cooked, and pickled vegetables including ginger, seaweed, carrot, spinach, okra, cabbage, and daikon; a small rectangular plate holding snipped *nori* (dried seaweed) and tempura crispies; and a bowl of sesame seeds to sprinkle as you see fit. The menu is dominated by four prix fixes—seasonal, sashimi, tempura, and Japanese steak—each of which is rounded out with many small dishes of vegetables and your choice of udon or rice, but the à la carte section offers many options as well, including the udon, rice with shiso (a mintlike green leaf) or broiled *anago* (sea eel), sashimi, and various types of cooked fish and meat. Many of the grains and legumes used are organic and grown in Japan, and Chef Mikio-san is particularly committed to using locally sourced ingredients as well, including the udon, which is made in Brooklyn.

The chiaroscuro setting, framed by dark wooden screens and large paper lanterns, fills the parlor floor of a narrow brownstone in Soho, and the exceedingly polite Japanese servers in red aprons are ready to respond to any request or to spirit your dishes away once you have laid down your *hashi* (chopsticks). You may feel reluctant to slurp your noodles in such an elegant and meditative space, but it is the best way to indicate your pleasure to the chef. Udon noodles are found on many Japanese restaurant menus in New York, but it is rare to find them prepared with as much care and taste as those of Omen.

Rai Rai Ken
East Village
214 East 10th Street, between First and Second Aves.
(212) 477-7030
$ (Cash only)

Ramen shops in Japan are like American diners: unpretentious, often family-run, with efficient service and minimal amenities. But beyond the obvious similarities, the best examples of both genres often make everything from scratch, have regional specialties, and above all pride themselves in making robustly flavored, simple yet soulful food. How could this possibly have anything to do with the freeze-dried packages of ramen so common in convenience stores, sold at six for a dollar? Well, it doesn't. The ramen noodles at Rai Rai Ken are another breed entirely, and the shop stands out as one of the few in New York that specialize in ramen, and do it well. Chef-manager Hirokazu Yoda manages a tiny shop (that seats barely 10) in the East Village and proudly carries on the flavors and traditions that he learned in his family's ramen shop in Tokyo.

The short menu includes three kinds of ramen, *gyoza* (pan-fried dumplings), fried rice, and *yakisoba* (stir-fried noodles), but the ramen is the *raison d'être*. Made fresh every day, the witchy-looking stock burbles on the stove behind the counter, drawing its flavor from chicken, fish, pork, vegetables, aromatic herbs and spices, and even apples bobbing in the steamy brew. Chef Yoda also makes all three soup flavorings, which are typical of Tokyo-style ramen, by hand in small batches: *shoyu* (soy sauce), *shio* (salt), and *miso* (bean paste). The flavorings are then combined with the stock for each order, ladled on top of freshly boiled ramen, and generously garnished with a variety of vegetables, meat, and seasonings such as seaweed and scallions. The roast pork that garnishes the shoyu and shio ramen (and can be ordered extra with any other dish) is also house-made: tender, moist, and meaty, with just the right amount of sweet fat on the rind. Noodle-eaters perch on stools along a counter that faces the kitchen area, slurp contentedly from their hot bowls, and then call out *"Gochiso sama"* to the cooks as they leave—which means, "Thank you for the feast!"

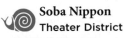

Soba Nippon
Theater District

19 West 52nd Street, between Fifth and Sixth Aves.
(212) 489-2525
$$

Soba Nippon blends in with other modern, glass-encased stores and buildings in Midtown, but after your eyes have adjusted to the interior light, the room takes the shape of a modern yet informal dining room: A long, undulating, hourglass-shaped communal table anchors the space, flanked on one side by a sushi bar and on the other by a wall of banquette seating framed by sprays of bamboo that reach the ceiling and a striking, wall-sized color photograph of a field of flowering buckwheat. The photograph is of owner Nobuyoshi Kuraoka's buckwheat farm near Montreal, which provides the main ingredient for Soba Nippon's signature dish: *soba*. Mr. Kuraoka started growing buckwheat using the seeds and guidance of a Japanese farmer from the island of Hokkaido (whose climate is similar to Montreal's) in order to fill the restaurant's need for high-quality buckwheat flour without having to pay exorbitant prices to import it from Japan. The buckwheat is grown without the use of chemical pesticides or fertilizers, and the restaurant is also focused on using many organic ingredients.

The noodles are made fresh every day in the restaurant, according to a traditional formula of 80 percent buckwheat and 20 percent wheat (which adds a little elasticity to the gluten-lacking buckwheat and tempers its natural bitterness). The menu includes cold and hot *soba*, udon, sushi, and various *don* dishes (dishes with rice), along with a good showing of appetizers, but the simplest and best dish is cold *soba*, plain or with grated daikon or *tororo* (Japanese yam). When you are close to finishing your cold *soba*, the waiter brings a lacquered box shaped like a teapot that is filled with the hot broth used to cook the *soba*—this is to be swirled into the remaining dipping sauce that you have in your cup and savored like the broth at the end of any good bowl of soup. The service is solicitous and prompt, with the proud Mr. Kuraoka often on hand to greet the largely Japanese clientele.

Sushi of Gari
Lenox Hill
402 East 78th Street, between First and York Aves.
(212) 517-5340
Dinner only
$$$

The art of sushi is subtle. Sushi is not just raw fish on a ball of rice; it is much more than that. It is the culmination of a skillful chef, quality ingredients, combination of flavors, and, most important, the *shari*, which is vinegar-flavored rice (if the vinegar is too strong, it ruins the sushi). Sushi of Gari possesses all these elements, and Gari-san, the head chef, creates wonderful sushi with finesse. The *shari* has a pleasant flavor of vinegar with just the right amount of air incorporated, and it is always the perfect size. So, when the sushi hits your mouth, everything falls apart effortlessly. (Sushi is supposed to be eaten in one bite! Despite the colossal sushi you may encounter in some New York City restaurants, bigger is not better.) Gari-san and his associates also craft some unusual toppings, such as smoked salmon, onion, and tomato with a cream-cheese sauce; fried oyster and thinly sliced avocado drizzled with a special sauce; broiled sea eel sprinkled with Okinawa sea salt; and countless other combinations. It may be helpful to keep in mind that Gari-san strongly disapproves of the use of soy sauce! Usually customers are advised not to dip their sushi in it. Honestly, there is no need for it; each piece of sushi is brushed with a "sauce" enhancing the beautiful flavor combinations that may be masked by the use of the "dark stuff." But most important, his technique and unlimited ideas for making one-of-a-kind sushi is a natural wonder. If you are lucky enough to get a seat, you're definitely in for a treat!

NOTABLE

Sugiyama
Theater District
251 West 55th Street, between Broadway and Eighth Ave.
(212) 956-0670
Dinner only; closed Sunday–Monday
$$$$

Chef Nao Sugiyama has earned accolades for his modern *kaiseki* menu, a pricey but poetic form of haute Japanese cooking inspired by the traditional Japanese tea ceremony. *Kaiseki* is not just seasonally influenced; it goes further by using the seasons and the natural world, including a different "spirit" each month, as a conceptual platform to present seasonal ingredients, from green onions in the spring to chestnuts in the fall, as symbols of the season themselves—a kind of edible trope. The real-life ingredients also live up to the restaurant's concept, as many are organic and seasonally chosen.

Taka
West Village
61 Grove Street, between Seventh Ave. South and Bleecker St.
(212) 242-3699
Dinner only; closed Monday
$$

It is rare to find a female sushi chef (some claim that womens' naturally warmer hands preclude such a career), but in the case of Taka, Takako Yoneyama is both chef and owner, as well as resident artist, with her own handmade traditional Japanese earthenware gracing the tables and a painterly aesthetic evident in handling exceedingly well-prepared fresh fish. If you're feeling adventurous, opt for the crunchy and sweet grasshoppers that provide an unexpected arthropodal thrill.

KOREAN

Hangawi
Murray Hill
12 East 32nd Street, between Madison and Fifth Aves.
(212) 213-0077
$$

Hangawi is located on the same street as the rest of Manhattan's bustling, neon-lit Koreatown, but it stands apart, to the east of Fifth Avenue, as an elegant vegetarian haven clothed in enameled wood, tatami floors, and paper lamps. After you surrender your shoes at the entrance, a robed waiter leads you to a table at shin level, in the style of traditional Japanese restaurants, but with the comfort of a well to slide your legs into instead of folding them underneath you, tea-ceremony-style, only to lose them to numbness ten minutes into the meal.

As a Korean restaurant, Hangawi is not among the most traditional, but as a vegetarian, dairy-free restaurant the choices are far superior to those at a typical vegan enclave that harps repeatedly on the themes of raw vegetables, seitan, and tofu. The prix fixe Emperor's Meal offers a wide variety of flavors, textures, and temperatures, playing with sweet and savory in the same dishes—from a cool and crisp mushroom salad with miso dressing, to an apple stuffed with fresh sweet relish, to rich and tender stuffed Portobello mushrooms with sesame leaf. The Steamboat Soup is a special addition to the prix fixe, and it is worth the extra few dollars for a complex broth swimming with watercress, radish, onion, tofu, oyster and straw mushrooms, scallions, carrots, walnuts, and red dates. Mushrooms and tofu dominate the regular menu, but not without other more original ideas such as acorn noodles, pumpkin noodles, and mountain roots and greens. Tea provides an aromatic finish to the meal, served ceremoniously in delicate earthenware pots (and tea leaves and accessories are also available for sale in the front of the dining room).

Kang Suh
Garment District/Koreatown
1250 Broadway at 32nd Street
(212) 564-6845
Open 24 hours
$$

What sets this barbecue joint apart from the others in Koreatown is twofold: Most of the grills are fueled by real hardwood charcoal embers (most other such restaurants use gas), and the place is open 24 hours. Should you have a craving at an indecent hour for barbecued Korean beef, accompanied by pungent pastes, hot mustard, and myriad *panchan* (the little appetizer-type dishes that typically accompany Korean barbecue), this is where to satisfy it.

Furnished in an unremarkable modern decor, the restaurant almost has the feeling of a diner at peak hours: noisy, bustling, with efficient waiters striding between tables and designated charcoal men swooping through the aisles bringing braziers of live coals to tables outfitted with built-in grills as the centerpiece. *Kalbi* (marinated boneless short ribs) and *bulkoki* (marinated prime rib eye) are good bets on a list of fourteen barbecue options that also includes ox tongue, squid, and shiitake mushrooms. *Nang myun,* a vinegary, cold, clear beef broth soup with chewy buckwheat noodles, scallions, and slices of *nashi* (Asian pear), provides a refreshing counterpoint to the smoky hot meat you'll likely be ordering, and a decent *bibim bob* (rice mixed with ground beef, vegetables, egg, and chile paste) can satisfy the biggest appetites. The smell of the grill stays with you (and your clothes), though no more than if you had stood over a smoking kettle of charcoal on a hot summer day.

Mandoo Bar
Garment District/Koreatown
2 West 32nd Street, between Fifth Ave. and Broadway
(212) 279-3075
$

Mandoo means "dumpling" in Korean, and the Mandoo Bar is full of fresh and tender dumplings, made daily by hand in the front window. While most Korean restaurants in this neighborhood specialize in barbecue, Mandoo Bar provides a refreshing and delicious alternative with pan-fried, boiled, or steamed dumplings filled with myriad ingredients, including pork, vegetables, *kimchi,* and seafood, combined with scallions and tofu. Pan-fried dumplings, which are actually double-cooked—steamed, then pan-fried, to retain their moisture and a tender crust—are especially juicy. While not quite like Chinese soup dumplings, these *mandoo* will squirt when you bite into them!

Mandoo Bar also makes an excellent selection of other hearty Korean dishes, including *bibim bob* (rice with assorted vegetables, ground beef, egg, and chile paste) that in its hot form (you can also order it cold) continues to cook while you eat it, forming a flavorful crust against the inside of the sizzling hot stone pot it arrives in. The service is friendly and efficient, and the sizzling *bibim bob* gets a rigorous mixing by the waitress upon presentation, with the level of spicy paste that you indicate.

New York Kom Tang Sot Bul Kalbi House
Garment District/Koreatown
31 West 32nd St., between Fifth and Sixth Aves.
(212) 947-8482
$$

With the distinction of being New York's first Korean restaurant, the three-story New York Kom Tang continues to serve some of the area's most authentic Korean cuisine. Forget the decor, circa opening day 1979. The draw here is the lusty cuisine, fiery and uncompromised for Western palates. The excitement starts with *panchan*, a half-dozen or so small dishes that serve as appetizers and condiments. The pride of the *panchan* chef and unique to the restaurant is *kae jang* (spicy crab), consisting of uncooked hard-shell crabs, quartered and marinated in an addictively spicy chile sauce. Opening volleys include *hae mool pajun* (seafood rice flour pancake); fried beef *mandoo* (dumplings) with greaseless, paper-thin skins; and *jap chae* (rice vermicelli with beef, vegetables, and sesame oil). Barbecue is the main event. Despite the presence of ventilator hoods, it is a smoky affair using real hardwood charcoal; it is sublime. *Kalbi* (marinated short ribs of beef) or *bulgog* (marinated rib eye) are excellent choices, as is *jae yuk guwi* (spicy pork). The beverage of choice is *soju*, Korea's favorite spirit. Ask for it in a kettle with cucumber or lemon slices. It's a flavorful infusion with an equally potent kick.

NOTABLE

Cho Dang Gol
Garment District/Koreatown
55 West 35th Street, between Fifth Ave. and Broadway
(212) 695-8222
$$

Homemade tofu is the specialty at Cho Dang Gol, where traditional flavors are well executed in satisfying country-style fare, including excellent *bibim bob* and many vegetarian options.

Gam Mee Ok
Garment District/Koreatown
43 West 32nd Street, between Fifth Ave. and Broadway
(212) 695-4113
Open 24 hours
$-$$

The menu at Gam Mee Ok includes about ten items, all of them vividly illustrated in laminated color, from punchy and sweet *kimchi* to ox bone soup with rice, noodles, and beef (a traditional comfort food favorite), and a gluttonous platter with raw oysters, sliced beef, and fresh cabbage. The portions are hearty, cheap (for the size), and satisfying.

Han Bat
Garment District/Koreatown
53 West 35th Street, between Fifth and Sixth Aves.
(212) 629-5588
Open 24 hours
$$

Han Bat has an extensive menu of Korean country dishes and offers a nice late-night alternative to Korean barbecue places, though you can get barbecue here, too, if that's what you're in the mood for in the wee small hours.

Korea Palace
Midtown East
127 East 54th Street, between Park and Lexington Aves.
(212) 832-2350
$$

Korea Palace might be written off as a Midtown tourist trap were it not for its flavorful barbecue and abundant *panchan* (appetizers). The encyclopedic menu has something for everyone, and the staff is professional and helpful.

Kum Gang San
Flushing, Queens
138-28 Northern Boulevard, between Maine and Union Sts.
(718) 461-0909
Subway: 7 to Flushing–Main St.
Open 24 hours
$$

A large Korean restaurant that serves fantastic barbecue as well as straight-up Korean fare: high volume but also high quality. If you can, try to get to the Queens location.

Other Location
49 West 32nd Street at Broadway, Manhattan; (212) 967-0909

Seh Ja Meh
Financial District
26 John Street, between Broadway and Nassau St.
(212) 766-5825
Closed Saturday–Sunday
$–$$

Owner Danny Min opened Seh Ja Meh in 1999 in this downtown location far from Koreatown. Like many other restaurants in Lower Manhattan, the place is jumping at lunch, when you might want to order a Korean soup, dumplings *(mandoo)*, or a bento box. But it's also great, and much less crowded, for an early dinner (with an emphasis on early—the restaurant closes around 9:30 P.M.).

PATRICK MARTINS

LATIN AMERICAN

Casa   *(Brazilian)*
West Village
72 Bedford Street at Commerce St.
(212) 366-9410
$$

Aside from having the best-translated menu, Brazilian or Portuguese, the friendly staff at Casa offers a genuine example of Brazilian regional home cooking. There are lace place mats, homemade green chile paste, perfectly cooked beans, and a decent selection of *cachaça* (Brazilian sugarcane liquor) at the bar. The low-lit dining room is modest and matches with the simple, clean plates that the kitchen produces. Outstanding fixtures on the menu include *xinxim de galinha* (an organic chicken and shrimp stew), *moqueca de frutos do mar* (a seafood stew made with coconut milk and *dende* palm oil), and, of course, Brazil's national dish, *feijoada* (hearty black bean stew made with pork, beef, and sausage). Some desserts not to be missed are *manjar branco,* a coconut pudding with a plum sauce, and the *mousse de maracuja,* a passionfruit mousse. Casa's Sunday brunch also offers some classic Brazilian selections such as *cestinha de salgadinhos sortidos,* an assortment of typical finger foods made from shrimp, chicken, and cheese, and *cuzcuz paulista,* a kind of polenta with shrimp, olives, hearts of palm, and tomatoes. Finally, the wine list includes Chilean, Argentine, and Portuguese selections.

Churrascaria Plataforma   *(Brazilian)*
Theater District
316 West 49th Street, between Eighth and Ninth Aves.
(212) 245-0505
$$$$ (prix fixe)

Churrascaria Plataforma is a New York version of a Brazilian "grilled meats" restaurant. The restaurant is not ideal for a romantic dinner for two, but better suited for larger groups who do not mind the high noise level that includes numerous renditions of "Happy Birthday" and a live band on weekends. *Caipirinha* (a cocktail made with *cachaça,* or sugarcane liquor), *maracuja* drinks, and other Brazilian delights are served over and above the prix fixe dinner, which features an immense self-serve buffet table of Portuguese and Brazilian appetizers, both hot and cold, that are well prepared and constantly replenished. But don't fill up on the shrimp and salads at the salad bar, for when you give the waiter the "green light" by turning over a placecard, a parade of grilled meats, sausages, chickens, hams, and fish are brought to you on skewers and sliced or cut onto your plate. Spicy condiments, rice, French fries, fried bananas, and black beans are all included. You must pace yourself to be able to get your money's worth and still find room for their very sweet desserts. When you leave you should either drive straight to the doctor to get your arteries declogged or go to bed, for you will be tired from all the action—both in the restaurant and inside your stomach!

Delicia   *(Brazilian)*
West Village
322 West 11th Street, between Greenwich and Washington Sts.
(212) 242-2002
Closed Sunday–Monday
$$

We stumbled across this tiny Brazilian restaurant, sitting discreetly on a West Village tree-lined block, by chance. Its street-level windows are hardly noticeable, and the decor inside is utterly simple: white-washed walls, half a dozen wood tables, a few plants, and a bunch of South American knickknacks lying around. But we urge you to try this little gem of Brazilian home cooking, fairly priced and so distinctive from all the neon-lit carioca cantinas on 46th Street. Plan to spend some time there, as friendly owner José and his mother (in the kitchen) are never in a rush. Just pretend you are sitting in a Rio joint, enjoy the subtle samba tunes while sipping some freshly made *caipirinha* cocktails, until the food finally arrives at your table. The *bolinho de bacalhau* (crispy cod balls) is a mouth-watering starter; main dishes include a perfect *feijoada* (Brazil's national dish—a pork and black bean stew sprinkled with manioc flour) and a creamy *moqueca de camarao* (shrimp and vegetables fricasseed in coconut milk). And be prepared: After the *café zinhou,* José might shove maracas and tambourines in your hands for an improvised dance session.

Flor's Kitchen   *(Venezuelan)*
East Village
149 First Avenue at 9th St.
(212) 387-8949
$

Since thumbs-up reviews in the *New York Times* and *Post,* Flor's Kitchen has expanded—from 12 colorful chairs to 15, and finally to the current 19. But don't worry, the whopping increase in seating capacity hasn't changed Flor's Venezuelan home cooking. One bite of any dish that features corn (happily, half of the menu) will dissolve any doubts about the kitchen's commitment to freshness.

A Frisbee-sized *cachapa* (loosely knit corn pancake) bursts with sweetness, although the cheese and lunch-meat ham that top one version is simply not on par with the other ingredients. Other entrées, such as *pabellón criollo* (a popular shredded meat dish served with rice, beans, and fried plantains) and *arroz con pollo,* are so satisfying that appetizers might seem unnecessary. Don't be fooled. Compact *arepas* are corn-cake pockets whose exuberant contents burst from one side. Spoon the accompanying avocado, olive oil, and lemon emulsion atop these or the *empanadas criollas,* which offer similar stuffing in a very different package. Breaking through the first crisp layer, then the mealy, soft dough, a heady aroma of fish rises from the *pescado* version. The shredded beef and black bean fillings are also outstanding. Flor's covers all the meal bases by offering wine and fruit juices, breakfast for the East Village's late-risers, and an assortment of dessert puddings and sugar cookies.

Inti Raymi   *(Peruvian)*
Jackson Heights, Queens
86-14 37th Avenue, between 86th and 87th Sts.
(718) 424-1938.
Closed Tuesday
Subway: 7 to 82nd St.–Jackson Hgts.
$$

It is worth a visit to Jackson Heights, the predominantly Latin neighborhood of Queens, for Inti Raymi's Peruvian cuisine. Inti Raymi, the name of an ancient Incan festival of the Sun, serves flavorful food in a comfortable environment. Peruvian food is based on the core ingredients of corn, potatoes, and beans, and accented with chiles. Meat and seafood are the important sources of protein. As the menu informs, traders and invaders from Spain, Italy, China, and Japan all influenced the development of Peruvian food. These contributions are apparent in Peruvian cuisine, as well as Inti Raymi's menu.

This traditional, family-run restaurant has been open since 1976. Chef Carlos Astorga imports ingredients, such as the *huacatay* (the native herb used in *papas ocopa,* a potato appetizer), directly from Peru. Ceviche is another interesting appetizer and has a fresh, balanced flavor. It is accompanied with thinly sliced pickled red onions, a slice of sweet potato, and roasted corn. The *papa relleño* is composed of ground beef mixed with olives, garlic, onions, and raisins, then encrusted in mashed potato. The *lomo saltado,* strips of beef and potato cooked with tomato, onions, and served with rice, is good, but not as good as the *picante de mariscos.* This mix of octopus, shrimp, squid, scallops, and potatoes is evenly cooked and settled into a rich, slightly spicy tomato broth. *Alfajores,* dense cookies that sandwich a rich caramel spread, are a fun treat for dessert, and a better choice than the *crema volteada,* which can be a bit overcooked.

Even when the restaurant is busy on weekends, the servers handle the crowd with ease. In terms of alcohol consumption, you have your choice. You can either bring your own or sample the restaurant's sangria, beer, or wine. A traditional Peruvian brunch is served on Saturday and Sunday.

Malagueta   *(Brazilian)*
Astoria, Queens
25-35 36th Avenue at 28th St.
(718) 937-4821
Subway: N, W to 36th Ave.
Closed Monday
$$

This small Brazilian restaurant sets itself apart from the others by its inviting atmosphere and tropical expression of chef-owner Herbert Gomes. The dining room hints of his hometown of São Luis de Maranhão in northern Brazil, with original artwork hanging on the walls and mellow tunes setting the atmosphere. Meanwhile, the presentation of the food speaks of Herbert's training with Claude Troigros.

At Malagueta, you'll find traditional Brazilian dishes finished in a French manner. The casual hospitality and reasonable wine list pair well with the menu. Herbert "permits" his French flair to show itself on the daily specials. His menu also carries Brazilian classics such as *feijoada* (on Saturday only), a black bean stew made with dried meats, pork, sausage, and bacon, and *moqueca de camarão,* a shrimp stew made with palm oil and coconut milk.

NOTABLE

Chicama   *(Pan-Latino)*
Gramercy Park/Flatiron District
35 East 18th Street at Broadway
(212)-505-2233
$$$

A haven for diners who love to try new and exciting interpretations of Latin American food, sampling national cuisines from Mexico to Argentina. Try the excellent ceviches.

Lima's Taste   *(Peruvian)*
East Village
432 East 13th Street, between First Ave. and Ave. A

(212) 228-7900
Open for dinner; brunch Saturday–Sunday
$$

Outstanding service, friendly, and helpful! Try the tender pork chops or the flavorful *lomo saltado,* a filet mignon that is cooked with tomatoes, onion slices, and fried potatoes.

Novecento   *(Argentine)*
Soho
343 West Broadway, between Broome and Grand Sts.
(212) 925-4706
$$$

Some people say that Novecento serves up the best marinated skirt skate in the city. And the other cuts of meat ain't bad either.

Paladar   *(Pan-Latino)*
Lower East Side
161 Ludlow Street, between Houston and Stanton Sts.
(212) 473-3535
Dinner only
$$ (Cash only)

Chef-owner Aaron Sanchez, who appears on the Food Network show *Melting Pot,* serves his Pan-Latin food until 2:00 A.M. on the weekends to the night owls prowling the Lower East Side. Sanchez first worked in San Francisco at Rose Pistola before coming home to New York to cook at Patria. His interpretation of the cooking of the barrio with its spicy appetizers, light entrées, and fruity drinks make Paladar definitely worth a stop!

Pampa   *(Argentine)*
Upper West Side
768 Amsterdam Avenue, between 97th and 98th Sts.
(212) 865-2929
$$ (Cash only)

With the recent closing of its nearby rival Campo, Pampa is the undisputed king of Argentine grills on the Upper West Side. In addition to the steaks and assorted organ meats, try the steak or chicken *empanadas.* The restaurant is usually crowded, and the service is slow, but the wait is invariably worth it.

Patria   *(Pan-Latino)*
Gramercy Park/Flatiron District
250 Park Avenue South at 20th St.
(212) 777-6211
$$$

Patria may not be the "slowest" or most traditional restaurant, but it is definitely getting better over time. My friend Natalia orders the suckling pig on every visit, without fail. The ceviche is well balanced and creative, particularly the salmon soy ceviche. For a light finish, try the apple mango ceviche with tarragon sorbet.

Rinconcito Peruano   *(Peruvian)*
Clinton
803 Ninth Avenue, between 53rd and 54th Sts.
(212) 333-5685
$ (Cash only)

Peruvian specialties including ceviche and potato-based dishes, many with a startling yellow cheese sauce. Christmas lights can't salvage the atmosphere in this storefront restaurant, but the staff is very nice.

Ruben's Empanadas   *(Argentine)*
Financial District
64 Fulton Street, between Cliff and Gold Sts.
(212) 962-5330
$ (Cash only)

Empanadas are what "fast food" would be like in a Slow world: flaky pastries filled with savory ingredients, such as judiciously spiced beef with sautéed onions and raisins. Ruben's, an Argentine takeout institution since 1975, sells this kind of *empanada,* as well as around 20 others, such as chicken, turkey, potato, chile, and mushroom. And at around $3 apiece, you can afford to try them all.

Other Locations
15 Bridge Street, between Broad and Whitehall Sts.; (212) 509-3825
505 Broome Street, between Thompson St. and West Broadway; (212) 334-3351

MALAY & INDONESIAN

Bali Nusa Indah *(Indonesian)*
Theater District
651 Ninth Avenue, between 45th and 46th Sts.
(212) 265-2200
$$ (Cash only)

Indonesian food and Malaysian food are nearly identical. The most noticeable difference is that Indonesian food does not incorporate the Chinese influence that produced *Nyonya* cuisine in Malaysia. At Bali Nusa Indah you can sample a very traditional Indonesian and/or indigenous Malay meal. Bali Nusa Indah serves a long list of dishes to be eaten with steamed white rice, often called *Rijstaffel* (from the Dutch, rice table); the Indonesian term is *nasi rames.* You'll commonly find *krepok* (shrimp crackers), *gado-gado* salad, deliciously tender beef satay with a peanut dipping sauce, *achar* (Indonesian pickled vegetable), *kari ayam* (chicken curry), beef *rendang* (beef slow-cooked in a mix of coconut milk, shredded and toasted coconut, lemongrass, chiles, turmeric leaf, and kaffir lime leaf), *sambal ikan bilis* (a mix of shrimp paste, onions, chile, tomato, and dried anchovies), and either beans or a leafy green vegetable cooked with chile and shrimp paste. You'll find the food fresh and hot, which ironically is the only aspect of Bali Nusa Indah that may not be so traditional, because, in Indonesia, by lunchtime most of the items you find on your plate have been sitting in the hot sun on the sill of the storefront window since morning.

Nyonya *(Malay)*
Chinatown/Little Italy
194 Grand Street, between Mott and Mulberry Sts.
(212) 334-3669
$$ (Cash only)

In the first half of the twentieth century, Chinese laborers migrated to the tin mines of Malaysia. A major growth industry at the time, the work provided a steady income, and many Chinese settled there permanently. In the process of settling down, Chinese men married Malay women. Yearning for a bit of nostalgia, these laborers tried to teach their Malay wives how to cook the dishes the men grew up with in China, and the result was a new cuisine called *Nyonya*, or "grandmother." *Assam laksa* or *laksa Penang* (Penang province was a hotbed for these cross-cultural marriages); *kari kapitan* (spicy red curry chicken—ask if they have it, sometimes it is not on the menu); *nasi ayam* (chicken rice); *hokkien mee* (thick noodle fried with squid, fried pork skin, shrimp, and *kecap manis*; and *young tau fu* (tofu stuffed with fish paste and served in chicken or coconut curry broth) are all part of the *Nyonya* culinary lexicon. Nyonya the restaurant makes fine examples of these dishes as well as traditional Malay dishes and some that are not so traditional, such as *sarong burong* (seafood and veggies in a fried taro cup), braised duck, and yam-fried rice. Always packed, especially on Friday and Saturday nights, expect to wait, but the buzz and the food are definitely worth it.

Sentosa   *(Malay)*
Chinatown
3 Allen Street, near Division St.
(212) 925-8018
$$

Sentosa, like all other Malaysian restaurants in New York, serves a mix of traditional Malay, Chinese, Indian, and *Nyonya* (see the preceeding review) cuisines. This is appropriate, as these cultures have helped to shape and influence Malaysia as it is today. Thankfully, the Malays never adopted Marmite on toast.

Sentosa is a small, storefront-type place located at the southernmost end of Allen Street, at the confluence of the Lower East Side and Chinatown. Being in this neighborhood makes you feel as if you've left Manhattan for parts unknown, and sampling some of the more exotic items at Sentosa only adds to the illusion. *Ikan panggang* (skate, marinated in a turmeric, chile, and lemongrass sauce, then wrapped in banana leaf and grilled) is Sentosa's version of a classic Malay dish; *mee goreng* (a yellow, wheat-flour noodle with Indian spices, shrimp, and vegetable) is a nod to Indian influence; and the *ba kut teh* (pork broth and Chinese herb soup) is the result of a strong Chinese influence. The *assam laksa* (rice noodles, flaked fish, fish broth, shrimp paste, chiles, and herbs) is pungent and spicy, a fine representation of the *Nyonya* cuisine stemming from Penang province. The okra with shrimp paste and chiles is a delicious addition of green to the colorful array of food available at this Malaysian getaway.

Taste Good   *(Malay)*
Elmhurst, Queens
82-18 Forty-fifth Avenue, between 82nd and 83rd Sts.
(718) 898-8001
Subway: G, R, V to Elmhurst Ave.
$

"This is great. I feel like I'm in Asia," my wife said, gazing at the squat row houses, terraces jammed with drying laundry, and women preparing food away from the heat of the kitchen. Taste Good Malaysian Restaurant is tucked into a small, predominantly Asian neighborhood in Elmhurst, Queens; and, like many Asian cities, Elmhurst is crowded and it's almost impossible to find parking. The restaurant is like a railroad apartment, long and narrow, and the only design element is a Buddha in the back corner.

Having lived and cooked in Malaysia, I've found that testing the *assam laksa* is the best indication of the quality of a Malay restaurant. *Assam laksa* is classic street food throughout Malaysia. It is also called *laksa Penang* after the province in which it was reputedly created. It's composed of a sour-and-spicy fish broth flavored with black shrimp paste, polygonum, and torch ginger; *laksa* noodles (round rice-flour noodles); and garnished with pineapple (a disputed condiment), cucumber, chiles, and mint leaves. The *assam laksa* at Taste Good does indeed taste great. Other classics are equally as good: *hokkien mee, young tau fu,* and *nasi lemak.* The staff is very proud of their food and they speak English quite well, so they are perfectly capable of guiding the novice through the lengthy menu.

An added bonus: Bordering Taste Good are two fantastic Asian markets, perfect for a casual stroll as you walk off the coconut curries and noodles devoured moments before at what may be New York's best Malay restaurant. Check out all the interesting produce at the Hong Kong Supermarket next door.

NOTABLE

Borobudur   *(Indonesian)*
East Village
128 East 4th Street, between First and Second Aves.
(212) 614-9079
$ (Cash only)

An East Village Indonesian storefront, featuring spicy *sambals* and authentic *petai* (Indonesian/Malaysian stinky bean).

Curry Leaves Malaysian Restaurant   *(Malay)*
Flushing, Queens
13531 40th Road, between Prince and Main Streets
(718) 762-9313
Subway: 7 to Flushing-Main St.
$ (Cash only)

Malaysian Rasa Sayang   (Malay)
Jackson Heights, Queens
75-19 Broadway, between 75th and 76th Sts.
(718) 424-9054
Subway: E, F, G, R to Jackson Hgts.–Roosevelt Ave.; 7 to 74th
  St.–Broadway
Closed Tuesday
$$ (Cash only)

The food here tends toward the Chinese end of the Malay food spectrum, but the shrimp *laksa* and other dishes are delicious.

Proton Saga   (Malay)
Chinatown/Little Italy
11 Allen Street, near Canal St.
(212) 625-1163
$$ (Cash only)

Next door to Sentosa, Proton Saga's decor is a little slicker, but the food is authentic.

Warteg Fortuna   (Indonesian)
Woodside, Queens
51-24 Roosevelt Avenue, between 51st and 52nd Sts.
(718) 898-2554
Subway: 7 to 52nd St.
$

A tiny café with counter seating, eating here is just like dining in Indonesia.

ELIZABETH LITTLES

MEXICAN

Café Habana
Chinatown/Little Italy
17 Prince Street at Elizabeth St.
(212) 625-2002
$

If you want a hip dining experience with flavor, then Café Habana is your place. This luncheonette's predecessor still exists in Mexico City and is famous for being frequented by great musicians. Here in the New York café, you can perch at the bar, sit at a table, take your food to go, or get it delivered. The delivery menu is a little different, so for your first visit go to the restaurant, sit by an open window, order a $5 Sauza margarita, and people-watch. Skewered chicken marinated in *achiote* is complemented by the flavor of mango. The *mole Poblano* has a strong chile presence and a bit of sweetness; it not only tops the enchiladas but is mixed with the chicken filling. Sides of black beans and Mexican rice make it a perfect entrée. For dessert, you have your choice of flan: coconut, cheese, or Kahlua-espresso.

Other Location:
Café Habana to Go, 229 Elizabeth Street, between Houston and
    Prince Sts.; (212) 625-2002

Castro's Autentico Restaurante Mexicano con Sabor Casero
Fort Greene, Brooklyn
511 Myrtle Avenue, between Grand Ave. and Ryerson St.
(718) 398-1459
Subway: G to Clinton-Washington Aves.
$

Castro's serves breakfast, lunch, and dinner, so you could potentially eat Mexican food all day long here. It may be a bit of a trip into Brooklyn, but it is well worth the effort. The staff is incredibly friendly, but speaking Spanish doesn't hurt. If it is a nice day, sit outside on the patio, and you will feel like you are vacationing in a foreign country. If you do not want a beer with your meal, definitely try the *agua frescas* (fresh fruit waters). They also offer *batidos* (shakes), *atole*, and *jugos naturales*.

The menu is extensive, but it does not spread itself too thin. Tacos are filled with traditional meats that may not be so familiar, such as *carnitas* (deep-fried pork), *cecina* (salted beef), *lengua de res* (beef tongue), *chiccaron en salsa verde con arroz* (fried pork skin in a green sauce with rice), or *barbacoa de chivo* (goat meat), which is really worth the adventure. Entrées are also worth investigating. The *puntas de res en chipotle* (strips of beef that have been cooked with a chipotle chile sauce) are delicious.

Various regions of Mexico are well represented, with dishes ranging from *camarones à la Veracruzana* (shrimp in a tomato-based sauce with olives, Serrano chiles, cilantro, onions, and garlic) to chicken cooked in *mole Poblano.*

El Chile Verde
Bushwick/East Williamsburg, Brooklyn
222 Bushwick Avenue at Meserole St.
(718) 381-0346
Subway: L to Montrose Ave.
$

Many New Yorkers who have traveled to Mexico, Texas, or California complain that you can't find good Mexican food in New York. For those of us who are seriously committed to eating great food, we know that this is not true; it simply takes an adventurous spirit and a little perseverance. The bulk of the Mexican population in New York hails from the Puebla region of Mexico. Pueblans are known throughout Mexico as great cooks, famous for dishes such as *chiles en nogado, mole Poblano,* and the wonderful *cemitas,* to name but a few. In traveling through Puebla (or anywhere in Mexico), one might remark at how few upscale or conventional restaurants there are. And, after eating in a couple of these places, one might deduce that these large, upscale restaurants are not producing the best food in the country. The *comida con sabor Mexicano,* the real food of the country, is found in the ad hoc storefront dives and in the home. Apply this logic to your search for great Mexican food in New York (or anywhere else for that matter) and you're on the right track.

El Chile Verde was pieced together on a shoestring budget by the owner José (Chico to his friends), and you get the sense that he was doing whatever he could to get the doors open, working with a sense of urgency to educate palates on the delights of great Mexican cuisine. Everything Chico makes is loaded with flavor, from the bright, crisp salsa to other salsas that are complex, spicy, and slightly smoky. He has fresh *popolo* growing on the counter of the small retail shop that is adjacent to the dining room. *Popolo* is an herb used in the Pueblan *cemitas,* which are sandwiches often layered with a fresh, stringy cheese, beans, avocado, jalapeños, a variety of meat choices, and sometimes even eggs mixed with jalapeños. The *huitlacoche* (corn fungus) and *flor di calabaza* (squash blossom) quesadillas are delicious, delicate, and robust with light textures playing off smoky and funky mouth-filling sensations, all framed by a balanced piquancy. The *adobado,* a rich, earthy sauce that Chico uses with slow-cooked chicken, stimulates compulsive eating. The *mole Poblano* (chocolate-based sauce with a dizzying number of ingredients) is sweet, bitter, and warming with a driving, salty undercurrent that keeps reminding you it is a savory dish.

Well worth the trip, El Chile Verde is a sure sign that great Mexican food is alive and well in New York.

La Palapa Cocina Mexicana
East Village
77 Saint Marks Place at First Ave.
(212) 777-2537
$$

La Palapa is a beautiful restaurant with plenty of open-air and patio seating, making it the perfect summer spot. Sit by a window and enjoy a pitcher of white hibiscus sangria. Snacking is easy with a multitude of rustic street-food selections; sample the *elote del mercado* (market corn), finished with lime, chile pequin, mayonnaise, and *queso fresco*. La Palapa is trying hard to teach New Yorkers about Mexican ingredients. The extensive menu features *epazote, achiote, jicama, palmitos,* and a variety of chiles. They serve a variety of sauces from a basic *mojo de ajo* (olive oil, garlic, and lime) to *pipian verde* (based on green pumpkin seeds), to more complex Oaxacan *mole negro* and classic *mole rojo*. The appetizers are impressive. *Pozole* (pork and hominy soup) is rich and comes with a plate of garnishes, including radishes, lime slices, avocado, and oregano. Choose your entrées wisely; the *albondigas* (Mexican meatballs) are a bit too dry, and the *chile relleno* is swimming in grease. For a dessert adventure, the parfait is perfect with corn ice cream, macadamia nuts, and *cajeta* (a goat's-milk-based caramel sauce).

Matamoros Puebla Grocery Corp.
Williamsburg, Brooklyn
193 Bedford Avenue at North 6th St.
(718) 782-5044
Subway: L to Bedford Ave.
$ (Cash only)

For the best tacos in the New York City area, run, don't walk, to Matamoros Grocery and Taqueria—just be careful not to run right by it. When you walk into the grocery store, if you look all the way down the aisles you will see three tables in the back. Browse through the store and pick up a few must-have items, such as dried herbs and chiles. Then, when you reach the back, you will notice four women behind a tiny counter using fresh *masa* to make tamales and *sopes* (*masa* "boats" that are filled with a variety of toppings such as black beans, aged cheese, and sour cream). Choose from the selection of tacos and *tortas,* and place your order, whereupon it is written down on a Post-it, called out in Spanish, and rapidly executed. You cannot go wrong with tacos here, especially the *tacos al pastor,* which are made with chile-rubbed roast pork and fresh onions and cilantro. The *torta milanese* is outstanding as well; the pork is pounded thin, breaded, and deep-fried, then used to fill a taco. On the weekends, tamales, *atole champurrado* (a very thick, masa-based Mexican drink), *arroz con leche* (a milk-and-rice-based beverage that is sometimes thicker, more like rice pudding), and *pozole* (soup, usually pork based and often served with hominy, chiles, and fresh garnishes such as onion and cilantro) are available, so go for brunch.

Maya
East Side
1191 First Avenue at 64th St.
(212) 585-1818
Dinner only
$$

For a more upscale Mexican dining experience, Maya is a good bet. If you have a large party, Maya is designed so that each table is almost partitioned, so it feels similar to a private room. The Margaritas are just okay here, but they do have an interesting wine list. The menu provides so many appealing choices that it is difficult to make decisions. If you choose not to decide, try the sampler appetizer with *tamal al chipotle* (*masa* filled with shredded chicken, served with a chipotle chile sauce, *crema fresca,* avocado, and cilantro oil), *chile relleno, quesadillas surtidas* (*masa* stuffed with Oaxacan cheese, *rajas,* and zucchini blossoms), and *tacos de camarron* (filled shrimp sautéed with habañero chiles and tamarind).

Chef Sandoval uses entrées as a stage to showcase Mexican dishes with fresh, seasonal produce, such as salmon *olmeca,* served over artichokes, swiss chard, and fingerling potatoes. Traditional *pechuga adobada* (adobo-marinated chicken) is topped with roasted corn, *huitlacoche* (corn fungus), and manchego cheese dumplings. Other good choices include the *mole Poblano* and *pipian de puerco* (tamarind-marinated pork tenderloin served with pumpkin seed sauce and roasted corn purée). There are big flavors, coastal influences, and fresh produce all over the seafood-centric menu.

Dessert tends to fall flat after the bold impressions that the appetizers and entrées make. Cinnamon ice cream and *café de olla* are good options.

The servers will even sing an accented "Happy Birthday" for anyone celebrating. This is creative Mexican cuisine.

Mexicana Mama
West Village
525 Hudson Street, between Charles and West 10th Sts.
(212) 924-4119
Closed Monday
$$ (Cash only)

Many options for Mexican food in New York are either high-end fancy eating establishments or plain lunch counters at the back of a neighborhood grocery store. Mexicana Mama fits somewhere in the middle. Located in the West Village, this tiny, one-room establishment has been bringing lively Mexican treats, both classical and innovative, to the neighborhood for the past few years.

With its cobalt-blue walls, open cooking views, and mere 21 seats (including 5 at the counter), the restaurant is reminiscent of a home kitchen in the heart of Mexico City. While the menu may contain items familiar to everyone, they are executed much better than usual and include a rich chicken with *mole,* pork tacos with Cascabel chile sauce and the classic slow-stewed beef known as *barbacoa.* Their dessert menu includes a classic flan as well as *pastel tres leches,* a white sponge cake soaked in three kinds of milk. While it does not have a full bar, Mexicana Mama offers a small list of Margaritas, beer, wine, and a limited selection of tequilas. They do not accept reservations, so, due to its size, there is usually a wait for dinner. However, they do offer delivery and takeout— great options for those who can't wait until *mañana.*

NOTABLE

El Paso Taqueria
Upper East Side
1642 Lexington Avenue, at 104th St.
(212) 831-9831
$ (Cash only)

To eat with fellow Mexicans and watch a *novella* or two on TV, visit El Paso. Craving beef? Choose the steak tacos, and top them with the fresh, delicious salsa verde. Homemade *sopes* are another good choice.

Hell's Kitchen
Theater District
679 Ninth Avenue, between 46th and 47th Sts.
(212) 977-1588
$$

Chef Sue Torres uses traditional Mexican ingredients to create an exciting Nuevo Mexicano cuisine.

Rosa Mexicano
East Side
61 Columbus Avenue at 62nd St.
(212) 977-7700
$$$

In 1984, Josefina Howard brought Mexican food to New York City, where she designed her restaurant with an open grill, rustic furnishings, and a vibrant color scheme. The Lincoln Center location opened in 2000 with a beautiful "diver" sculpture and water wall. The bars at both places can be crowded, but also casual and fun. Try the made-at-table guacamole, homemade tortillas, and frozen Margaritas, which are fantastic!

Other Location
1063 First Avenue at 58th St.; (212) 753-7407

Super Tacos
Upper West Side
Corner of 96th Street and Broadway
(917) 837-6052; beeper: (917) 827-9726
$ (Cash only)

The Super Tacos truck has been serving customers for ten years. Go for any of the tacos, then try the *tortas,* quesadillas, and *agua frescas.*

Taco Taco
Upper East Side
1726 Second Avenue, between 89th and 90th Sts.
(212) 289-8226
$ (Cash only)

The daily specials are particularly good, such as the *quesadillas con huitla-coche.* Try the "Taco Taco" tacos (pork marinated with smoked jalapeños).

Zarela
Midtown East
953 Second Avenue, between 50th and 51st Sts.
(212) 644-6740
$$

Located in a townhouse in midtown Manhattan amid Irish pubs and singles bars, Zarela has been bringing imaginative and lively Mexican cuisine to New Yorkers for more than fifteen years. The menu includes original offerings such as *salpicon de pescado* (red snapper hash cooked with jalapeño, tomatoes, cinnamon, and cloves), *pollo borracho* (chicken braised with tequila, green olives, and golden raisins), and *arroz con crema* (rice baked with cream, corn, and roasted Poblano chiles). The atmosphere is fun and festive, with "killer" Margaritas and snacks at the bar, and live music most nights.

ELIZABETH LITTLES

TAMALES

It makes me inordinately happy to pick up the phone at my restaurant and hear somebody ask, "What's the tamal of the day?" It wouldn't have happened when we opened fifteen years ago, because people thought all Mexican tamales were the same thing: blobs of some kind of wrapped-up cornmeal mush with a few shreds of meat in an anonymous red sauce. Now most diners understand that tamales exist in countless wonderful varieties.

All the parts of a tamal have to be lovingly crafted by hand. Its soul is *masa*—a luscious corn dough not at all like cornmeal mush—skillfully beaten with very good, flavorful lard (preferably home-rendered, which has less saturated fat than butter) to a delicate lightness. Its heart is a filling—anything from turkey in *mole* to a savory vegetarian bean mixture—either folded into or cradled on the *masa*. And the garment that surrounds both is a wrapping, usually of either dried corn husks or banana leaf, that imparts its own taste to the tamal. Finally, the finished tamales are steamed. As they cook, all of the layers of flavors come beautifully together.

Because each of the main elements has many possible variations, there's immense diversity beyond the deceptive simplicity of tamales. At Zarela, for example, we may play with the layer of corn *masa* by folding in the elusive southern Mexican herb called *chipilin,* or a subtly spiced roasted pumpkin mixture, or fresh corn kernels and roasted Poblanos with the musky accent of epazote. Sometimes we'll make tamales from my childhood—pork in red chile sauce that we always ate at Christmas, or chicken with green olives and raisins that my grandmother used to make—as well as sophisticated versions with shrimp and jalapeños or earthy *huitlacoche,* the corn fungus that Mexicans prize like truffles. We may cap a filling with the anise-scented herbs *hoja santa* or avocado leaf.

As for the wrapping, we might experiment with regional variations such as fresh cornstalk leaves used instead of corn husks for *corundas,* the triangular tamales that I ate on my recent visit to Michoacan state. We might tie tamales with a twist like party favors, or make them in varied shapes like elegant gift packages (which for Mexicans is what they are!).

The payoff of all this loving care is the moment when the steaming hot tamale is brought to the table and the leaf "gift-wrap" is undone to release the heavenly aroma. The *masa* will be a light, fluffy foil for the deep-flavored filling, and at one bite you will understand why tamales have been the Mexican food of celebration since time immemorial.

—*Zarela Martinez*

Al Bustan   *(Lebanese)*
Midtown East
827 Third Avenue, between 50th and 51st Sts.
(212) 759-5933
$$$

The lack of truly outstanding Middle Eastern and North African restaurants creates a big vacuum in the New York restaurant scene. That's a shame, because this cuisine is so ancient and extraordinary. And while the French *Guide Michelin* lists no fewer than thirteen such restaurants as among the best in Paris, only Al Bustan in New York is widely considered to be worthy of the "Best Lebanese" title.

Al Bustan's very impersonal and uninviting decor is a turn-off, but the food here is well prepared. The selection of *meze* (appetizers) is very good, and if price is no issue, the Royal Meze at $35 per person (minimum four people) with hot and cold appetizers, including the tartare-like delicacy *kibbe nayeh* (finely ground seasoned lamb) makes for a very interesting meal. The *mahashi,* vegetables that are individually stuffed with meat, rice, and spices, as well as the grilled meats are good and served in generous portions. The Lebanese desserts and Middle Eastern coffee are all very authentic.

Someday, we hope, there will be a Middle Eastern restaurant in New York like San Francisco's Mammounia, where you walked into an elegant ambience of low tables, cushions, and copper trays, and a waiter poured rose water over your hands. It all made for an extraordinary and unforgettable dining experience, great food included.

Dalga Seafood Grill   *(Turkish)*
East Side
401 East 62nd Street, between First and York Aves.
(212) 813-1790
$$$

Although the atmosphere at Dalga Seafood Grill is casually simple—comprised of blue and green Mediterranean-style decor with a bar in front, and dining in back—the slow-cooked food is anything but. You might start with *dolma,* grape leaves stuffed with Turkish rice, dill, currants, cinnamon, and pine nuts, or the yogurt *yayla,* a hot yogurt, rice, and mint soup flavored with homemade chicken stock. Other appetizers included grilled octopus, seafood *borec* (a phyllo dough pouch stuffed with crab, shrimp, and scallions), and *iman baylldi,* or stuffed eggplant. With so many entrées on the menu, it can hard to decide, but on the waiter's suggestion we tried the *karides guvec,* a traditional shrimp and vegetable stew served in a clay pot and topped with Turkish Kosar cheese. The chicken *sis kebap* is succulent and served with Turkish *baldo* rice and *cacik,* a yogurt, cucumber, and garlic sauce.

True to its name, Dalga Seafood also has a host of daily fish specials, ranging from mahi mahi to swordfish, sea bass, or halibut. All fish can be ordered sautéed, broiled, or grilled, and comes with a root vegetable remoulade on a bed of arugula. For dessert, don't even think of leaving without trying the baklava. We found it to be the best we've ever had, with a mild sweetness that was by no means overwhelming.

Superbly blended flavors are the common theme that runs throughout the whole Dalga experience. The ingredients are numerous and complex, yet the food consistently proves full of intricately woven tastes. No single spice jumps out to steal the show, yet the richly delicate seasonings each made an appearance on the palate. Go to Dalga and enjoy some of the finest, most authentic Turkish cuisine you'll ever encounter.

Mamlouk   (*Mediterranean*)
East Village
211 East 4th Street, between Aves. A and B
(212) 529-3477
Closed Monday; two seatings nightly, at 7:00 and 9:00 P.M.
$$$$ (prix fixe)

Mamlouk is an extreme dining experience. From the moment the light of the lantern hits you as you enter the small restaurant, you are "received" into the capable hands of the staff. They expertly guide you through the myriad tasting menu, explaining each of the chef's creations. The menu changes daily and touches all cuisines of the region. Some days you might be served a lamb *tajeen,* on another a *moussaka.* Whichever way the chef leads you, you'll find that the plates complement each other and lead you to another taste experience.

Friendly, but not overwhelming, the staff checks in with you as your culinary journey transports you. The decor, including the copper-topped oven hood in the open kitchen and the handcrafted plates, contribute to the enjoyment. A downstairs room is available for larger parties. After several courses, you can round out the evening by puffing on a hookah. Mamlouk sets a Slow standard that everyone should aspire to.

Mombar   (*Egyptian*)
Astoria, Queens
25-22 Steinway Street, between 25th and 28th Aves.
(718) 726-2356
Subway: G, R, V to Steinway St.

Dinner only; closed Monday
$$ (Cash only)

Mombar is the haunt of artist and chef Moustafa El Sayed, whose brother, Ali, runs the nearby Kabab Café (also well worth a visit). Outside you won't find any sign with the restaurant's name (*mombar* is the name of an Egyptian sausage stuffed with meat and rice), but only a huge pair of eyes over the door—one made of stucco, the other of mosaic tiles. Inside the small storefront space, there are more expressions of El Sayed's creativity, with tile designs on the walls, stained glass in the window, and an elaborate mosaic on the floor. The tables are mismatched and decorated with antique and recycled items that the chef-owner has turned into art.

Moustafa's talent, however, is not restricted to visual arts. In the tiny kitchen he cooks everything to order. There's no menu, and choices vary daily, but you will find examples of the stewed meats typical of southern Egyptian cooking, such as chicken, lamb, or rabbit cooked with a variety of vegetables and dried fruits, served with couscous or pilaf. One of Mombar's signature dishes is a half duck with a dark, nutty-tasting molasses glaze, as delicious as it is unusual. Dessert is likely to include some type of cake (date, pound, or *ravani*, made with semolina flour and dried fruits), typically served with yogurt and fresh fruit.

Not at all stuffy, pretentious, or predictable, the dining experience at Mombar is a delight for both the eyes and the taste buds.

NOTE: Moustafa's brother, Ali El Sayed, runs the Kebab Café down the street at 25-12 Steinway Street (718-728-9858), which serves very good Egyptian food.

Moustache   (*Mediterranean*)
West Village
90 Bedford Street, between Barrow and Grove Sts.
(212) 229-2220
$ (Cash only)

There are no more than a dozen small tables, and, yes, more often than not, you have to wait in line on the narrow sidewalk. But among other things a most wonderful lentil soup awaits you, prepared with all the right spices. The pita comes right from the oven and is brought to your table still blown up like a balloon. The magnificent *ouzi* is a dish of basmati rice, chicken, vegetables, roasted almonds, and raisins, wrapped in a phyllo pastry and served with a yogurt sauce. The *meze*, or appetizers, are impeccably prepared. The sandwiches, falafel, and lamb are all good and always seem to hit the spot. Among Moustache's specialties are the

Middle Eastern "pitzas": the *lahm bi'Ajin* is especially recommended, with lamb, onions, and secret mixture of spices. *Laomi,* Moustache's citrus drink, and *ayran,* their yogurt drink, are very typical, and all of their desserts are first-class. The quality of the food and the unpretentiousness of the restaurant make Moustache a little jewel of a place in this busy metropolis.

Other Location
265 East 10th Street, between First Ave. and Ave. A; (212) 228-2022

Salam Café & Restaurant   *(Mediterranean)*
West Village
104 West 13th Street, between Sixth and Seventh Aves.
(212) 741-0277
Dinner only
$$

Salam is set in a tranquil, hospitable location in the West Village. There are mosaic tables, tapestries on the walls, and North African lanterns illuminating the restaurant. Friendly staff serve a Pan-Arabian menu including couscous, kebabs, curries, and coriander dishes. Stand-out dishes were the Couscous Royale, a kind of Moroccan paella served with *merguez* (lamb sausage), lamb, chicken, and shrimp, or any of the *ouzi* dishes, which are phyllo pastry pockets stuffed with sweet and savory rice and served with either lamb, chicken, shrimp, or vegetables. Also interesting is an assorted *meze* (appetizer) plate as a meal; if you order this, you can sample all of the various hot and cold appetizers. Salam's wine list includes some North African and Lebanese selections, which are little known in the West, but well worth trying.

NOTABLE

Al Baraka
See African, p. 3.

Bedouin Tent
Downtown Brooklyn (Boerum Hill)
405 Atlantic Avenue, between Bond and Nevins Sts.
(718) 852-5555
Subway: A, C, G to Hoyt-Schermerhorn
$$

Founded by the Moustache folks, Bedouin Tent is now an independent restaurant serving freshly made Middle Eastern food, including fantastic pita bread baked to order and all the usual spreads, plus specialties such as *dolma* and lamb *merguez*.

Colbeh   *(Persian)*
Garment District/Koreatown
43 West 39th Street, between Fifth and Sixth Aves.
(212) 354-8181
$$

A *glatt* kosher Persian restaurant serving authentic dishes such as *tahdig,* a crispy rice dish that's made by scraping the rice off the bottom and sides of the cooking pot, then topping it with a souplike vegetable or beef stew.

Other Location
68-34 Main Street, between 68th Dr. and 68th Rd., Flushing,
    Queens; (718) 268-8181

Fountain Café   *(Syrian)*
Brooklyn Heights, Brooklyn
183 Atlantic Avenue, between Clinton and Court Sts.
(718) 624-6764
Subway: F, G to Bergen St.; M, N, R to Court St.; 2, 3, 4, 5 to
    Borough Hall
$

One of the highlights at Fountain is the homemade stuffed grape leaves, served warm in a tangy tomato sauce. The rest of the food rises almost as high, with delicious kebabs cooked to order and interesting items such as the *kibbeh saneeya,* a meat pie made with lamb and pine nuts in a crust of cracked wheat, served with minted yogurt.

Hapina   *(Yemeni)*
Flushing, Queens
69-54 Main Street at Jewel St.
(718) 544-6262
Subway: E, F, to Briarwood/Van Wyck Blvd.
$

Three different hot sauces—green, red, and yellow (mango-based)—characterize Yemeni cuisine. They use them all to good advantage at Hapina. Try the Cornish game hen *schwarma* here, and soothe the spiciness at the self-serve salad bar, which features a range of raw and prepared vegetables.

Layla   *(Mediterranean)*
Tribeca
211 West Broadway at Franklin St.
(212) 431-0700

Belly dancers will greet you at Layla after 9:00 P.M., a nice perk to this
Drew Nieporent outpost with many specialties, including *babaganoush*
and phyllo-wrapped sardines. A nice wine list and great desserts are more
reasons to visit this trendy oasis.

Oznot's Dish   *(Mediterranean)*
Williamsburg, Brooklyn
79 Berry Street at North 9th St.
(718) 599-6596
Subway: L to Bedford Ave.
$$

Just like the decorations, the menu is filled with odd combinations of
ingredients that excel when they click: Some New Yorkers swear by it.

Persepolis   *(Persian)*
Lenox Hill
1423 Second Avenue, between 74th and 75th Sts.
(212) 535-1100
$$

Persepolis is known for its outstanding kebabs, which are marinated
overnight, and the exquisitely prepared basmati rice, which is infused
with flavor and seasonings.

SOUL FOOD

Great Jones Café
Noho
54 Great Jones Street, between Bowery and Lafayette St.
(212) 674-9304
$ (Cash only)

The beauty of living in an ethnically diverse city such as New York is that you can experience different cities and cultures simply by stepping through the doors of a restaurant. Such is the case with Great Jones Café in Greenwich Village. After a nocturnal meal of garlic mashed potatoes (real potatoes—I asked), perfectly seasoned grilled chicken with cilantro pesto, or fried Cajun-spiced catfish, I almost expect to walk around the corner onto Bourbon Street and see men throwing beaded necklaces. Don't expect to be given a dinner menu, though; since it changes daily, it is written on a small blackboard. But, of course, Southern/Cajun staples such as Cajun popcorn crawfish, filé shrimp gumbo, and red beans and rice are almost always available. The side dishes and brunch menu are more permanent, as they are painted on the wall. Great Jones offers outrageously good home cooking (grilled ham steak with brown sugar glaze, pecan pie, and Mississippi mud pie) and good drinks (try their smooth Electric Lemonade or a Cajun Martini) at good prices, along with great music to eat by. It really doesn't get much better—though it would be nice if more emphasis were placed on sourcing local products. While you might almost pass by this small box of a restaurant due to its no-frills facade the first time you visit, you'll leave with its address and location etched on your brain.

Jimmy's Uptown
Harlem
2207 Adam Clayton Powell Jr. Blvd. (Seventh Ave.) at 131st St.
(212) 491-4000
$$$

Now with three locations (Jimmy's Uptown, Downtown, and Bronx Café) Jimmy's Uptown, just blocks away from the Apollo Theater, gives guests a new, modern take on soul food with Latin underpinnings. The restaurant itself is sleek, with beautiful tables and chairs and sheer panels. If you are a party larger than five, make sure to reserve one of the luxurious booths. Jimmy's specializes in fish and seafood, which Chef Fiona Ruane serves with gusto. The shrimp hush puppies for an appetizer are very good but could do without the huge amounts of tartar sauce that come with them. The pecan-crusted catfish for a main course is served in its entirety and is delicious. The spinach and shrimp that is stuffed inside the catfish make the dish overly complicated, but does not take away from the fish itself. The coconut fish 'n chips (monkfish) is also special. Ruane's talent lies in preparing batter for her foods that is very light, which is good news for people who don't feel like committing to a hardcore soul food meal. Modernizing soul food in this way is perhaps the restaurant's greatest appeal. The service is stellar: If you are lucky you will have the pleasure of being served by head waiter Victor Adams. Hopefully, Jimmy's Uptown will soon be one of many more elegant restaurants in this historic and architecturally beautiful neighborhood.

Other Locations
Jimmy's Bronx Café, 281 West Fordham Road, between Cedar
   Ave. and Major Deegan Expwy., Bronx; (718) 329-2000
Jimmy's Downtown, 400 East 57th Street, between First Ave.
   and Sutton Pl.; (212) 486-6400

M & G Soul Food Diner
Harlem
383 West 125th Street at Morningside Ave.
(212) 864-7326
Open 24 hours; Monday–Thursday
$$ (cash only)

Don't let the bright, flashy-yellow, Las Vegas–like lights circling the sign fool you: M & G Soul Food Diner is not about show. While you may enter this small diner to the crooning of Stevie Wonder or Luther Vandross or Ella Fitzgerald, the smooth, sophisticated ambience stops there. Reminiscent of an African American version of the old television show *Alice* (the waitresses wear hairnets and uniforms that went out of style decades ago), M & G is your typical soul food joint—offering all the fondness of Southern-style memories and nothing more. A large breakfast of salmon or chicken with grits or homefries and toast will set you back no more than $6, while the dinner menu features beef short ribs, smothered pork chops, chitterlings, and more—none of which cost more than $12.

Having been in business for the past thirty-five years, not much has changed at M & G, including the flea market paintings that can be found in many a grandmother's home. The ribs, pork chops, warm cornbread muffins with butter, and carrot cake are uniformly good and filling.

Miss Mamie's Spoonbread Too
Upper West Side
366 West 110th Street, between Columbus and Manhattan Aves.
(212) 865-6744
$$

While many people might not know what spoonbread is, they do know good food when they eat at Miss Mamie's Spoonbread Too. Plenty of New Yorkers have had good food (it's not hard to find in this city), but great soul food with good service—service that's quick and pleasant? That's a rare commodity indeed. Miss Mamie's ribs are so tender that the meat falls off the bone, and they're basted in a tangy barbeque sauce that's neither too tangy nor too sweet. The macaroni and cheese still retains the corner shape of the glass Pyrex casserole dish it was most likely baked in, and the Spoonbread Punch (a combination of what seems like orange Kool-Aid, fruit juices, cinnamon, and cloves) served in canning jar glasses is perfect for summer days as an accompaniment to the good eats.

Started by former New York fashion model Norma Jean Darden, the Spoonbread dynasty has turned into two restaurants, a catering company, and a cookbook describing all the delicious secrets of spoonbread, strawberry wine, and more. Secret or not, the peach cobbler with its perfectly baked crust and homemade peach filling, and the *Best of Rick James* playing in the background are all anyone should need to know about Miss Mamie's.

Other Location
Miss Maude's Spoonbread Too, 547 Lenox Avenue, between 137th and 138th Sts.; (212) 690-3100

NOTABLE

Carmichael's Diner
Jamaica, Queens
117-08 Brewer Boulevard (New York Blvd.) at Foch Blvd.
(718) 723-6908
Public transit: F to Parsons Blvd., then Q111 or Q113 bus to Foch Blvd.
$ (Cash only)

Grab a booth and get ready for some solid Southern home cooking, with daily specials and old favorites like the homemade sweet potato pie. Good comfort food doesn't need any excuses—it's spectacular simply because it is so familiar and meets all our expectations.

Charles' Southern Style Kitchen
Hamilton Heights
2841 Frederick Douglass Boulevard (Eighth Ave.), between 151st
and 152nd Sts.
(212) 926-4313
Closed Monday–Tuesday
$

Charles' fried chicken is peerless and worth a trip uptown on its own, but
try the barbecued ribs, too, and other well-prepared soul food standards.

Copeland's
Hamilton Heights
547 West 145th Street, between Broadway and Amsterdam Ave.
(212) 234-2357
Closed Monday
$$

Copeland's offers large portions of authentic, well-prepared Southern
soul food. Their "gospel brunch" on Sunday is a popular destination for
post-sermon churchgoers in Harlem.

North Carolina Country Products
Brownsville, Brooklyn
1991 Atlantic Avenue at Saratoga Ave.
(718) 498-8033
Subway: C to Rockaway Ave.
$

Where do you find a really good Southern spicy sausage sandwich? Or
how about a great savory sage sausage sandwich? Ham steak? Ham hocks?
Okay, maybe just a pack of Black Mariah chewing tobacco, a tin of snuff,
and some horehound (a bitter herb) candy. At North Carolina Country
Products, these are just a few of the products you'll find. Commonplace
in the small towns of the Carolinas and places south, the products aren't
high-end, and they're not beautifully packaged, but they are certainly
authentic, and definitely out of the ordinary up here in Yankeeville. It's a
market that is easy to praise after finishing off a hearty breakfast of bis-
cuits and sausage gravy. Be sure to brush up on your please, thank you, sir,
and ma'am—the Southern hospitality here is contingent on proper
Southern manners.

Old Devil Moon

East Village
511 East 12th Street, between Aves. A and B
(212) 475-4357
Dinner only weekdays; brunch–dinner Saturday–Sunday
$

An old New York blues guitarist friend turned us on to the great Southern food at Old Devil Moon, and we're glad he did. Portions of delicious fried chicken, pork chops, and ribs are ample; the brunch menu and desserts are solid (try the peanut-butter or fruit pies); and, for the less carnivorous, they even do a Southern-fried version of tofu.

Pink Tea Cup

See Brunch, p. 175.

ELIZABETH LITTLES

Arharn Thai *(Thai)*
Long Island City, Queens
32-05 36th Avenue, between 32nd and 33rd Sts.
(718) 728-5563
Subway: N, R, W to 36th Ave.
$$

Astoria, once a stronghold of Greek culture and cuisine, today offers cuisines ranging from Yugoslavian to Egyptian to Thai. Arharn, a small, simple restaurant, serves well-balanced yet strongly flavored Thai food that stands up to the fare served in the couple of great Thai restaurants in nearby Jackson Heights. Try the *yum ped krob* (duck salad), which combines crispy, salty bits of duck with intense chiles, sour lime, aromatic basil, a hint of sweet palm sugar, and warming, earthy peanuts. It is a superb example of balancing flavors and textures that, when executed correctly, makes Thai food the envy of most other cuisines. Other dishes worth trying are the *massaman* curry (a dish most likely inspired by the Arabs who scoured Southeast Asia for exotic spices and other products to broker overseas), and the excellent *pad thai* and *som tam* (green papaya salad).

Arunee Thai *(Thai)*
Jackson Heights, Queens
37-68 79th Street, between Roosevelt and 37th Aves.
(718) 205-5637; (718) 205-5559
Subway: E, F, G, R, V to Jackson Hgts.–Roosevelt Ave.; 7 to 82nd
   St.–Jackson Hgts.
$ (Cash only)

In Asian cuisine, fried rice is as commonplace as the bread basket at a French restaurant. But just as that first squeeze, sniff, and bite of bread sets the tone for a meal and foreshadows the quality of the *bouillabaisse* and duck confit to come, so does the smell and fork-fluff of a dish of fried rice at a Thai restaurant. At Arunee Thai, the *khao pad prik* (fried rice) with crab is anything but pedestrian, and sets the tone for a long list of well-executed Thai specialties such as fried fish maw with pork belly, catfish red curry, and a sumptuous rice noodle with beef, basil, and chile. The two Thai women who run the small dining room are always willing to help customers navigate the menu, answering as many questions as they can; and the menu is indeed deserving of a thorough investigation. Try the Jungle Curry from northern Thailand, made without coconut milk. In addition to the menu, Arunee offers specials that often consist of seasonal ingredients. One special of fried softshell crab with a salad of julienned mango, lime juice, fish sauce, chile, coriander, palm sugar, and red onion was a skillful representation of elegant Thai cuisine.

If you are a true connoisseur of Thai food—that is, a believer in the gospel of "not spicy, not Thai food"—then be sure to ask the waitress to turn up the heat, because the kitchen has been known to use a light hand on the chile from time to time.

Nam   *(Vietnamese)*
Tribeca
110 Reade Street, between West Broadway and Church St.
(212) 267-1777
$$

Nam is a statistical outlier among Vietnamese restaurants, and, for that matter, among most Asian restaurants in New York. With tastefully presented old pictures of Vietnam; candles; soft, stylish chairs; and white tablecloths, Nam has an elegance and upscale setting of which Vietnamese food is worthy, but this is treatment it rarely receives. Complementing the design is a culinary triumvirate of women ranging in age from their mid-forties to around seventy. These women produce delicate and highly flavored food from traditional recipes that are by no means run-of-the-mill. *Banh la* (rectangular rice-flour dumplings stuffed with minced shrimp, wrapped in banana leaves, and steamed) was something completely new for me: dense, salty, and delicious. *Ca bam* (monkfish, mint, and cilantro served on rice crackers) is a skillful play of textures and aromas, and *banh xeo* (a crisp crêpe with chicken, shrimp, and rice) was delicate and warming. The thinly sliced, barbequed pork chops, curry chicken, and the *ca chien* (fried red snapper), are all good choices from the main course category. Even in the most humble dishes, the kitchen brings a level of refinement that, when combined with the atmosphere in the dining room, makes for one of the most civilized Vietnamese dining experiences in the city. Maybe a little more of the French influence is beginning to show itself.

Nha Trang   *(Vietnamese)*
Chinatown/Little Italy
87 Baxter Street, between Walker and White Sts.
(212) 233-5948
$ (Cash only)

Always busy, Nha Trang is an example of the classic Chinatown fixture: unchanging (particularly the uninspired decor); comfortable in serving the same simple, straightforward menu day after day, year after year; and always confident that the throngs of people will continue to spill in from the street. As long as the *cha gio* (fried pork and vermicelli spring rolls served with lettuce and mint leaves for wrapping) are still crispy and well seasoned, and the grilled pork chops (glazed with a balanced mixture of fish sauce and palm sugar) are still nicely charred and addictively delicious, there's no doubt the place will be full. The clientele is mostly Western, often reason enough for second-guessing an Asian restaurant; but the *banh xeo* (rice crêpes stuffed with ground shrimp and pork) and the chicken or frogs' legs with chile and lemongrass will quickly assuage any fears you might have had. The clientele is simply proof that Nha Trang is not an undiscovered gem, but it still shines brightly.

Other Location
148 Centre Street, between Walker and White Sts.; (212) 941-9292

Sripraphai   *(Thai)*
Woodside, Queens
64-13 39th Avenue, near Roosevelt Ave.
(718) 899-9599
Subway: 7 to Woodside–61st St.
$

Like most good ethnic joints, Sripraphai has a decor that leaves much to be desired. Fortunately for the diner, any attention paid to the mirrored walls and fluorescent lighting ends immediately upon the arrival of the first dish. Not much compares to the aroma of sliced fresh kaffir lime leaf, pickled chiles, and rich, complex coconut curries. There are no jarred or canned curry pastes being used here.

I have spent some time traveling and cooking in Thailand. *Moo choom*, one of my favorite dishes from northern Thailand, is a spicy/citrusy pork broth, heated at the table, in which one dips thin slices of raw pork, cooks the pork in the broth, and then ladles a little broth and cooked pork into a bowl and consumes it with fresh herbs. I have never seen it on a menu in the States. When I spoke to the owner, she told me she had eaten the dish when she was in Thailand, but sorry, no, it was not on the menu.

Unperturbed, we ordered a wonderful *khao soi* (crispy fried egg noodles topped with a deep, soul-satisfying chicken curry), crispy catfish salad (light, crispy catfish with some sliced green papaya, chile, red onion, fish sauce, lime juice, and palm sugar), a shrimp salad, and rice noodles with ground beef and chile. A few minutes into our meal, the owner appeared from the kitchen, carrying a bubbling dish, set it down on our table, smiled humbly, and apologized for the poor quality of her *moo choom*. I knew then that I was eating in the best Thai restaurant in New York City.

Ubol's Kitchen   *(Thai)*
Astoria, Queens
24-42 Steinway Street at Astoria Blvd.
(718) 545-2874
Subway: N, W to Astoria Blvd.
$

A common theme in Thai restaurants, and throughout Thailand, for that matter, is friendly service. The staff at Ubol's exceeds the Thai standard for courtesy. They are just flat-out super-nice. So nice, you want to eat more than you should, which is a sure way to torture your stomach with an overdose of chiles. While Ubol's offers plenty of traditional Thai selections, there are also innovative house specialties that are worth trying. One in particular is the shredded fried duck with fried basil—a balanced blend of savory, crunchy, aromatic, and spicy taste sensations that's certain to get you drinking a Singha beer before you can say *prik kee neuw* (Thai chile). If you're a fan of *prik kee neuw,* you'll certainly be singing the praises of Ubol's, as the liberal use of chiles is employed here.

There's a good deal of hype surrounding Ubol's: Claims are made that the food here is spicier than any other Thai restaurant in the city. The verdict is still out on this, but order the spicy green curry chicken or a sliced beef *yum* (salad) and you'll find the use of chiles far from subtle. If you do find your stomach rumbling from too much chile and ordering too much food from a staff that is so damn nice, wander down Steinway Street and grab a stomach-settling smoke from a hookah at one of the many Egyptian cafés; and feel fortunate you can delight in such multicultural pleasures all on one street.

The Vietnamese Sandwich   *(Vietnamese)*
Chinatown/Little Italy
Banh Mi Saigon—Under the Manhattan Bridge
108 Forsyth Street
(212) 941-1541
$ (Cash only)

Viet-nam Banh-mi So 1, Inc.
Chinatown/Little Italy
369 Broome Street, between Elizabeth and Mott Sts.
(212) 219-8341
$ (Cash only)

The Vietnamese may not have appreciated French imperialism, but food lovers definitely appreciate its results. One of the clearest representations of these two distinctive culinary cultures colliding is the *banh mi*. From the French we have baguette, the base of this fresh and delectable sandwich, and we have pâté and aioli (some use aioli, others use mayonnaise). From Vietnam, we have shredded daikon and carrots, coriander, chile, sweet marinated and roasted pork sausage, and the inimitable Sri Racha red chile sauce. Together, these components are combined to make one of the most satisfying and inexpensive meals in town. And at $2.75 to $3.00 for a sandwich, the value cannot be beat. Both locations listed above prepare all the ingredients fresh daily. In fact, Anthony, a Vietnamese native with a not-so-Vietnamese first name, says he makes his mayonnaise fresh every day because he is skeptical of the store-bought brands that have infinite shelf lives. You can be confident that you're in for a special treat when a man takes that much pride in producing a dish so simple and fresh. At both spots you can buy other premade goodies, such as sticky rice wrapped in banana leaves and stuffed with chicken, as well as a variety of rice-flour-based desserts and other Vietnamese specialties.

NOTABLE

Ba Xuyjen   *(Vietnamese)*
Park Slope, Brooklyn
6011 7th Avenue, between 60th and 61st Sts.
(718) 765-0037
Subway: N to 8th Ave.
$

A *banh mi* Vietnamese sandwich shop. Some interesting alternatives to the regular chicken or roast pork are the sardines and meatballs.

Cambodian Cuisine   *(Cambodian)*
Fort Greene, Brooklyn
87 South Elliot Place, between Fulton St. and Lafayette Ave.
(718) 858-3262
Subway: C to Lafayette Ave.; G to Fulton St.
$

You'll find home-cooked Cambodian specialties in this small, family-run restaurant. After dinner, stroll around the growing neighborhood of Fort Greene with its beautiful brownstones and the new restaurants and shops that are popping up every week.

Pam Real Thai Food *(Thai)*
Theater District
404 West 49th Street at Ninth Ave.
(212) 333-7500
$ (Cash only)

Hole-in-the-wall digs keep prices low at this Midtown authentic Thai restaurant.

Pho Cong Ly *(Vietnamese)*
Lower East Side
124 Hester Street, near Chrystie St.
(212) 343-1111
$ (Cash only)

Great *pho* (aromatic beef-based soup) in this little café.

Temduang *(Thai)*
Theater District
644 Tenth Avenue, between 45th and 46th Sts.
(212) 307-9388
$

Fresh and authentic Thai. The best thing to do is eat here and afterward stroll over to the Thai grocery a block away and shop for the ingredients to cook your own Thai food at home.

Village Mingala *(Burmese)*
East Village
21-23 East 7th Street, between Second and Third Aves.
(212) 529-3656; (212) 260-0457
$

A mix of several Southeast Asian cuisines, Mingala is a real palate pleaser. Try the spicy sour fish with basil sauce.

SPANISH & PORTUGUESE

Alphabet Kitchen   *(Portuguese/Spanish)*
East Village
171 Avenue A, between 10th and 11th Sts.
(212) 982-3838
$$

The open kitchen and garden with a waterfall are certainly a draw to this East Village restaurant, but their "Iberian" menu offers another sensation to be appreciated. From traditional *tapas,* to Brazilian avocado salad, to seafood *paella,* the dishes complement each other. The *pastel de conejo,* a rabbit pastry with spinach, pistachio, and basil-peach chutney starts off an inspirational menu that offers insight into the emerging culinary magic across the peninsula. *Vieras y hongos* (bay scallops, watercress, and oyster mushrooms in a lemon-truffle sauce) is another delicious seller. In addition, try the free-range Portuguese-style chicken, Cuban-style pork chops, or Moroccan-spiced tuna. With a friendly, informed staff and an approachable wine list, strong on Spanish selections, Alphabet Kitchen offers a promising dining experience.

El Cid   *(Spanish)*
Chelsea
322 West 15th Street, between Eighth and Ninth Aves.
(212) 929-9332
Closed Monday
$$

Most Spanish restaurants in New York seem to reflect the traditional standard *tavernas* found on every block from Madrid to Valencia. El Cid, a cramped and crowded Chelsea spot, is no different. However, while the place screams for a makeover, the kitchen turns out top-notch Spanish food. Although the menu includes a small selection of entrées, the real specialty of El Cid are its *tapas.* Their cold selections include perfectly cooked tortilla Espanola, garlicky *escalibada,* a salad of roast eggplant, peppers, and codfish, and *pulpo a la Gallega* (Galician-style octopus). Some of their better hot selections are *angulitas* (baby eel), *gambas a la plancha* (simply grilled head-on shrimp), and *codorniz* (roasted quail served with a sweet prune and raisin sauce).

While El Cid serves lovely sangria made with white or red wine, their wine list lacks imagination. Of the 20 bottles listed, 15 of them happen to be from the Rioja region. This is unfortunate, considering that Spain produces one of the widest ranges of interesting and delicious wines available in the U.S. today. However, the wines and sherries offered are more than respectable. El Cid is hardly what you would call a culinary epiphany, but it is a great place to go when you have a craving for delicious and traditional *tapas,* fruity sangria, Old World–style service and memories of Spain. They must be doing something right—the place is always jammed!

Oliva *(Spanish)*

Lower East Side
161 East Houston at Allen Street
(212) 228-4143
$$

This little Lower East Side Spanish-Basque restaurant exudes "coolness" with every aspect of its existence: food, wine, people, and decor. The food is surprisingly authentic, with San Sebastian–style *tapas,* including the colorful *pintxosóan* assortment of five different *tapas* (changed daily), served atop small pieces of delectable bread. Other, more contemporary items—such as half an artichoke grilled with olive oil and paprika and served on a bed of spinach, white beans, and giant olives—will also not disappoint.

Less adventurous sorts are sure to find the all-time Spanish classic *jamon serrano* served on a cutting board with two types of Basque cheeses more appealing. Don't miss the desserts, as the homemade flans and chocolate tortes serve to finish off a delightful meal along with a nice digestif.

Following in the strictest Spanish tradition, Oliva offers sangria along with a solid wine list and a full-service (and quite hip) bar. The drinks go down especially well with fresh sounds being spun by in-house DJs, not to mention the free live Latin Jazz session on Sundays. The restaurant itself infuses a nice mix of 1960s decor with an ensemble of stylish servers dressed in all black. Needless to say, Oliva's magnetism may keep you there for long hours, especially once the wine starts flowing.

Pão *(Portuguese)*

Soho
322 Spring Street at Greenwich St.
(212) 334-5464
$$

Pão is the name of the country bread of Portugal, and this restaurant lives up to it, by serving fresh, tasty Portuguese bread in a terra-cotta plant pot. The whirring ceiling fan, worn wooden floor, and exposed brick wall puts you somewhere in the Bairro Alto in Lisbon. On this hip strip of Spring Street, Pão attracts casual diners and an elegant bar crowd. In fact, the full bar is worth a visit on any weekend night. The cooking doesn't let you down either: The simple, clean, authentic food and reasonably priced Portuguese wines will delight your palate. Pão's menu carries classics such as the *bacalhau à braz* (cod with egg, onion, and potatoes), *cataplana de mariscos* (steamed shellfish and sausage), and *pasteis de bacalhau* (codfish cakes). There are also more contemporary dishes, such as the *tamboril assado* (monkfish with saffron potatoes and Madeira sauce) and *gambas com acorda* (shrimp on a lemon-shellfish bread pudding).

Pico   (Portuguese)
Tribeca
349 Greenwich Street, between Harrison and Jay Sts.
(212) 343-0704
Closed Sunday
$$$

Pico is a real New York version of a Portuguese restaurant. It crosses borders, just as the Portuguese themselves once did as one of Europe's first imperialist nations. Chef and co-owner John Villa uses fresh local products to create dishes that pull inspiration from all the former Portuguese colonies. Macao and Goa are two that stand out when you feel a little spice on your tongue or get a faint whiff of anise from the kitchen. The octopus terrine, a gorgeous mosaic of tentacles, is spiced with cumin and fennel and served with a miniature salad of bright, pickled vegetables. The crisped *bacalhau* (cod) cakes are served with a lively salad of blood oranges, beets, radishes, parsley, and cilantro. And the suckling pig, the signature dish of the house, served with crisp skin and wildflower honey, is sure to please the most demanding patrons.

Another aspect of Pico that exceeds one's expectations is the drink list. Bartender Eben Klemm, a former manager of an M.I.T. laboratory, has created some of the most exciting cocktails in the city: The Cujo is a *caipirinha* of kumquat, cucumber, and cumin, and the Ann Hester is a elegant blend of calendula, gin, and a Campari-grapefruit foam. Moving on from cocktails, Pico offers the most exciting Portuguese-focused wine list in New York. All the diversity may seem overwhelming, but Pico's staff is knowledgeable, courteous, and eager to guide customers through all the wonderful choices.

Pipa   (Spanish)
Gramercy Park/Flatiron District
38 East 19th Street, between Broadway and Park Ave. South
(212) 677-2233
$$

Founded by, but no longer with Pipa, Chef Douglas Rodriguez did his best in articulating the Nuevo Latino movement through the bold expression that Pipa represents. Classic ingredients found in everyday Spanish cuisine clash with twists of contemporary furor. The harmony of the food and the atmosphere demonstrate a unique combination of traditionalism enhanced by a touch of modernity, of ethnic roots succumbing to a larger process of globalization—all presented in a neat and tidy minimalist structure.

Traditional *tapas* are extensive in the menu, although they have been slightly modified in the restaurant's nouveau style. *Sopa de ajo blanco* is made in the same manner as traditional cold gazpacho soup, but it combines Mediterranean ingredients such as almond and garlic in an entirely new way. The way the classic *buquerones,* small fillets of pickled anchovies, are served is more reminiscent of a Picasso than a stuffy, old Spanish tavern: two small fillets served on top of a Yukon Gold potato with a pepper-and-olive salad.

Although one might think that the deep-red velvet curtains, the pale exposed brick walls, and the extravagant chandeliers hanging from the ceiling would create a stiff atmosphere, the low lights, copious amounts of wine, and the soft Spanish-inspired music (including, of course, the never-missing Gipsy Kings), give a much warmer touch to the eating experience.

Finally, the tension between tradition and modernism found in this restaurant is best summed up by a small statement in the menu that makes it very clear that smoking of cigars or pipes is prohibited—even though the restaurant is called Pipa, which means "pipe" in Spanish.

Rio Mar   *(Spanish)*
West Village
7 Ninth Avenue at Little West 12th St.
(212) 242-1623
Open to 2:00 A.M.
$$

This spot has been written up favorably by just about everyone—from *Time Out New York* to Zagat to Japanese *Esquire.* Rio Mar just keeps going, with it's no-nonsense sangria, friendly smiles, and tasty treats. Garlic is definitely a predominant thread throughout the menu, which includes a separate list for *tapas.* The place is rustic and maintains an old-school Meatpacking District feel. Upstairs you'll find sit-down dining along with serenading musicians; downstairs there's the bar and several tables with a jukebox tucked away by the kitchen. The food here tends to concentrate on large portions of standards such as *arroz con pollo* and *paella.* The broad smile and uniform of the Spanish-accented bartender lends an

Almodovarian ambience. Rio Mar is definitely not a chic newcomer to the neighborhood; this place has been around for a while for a reason.

NOTABLE

Allioli   (*Spanish*)
Williamsburg, Brooklyn
291 Grand Street, between Havemeyer and Roebling Sts.
(718) 218-7338
Subway: L to Bedford Ave.
Dinner only; closed Tuesday
$$

Chef-owner Diego Gonzalez focuses on Galician cuisine in his new restaurant. Enjoy delicious *tapas* and great seafood specials either inside or outdoors in the shady backyard. Flamenco performers add to the atmosphere every other Thursday.

El Faro   (*Spanish*)
West Village
823 Greenwich Street at Horatio St.
(212) 929-8210
$$$

El Faro is a West Village institution, having served great food for decades. The interior too looks decades-old, but it's worth coming here for the *paella.*

Meson Asturias   (*Spanish*)
Jackson Heights, Queens
40–12 83rd Street, between Baxter and Roosevelt Aves.
(718) 446-9154
Subway: 7 to 82nd St.–Jackson Hgts.
Closed Tuesday
$$

The decor isn't impressive, but the food at this Jackson Heights restaurant is typical of rural Spain, with peasant-inspired dishes that utilize every part of the animal (blood sausage, organ meats) and well-prepared seafood specials.

Ñ.
See Bars, Pubs & Taverns, p. 170.

Pintxos   *(Basque)*
Soho
510 Greenwich Street, between Canal and Spring Sts.
(212) 343-9923
$$

Pintxos (pronounced "pinchos") means *"tapas"* in Euskara, the Basque language, and they are excellent here, especially the grilled chorizo sausage, with a glass of inexpensive red wine. Main dishes include squid in its own ink, and other seafood-focused specialties.

Xunta   *(Spanish)*
East Village
174 First Avenue, between 10th and 11th Sts.
(212) 614-0620
Open to 2:00 A.M. Friday–Saturday
$$

This place is pure *tapas:* a fertile meeting ground for East Villagers and those looking to experiment with the long list of varied items on Xunta's menu. In addition to the red and white sangrias, there are several regional red and white Spanish wines available by the glass or bottle. Xunta (pronounced "Zhoon-tah"), with the fishnets on the ceilings and wooden barrels serving as tables, is a good atmosphere to experiment with affordable Spanish *tapas* and wine.

ELIZABETH LITTLES

VEGETARIAN

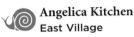

Angelica Kitchen
East Village
300 East 12th Street at 2nd Ave.
(212) 228-2909
$ (Cash only)

Angelica Kitchen is the godmother of vegan, organic cooking in New York City. For more than twenty years, owner Leslie McEachern has held true to the principles of community, sustainability, and traceability. The restaurant deserves its unanimous praise for demanding organic produce before it was widely available and for continuing to use seasonal ingredients purchased directly from local growers. Basic combinations such as the Dragon Bowl (rice, beans, tofu, and steamed vegetables) are unassailable; the housemade breads are dense and hearty (try them with the caramelized onion or curried cashew spreads); and green onions and carrot shreds add crunch to a yummy miso soup. But now that more restaurateurs are catering to the growing population of health-conscious and socially conscious diners, Angelica's competition has grown increasingly fierce. Other organic and vegan menus have gone for broke with creativity and seasonings while Angelica remains comparatively inhibited, though daily specials do tend to pump up the flavor. Bottom line: Angelica Kitchen was slow food before there was Slow Food. Make the pilgrimage.

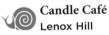

Candle Café
Lenox Hill
1307 Third Avenue at 75th St.
(212) 472-0970
$$

If you think you need an iron stomach to eat vegetarian food, you've never been to Candle Café. Walk in the door and you'll see the juice bar on your left, where you can take a seat and watch simple fresh ingredients (fruits, vegetables, herbs, juices, and soy and rice milks) being transformed before your very eyes (and nose) into delicious "cocktails" such as the Green Goddess (mixed greens, apple, lemon, and ginger) or my favorite, the Candle Colada (coconut sorbet, pineapple, lime, and rice milk).

The dining space is a long, gently flowing room with earth-tone hangings and no hard edges—very restful and understated. The food is fresh and nourishing, as you'd expect, with soy and wheat protein standing in for meat in dishes ranging from tempeh lasagna to a South American–style char-grilled seitan steak.

The most popular feature on the menu is the list of Good Food Side Dishes, where customers can "Choose Three" from daily vegetables, starches, and grilled tempeh or tofu. Save room for one of the tempting desserts. If you order organic tea or coffee here you won't get honey (it's an animal byproduct, in the strictest sense) but agave syrup to use as a sweetener.

With more than eighteen years in the business, and over eight at its present location, Candle Café is clearly doing something right. Co-owner Bart Potenza sources most of his organic produce from farmers in the tri-state area. Potenza jokes that his restaurant sits "between the devil and the deep blue sea," sandwiched between Hurricane Island, a seafood place, and Bistro Le Steak, where all manner of naughty and delicious things are done to our hoofed and finny friends.

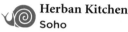

Herban Kitchen
Soho
290 Hudson Street at Spring St.
(212) 627-2257
Closed Sunday
$$

Co-owners Adam Ruderman and Jeanette Maier were dedicated to "eating clean," as their banner encourages passersby, years before they started Herban Kitchen as a catering and takeout business in 1994: he as an owner of Native Farms, an early all-organic market in New York; she as a private chef with a repertoire of tasty, mostly vegetarian recipes. Herban Kitchen has since developed into a full-flavored, full-service restaurant where strict vegans, seafood lovers, and red-meat eaters can enjoy creatively and carefully prepared organic meals.

A burger of ground Portobello mushrooms, carrots, and rice coexists on a menu with more traditional grass-fed beef and free-range turkey burgers; all come with a side dish choice such as chile "un-fries," baked wedges of oil-brushed, seasoned potato. For a lunch-on-the-run there are wrap sandwiches, available solo or in combination with a mixed baby greens salad with Thai peanut dressing or one of the special soups of the day. Dinner offerings include an unforgettably fresh harvest plate, and daily entrée and dessert specials feature seasonal and local foods that allow the inventive kitchen to really shine. Organic cheeses, wines, and beers round out the meal, which progresses at a gentle pace in the relaxed, earth-toned dining area or in the adjoining garden.

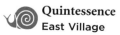

Quintessence
East Village
263 East 10th Street, between First Ave. and Ave. A
(646) 654-1823
$$

Nothing is as it seems at Quintessence, a "live food" (raw food) restaurant where the groundnut "meatballs" on your "pasta" and your dessert's groundnut "pie crust" taste suspiciously similar. But a unique vocabulary is the only thing that's missing from the dishes, which are mind-bogglingly original and packed with flavor. All organic, vegan, and completely uncooked and unprocessed (no tofu, no alcohol allowed), the theory behind live foods is that the enzymes contained in raw fruits and veggies establish and maintain mental, physical, and spiritual health. While the staff and some of the diners seem to take the restaurant's mission (explained in lengthy detail on the printed menu) more seriously than the food itself, there is ample reason for food lovers to visit one of Quintessence's three locations. Entrées include spaghetti marinara made from dehydrated strings of yellow squash, sprinkled with grated sesame seed "Parmesan cheese." Black olive, red onion, and mashed avocado tucked into pockets of nori seaweed should be added to sushi menus across the city; and nutty wild rice salad is both sweet and acidic, smooth and crunchy in every bite. "Nondairy, nonfattening, and cholesterol-free" desserts are less satisfying, so try an electrolyte lemonade. It's good for you.

Other Locations
566 Amsterdam Avenue at 86th St.; (212) 501-9700
353 East 78th Street, between First and Second Ave.; (212) 734-0888

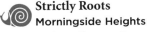

Strictly Roots
Morningside Heights
2058 Adam Clayton Powell Blvd. (Seventh Ave.) at 123rd St.
(212) 864-8699
$

It's a good thing that Strictly Roots is so inexpensive—after one visit you'll return repeatedly and obsessively to sample every dish on the mostly Caribbean, entirely vegan, organic menu. The steam table set-up may appear suspect, but Strictly Roots, which serves "nothing that crawls, swims, or flies," is as removed from bland cafeteria food and the commercial fast-food joints burgeoning around 125th Street as possible. Families lounge around the small tables, and at least one group of men, perhaps even the counter worker, will be shouting "Jab! Jab!" over a rousing chess game. But the food is worth getting really worked up about: creamy scrambled tofu, light and bitter collard greens with a clean, bright flavor, shredded tofu duck tossed with red pepper and onion, lima beans or chickpeas simmered with fragrant coconut milk, chewy barbecued seitan (wheat gluten) coated with sweet, sticky sauce, chunks of baked potato and yam in spicy oil . . . it's all tasty. Try the spicy drinks at the juice bar, too. There's a new selection every day and each one seems more delicious than the last.

NOTABLE

B&H Dairy Restaurant
East Village
127 2nd Avenue, near St. Marks Pl.
(212) 505-8065
$ (Cash only)

Known for its inexpensive, comforting soups and homemade challah bread, B&H is an old East Village institution that serves fish, but no meat. Go for the borscht, pierogies, and other kosher delights, along with the occasional helping of good-natured New York attitude from the countermen. "Wattah? Whaddaya want wattah for? There's wattah in duh soup!"

Caravan of Dreams
East Village
405 East 6th Street at First Ave.
(212) 254-1613
$$

Claiming to offer the "most progressive menu in the city," Caravan is kosher, vegan, organic, and about half raw. But unlike some restaurants where the mission seems to overwhelm the menu, Caravan aims to delight your taste buds, with selections such as a ginger curry stir-fry and the "Cuban Delight," with sweet grilled banana, Spanish rice, and black beans.

Hangawi
See Korean, p. 104.

Josie's
West Side
300 Amsterdam Avenue at 74th St.
(212) 769-1212
$$

With a second location in Murray Hill, there's more of Josie's to love. The restaurant is completely dairy-free, and all meats are free-range.

Other Location
565 Third Avenue at 37th St.; (212)490-1558

Spring Street Natural
Soho
62 Spring Street at Lafayette St.
(212) 966-0290
$$

The menu here claims that the vegetarian dishes contain all organic vegetables, though it does not vouch for the rest of the choices. Still, the American cuisine, with influences scattered from the Southwest to Asia, holds lots of possibilities for both vegetarians and their meat-eating friends, with salads being particularly popular.

Vegetarian Dim Sum House
Chinatown/Little Italy
24 Pell Street, between Doyers and Mott Sts.
(212) 577-7176
$ (Cash only)

This is a really fun place to take friends from out of town. For about $2 for each order of the assorted dumplings, buns, rolls, and cakes, you can order lots! Don't miss the monk dumplings, filled with rice and faux ham, and the extra-crispy spring rolls.

PART TWO

SPECIAL FOODS & NIGHTLIFE

BARS, PUBS & TAVERNS

Angel's Share
East Village
8 Stuyvesant Street, 2nd Flr., between Third Ave. and 9th St.
(212) 777-5415

To get to Angel's Share, you have to walk through a side door of Village Yoko Cho, a restaurant serving Japanese food in one part and Korean in the other. Founded in 1994, Angel's Share (the name is an old distiller's term for the evaporation and loss in volume that takes place in a spirits barrel during long aging—the missing portion is known as "the angel's share") boasts a lovely second-story view of the East Village with one whole wall consisting of windows. The Raphaelesque wall mural, great music, and cozy atmosphere make the bar a pleasure to sit in. There is no standing room here: You must find a seat at the bar, in a booth, or in the backroom. The bartenders and waiters take great pride in the crafting and serving of drinks. The menu reflects a true appreciation of whisky, brandy, spirits, and cocktail culture. At Angel's Share, alcohol is treated like royalty. Fried chicken wings *tatsuta,* roast beef *tataki,* and the Japanese satay assortment are a delicious accompaniment to the drinks. The only thing to beware of at Angel's Share is that you must follow the rules—no more than four at a booth. If you're in a big group, Angel's Share is not the place for you.

APT
West Village
419 West 13th Street, between Ninth Ave. and Washington St.
(212) 414-4245

Opened a couple of years ago in the booming Meatpacking District, APT was, at first, an absolutely trendy and confidential destination. It could only be found by word of mouth, since it is hidden between several completely unmarked building doors. Its popularity grew quickly, and the luxurious duplex bar finally allowed its address to be disclosed. It hasn't lost any of its allure, though, and it is still a treat to sip a perfect Cosmopolitan, a dizzying Sidecar, or a deliciously refreshing Pimm's Cup (adorned with a slice of cucumber) in these sleek, secluded digs, along with an elegant—but frugal—snack such as a bruschetta or homemade potato chips with *crème fraîche.*

The place is designed like an apartment (hence the name) with pastel-striped wallpaper, a large modern dining table, a wrap-around velvet banquette, many armchairs and coffee tables, and even a fluffy bed. For those who'd rather dance than linger, or who didn't make a reservation upstairs, the basement lounge is a happening—and sometimes overcrowded—place, with live DJs spinning trendy tunes every night.

Bemelmans Bar
Lenox Hill
Carlyle Hotel
35 East 76th Street at Madison Ave.
(212) 570-7189

When you are in the mood for New York "chic," go to the Bemelmans Bar at the Carlyle Hotel. From some of the best Bullshots and Martinis to sandwiches and snacks, the bar will make you feel very cosmopolitan. The walls and columns, painted by Ludwig Bemelmans in the 1930s, featuring depictions of dog walkers and other park scenes, have been restored to perfection with a feel of luxury that represents a bygone era. Live jazz has recently been very cool and well worth the cover charge. The late-night experience is very romantic—this is the place to go for a third date or an important anniversary. So even if you are not spending the night in a top-floor suite of the Carlyle Hotel, stop by the bar for a bit of "dreaming."

Blind Tiger Alehouse
West Village
518 Hudson Street at West 10th St.
(212) 675-3848

Is the Blind Tiger Alehouse the most comfortable pub in New York? It depends on your definition of "comfortable." There are certainly no buttery-soft green leather club chairs where you can nurse your snifter of brandy. No, the Blind Tiger is a rougher-hewn place, with its wide-plank wooden floor, a bar filled with both regulars and newcomers, and simple pine tables where you can hunker down and feel positively conspiratorial—maybe foment a workers' revolution over a pint or two after quitting time.

In other words, the Blind Tiger (the name comes from a Prohibition slang term for a speakeasy) is comfortable like your favorite pair of shoes, ones that are all broken in and fit just right. Everyone fits in here.

With 26 microbrews on draft, you could spend a long time sampling them all. If you do, you'll be rewarded with a membership in the Connoisseur's Club; after trying 51 beers (preferably not in one sitting), your name goes onto a brass plaque on the wall, celebrating your taste, discernment, and drinking prowess for the ages. If you're not in mood for beer, the bar also stocks a nice range of single-malt Scotches, specialty bourbons, and high-end tequilas.

There's no kitchen at Blind Tiger, and the food is of the packaged snack variety. But the fare improves on days when the bar features special tastings and events. Mondays usually feature New York foot-long hot dogs and Brooklyn Brewery's Pennant Ale. Wednesdays are often devoted to cheese tastings, with farmhouse cheeses from Great Britain, Vermont, and other regions paired with their local beers. And Sundays there's a free brunch featuring an assortment of Murray's Bagels, along with Blind Tiger's Bloody Marys.

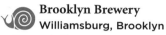

Brooklyn Brewery
Williamsburg, Brooklyn

Brewer's Row
79 North 11th Street, between Berry and Wythe Sts.
(718) 486-7422
Subway: L to Bedford Ave.
Open Friday 6:00–10:00 P.M., Saturday noon–5:00 P.M.

The Brooklyn Brewery's Brewhouse in Williamsburg, Brooklyn, has only been operating since 1996, but its roots in the community go much deeper. Brooklyn in the late 1800s was a dominant brewing center of America, with almost fifty operating breweries; today only Brooklyn Brewery remains. In addition to their award-winning Brooklyn Lager, you can also find Brooklyn East India Pale Ale, Brooklyn Brown Ale, Brooklyner Weisse, and Blanche de Brooklyn Ale served every Friday night and Saturday in the taproom, which is managed by Tom Grubb and which serves as a venue for special community events and for local artists to showcase their art. Brooklyn beers, which are crafted under the watchful eye of master brewmaster Garrett Oliver (author of *The Brewmaster's Table*) are made exclusively with American ingredients; all of them use the highest-quality traditional varieties of malts and hops. Cofounders Steve Hindy (a former foreign correspondent) and Tom Potter (a former lending officer) both admit, "Our primary goal is to invest in our community and we try to play a positive role in its development." A new organization founded by Hindy and Potter, the Open Space Alliance for North Brooklyn, encourages businesses to help purchase and develop parks in the area. But the primary reason you should share a drink here with the other hundreds of locals who come each week is not because of what the Brewery does outside, but because of what it does inside the depths of your mouth. The beer is delicious, and, best of all, it has only traveled a few feet from where it was made when you drink it!

The Chickenbone Café
Williamsburg, Brooklyn

177 South 4th Street, between Roebling and Driggs Sts.
(718) 302-2663
Subway: J, M to Marcy Ave., L to Bedford Ave.
Cash only

There are plenty of bars in New York that have great beers, and plenty of restaurants that have great food, but it is rare to find a great bar with great food. The Chickenbone Café has been designed to satisfy the hungriest drinker in town. Order a Newcastle draft and a roast beef, cornichon, shallot confit, and fontina sandwich, or have a glass of wine and a pancetta, fresh mozzarella, and roasted tomato sandwich. Other hardy and seductive offerings include a slow-roasted salmon, aioli, watercress, and black Lithuanian bread sandwich; wild mushroom, arugula, and toasted brioche salad; and the Greenpoint crostini, with kielbasa, pickles, dill, and spicy mustard. The high-spirited and accommodating managers, Koki and Brian, show genuine concern for the well-being of their customers, and will make it their mission to ensure you're having fun.

Located on the ground floor of a music rehearsal building in laid-back Williamsburg, the Chickenbone often plays host to impromptu jams, and there's a digital jukebox with more than one thousand CDs—something for every taste. Another unique feature of this convivial watering hole cum restaurant are the desserts: cookies and brownies from the owner's mother's secret recipes, roasted seasonal fruit served with honey and ricotta, and Brooklyn-made gelato panini, a specialty of Palermo, Italy, now served in Williamsburg. The great variety of offerings and entertainment is what the staff likes to refer to as Brooklyn Global cuisine. A true representation of the diversity of this far-out borough.

Chumley's
West Village
86 Bedford Street, between Barrow and Commerce Sts.
(212) 675-4449
Cash only

Since 1994, almost everyone who works behind the bar at Chumley's has been a firefighter. Current owner Steve Shlopak, with the bar since 1987, first developed a relationship with local firefighters when two separate fires engulfed the bar. The back wall features pictures of seventeen fallen heroes who once worked here.

Located in the very heart of the West Village on two of its prettiest streets, the building used to be a stable, and in the nineteenth century it became a "station" on the Underground Railroad. It continued its secret mission as a thriving speakeasy during Prohibition times. Even today it is hard to find, with no outside signage.

The bar was founded by Lee Chumley, a socialist journalist/labor organizer in the 1920s. Chumley's was a meeting place for a writers' movement at the time that included the likes of John Steinbeck, J. D. Salinger, Orson Welles, F. Scott Fitzgerald, and Jack Kerouac. Their portraits line the bar's walls, as do hundreds of dust jackets. Moving from the printed page to the silver screen, it's interesting to note that scenes from major films, such as Warren Beatty's *Reds* and Woody Allen's *Sweet and Lowdown,* were filmed here. Chumley's serves 11 quality beers, all of which are brewed in-house, ranging from a Pilsner and an Irish Red Ale to a Stout and a Blackberry Hefe-Weizen. The booths and tables are as inviting as the neighborhood people who frequent Chumley's. Looking at the wall decorations is a lesson in New York history—from the writers on the wall that helped make the place famous to the firemen who kept it alive for future generations to enjoy.

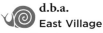 **d.b.a.**
East Village

41 First Avenue, between 2nd and 3rd Sts.
(212) 475-5097

Deep in the heart of the East Village, 41 First Avenue has been a bar for most of the past one hundred years, and the building that houses it dates from the 1870s. The small, narrow room has a dozen tables with marble tops and pews for seating, formerly from a local synagogue. You can also sit outside in a walled garden and deck. D.b.a. (an abbreviation for "doing business as") was established in 1994, and was the first bar in New York to offer cask-conditioned ales such as Fuller's, Brakspear's, and Bateman's. D.b.a. features 16 conventional draft lines and about 150 bottled beers, including one of the broadest selections of America's greatest craft beers, as well as single-malt scotches and numerous tequilas. Owners Dennis Zentek and Ray Deter (a former cab driver who also studied English literature, making him one of the few English-speaking cab drivers in New York City) had a goal from the beginning to run a "neighborhood corner joint that offers the best of everything." And if it's the best food you are looking for, d.b.a. allows you to order in from nearby restaurants.

Ear Inn
Soho

326 Spring Street, between Greenwich and Washington Sts.
(212) 226-9060

Today only within earshot of the Hudson River, the Ear Inn used to stand just five feet away from the original shoreline. The building was built in 1817 for James Brown, an African American aide to George Washington who was depicted in the Cass Gilbert painting of Washington crossing the Delaware. A city, state, and national landmark, the Ear Inn started serving booze when Thomas Cooke first brewed beer in the basement for sailors in the 1830s.

PATRICK MARTINS

The upstairs apartment served many purposes over the years including as a boarding house, smuggler's den, and brothel. No women were allowed into the Ear Inn (unless they were on their way upstairs) until 1970. After serving as a speakeasy during Prohibition, the bar never received an official name: To avoid the Landmarks Commission's lengthy review of any new sign, current owner Martin Sheridan simply painted over the neon BAR sign to read EAR. Today you will find a collection of century-old odds and ends above the bar, including containers of ashes of previous customers. Pictures of the old neighborhood the way it was in 1920 decorate the back room. The Ear Inn serves burgers and shepherd's pie, but what really makes it special is its history, sense of conviviality, special atmosphere, and the feeling you get knowing you are in one of the oldest bars in the city.

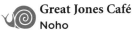 ### Great Jones Café
Noho

54 Great Jones Street, between Bowery and Lafayette St.
(212) 674-9304
Cash only

Great Jones Café is one of the best bars in New York City. It merits this title because of its continued dedication to making perfect drinks using perfect ingredients. Located just doors down from the Engine Co. 33 and Ladder 9 Firehouse, Great Jones makes among the best Bloody Marys and Margaritas you will find anywhere—the former being so spicy, its nice to know that firemen are in the vicinity. "The drink has been good here for so long its hard to remember who created our version," explains manager Bill Judkins, who has himself been here almost since the bar's founding in 1983. The Bloody Mary is not shaken and actually feels more like a meal than a drink—it is certainly treated that way by the bartenders, who put in copious amounts of Tabasco, horseradish, and Worcestershire sauce. The Margaritas are also among the best in New York, thanks to a special lime juice that is used (a bad lime juice leaves a metallic aftertaste). The Great Jones is always on the lookout for quality products. One of the more recent finds is Blenheim Ginger Ale, which is shipped to them ten cases at a time from the producer in Hamer, South Carolina. The very spicy ginger ale is the perfect complement to Goslings Rum—together they combine to make the Shaggy.

If you want some food to wash down your drinks, try some of Chef Mark Hitzges's mean soul food (see Soul Food, p. 133).

King Cole Bar
Midtown East
St. Regis Hotel
2 East 55th Street, between Fifth and Madison Aves.
(212) 339-6721

> Old King Cole was a merry old soul, and a merry old soul was he. He called for his pipe and he called for his bowl, and he called for his fiddlers three. Every fiddler he had a fiddle, and a very fine fiddle had he. Oh, there's none so rare as can compare with King Cole and his fiddlers three. ("Old King Cole")

Located in the St. Regis Hotel, the King Cole Bar is one of the prettiest in New York. One of the main reasons for this is the striking wall-sized mural by Maxfield Parrish of Old King Cole commissioned by Colonel John Jacob Astor in 1906. Originally designed for the Knickerbocker Hotel in Times Square, the mural traveled to the Chicago Art Institute and the New York Racquet and Tennis Club before it arrived at this 55th Street location.

Only men were allowed into the bar until 1950, when the fairer sex was permitted onto the premises for the first time. Starting in 1934, the St. Regis Hotel boasted Fernand Petiot as a bartender, the inventor of the Bloody Mary. At the time, the mixture of tomato juice and vodka was called a Red Snapper. While the original name never stuck, the drink did, as did the bar that introduced it for the first time to the United States. The cherry-oak bar creates an elegant atmosphere and, along with the mural, makes you feel like you are in old New York. The bar snacks are great as well!

Lenox Lounge
Harlem
288 Malcolm X Blvd (Lenox Ave.), between 124th and 125th Sts.
(212) 427-0253

The Lenox Lounge is a genuine piece of New York City history. Located just south of Martin Luther King Boulevard (125th Street) this music bar is a tribute to Art Deco design, with beautiful lamps and tables. Alvin Reed, Sr., who was born and raised in Harlem, bought the business in 1988 with the goal of reintroducing music to the Lounge after years of silence despite the fact that it used to be frequented by the likes of Billie Holiday, John Coltrane, and Muddy Waters. His efforts failed at first, but in 1996, thanks to better marketing to tourists and downtowners, great jazz was back for good, and can now be heard five days a week. I had the fortunate opportunity to hear Dakota McCloud and Night Hawk belt out fantastic tunes as I relaxed in my comfortable leather chair. The atmosphere is a textbook lesson in conviviality, with hugs and warm laughter all around. Soul food is served in the back, but it is the bar that is most special, with a nice selection of bottled beers. First founded in 1939, Lenox Lounge has appeared in numerous films including *Dead Presidents* and *White Lies*. Jazz festivals and Open Mike nights also make the Lounge a worthy place to visit.

McSorley's Old Ale House
East Village
15 East 7th Street, between Second and Third Aves.
(212) 473-9148

Founded in 1854 by John McSorley of Tyrone, Ireland, McSorley's Ale House is one of the oldest bars in New York. While some of the people there look like they have been drinking since 1854, it is hard to not appreciate the tradition.

Only two drinks are served at McSorley's, a dark ale and a light ale. And when you order one, you actually get it in two 8-ounce mugs, a tradition that's been maintained since the bar's founding. The ale is made especially for the bar by the Pabst Brewing Company in Wisconsin.

The bar has no stools (just a footrest), and sawdust carpets the floor. A mug of mustard sits on every ancient wood table. A huge furnace squats in the middle of the room. Old pictures and newspaper clippings line the walls. When I walked in with my Sicilian father-in-law, he asked me if we had gone back in time to the Wild West.

Some places go into this guide for maintaining the highest standards in quality, others for their commitment to sustainability; McSorley's goes in because it was founded when Franklin Pierce was president. It has also managed to hold on to a charm and energy that makes one feel that perhaps not that much has changed after all these years: A mug of ale and a place to rest will always exist for New York's busy residents.

The Oyster Bar at the Plaza Hotel
East Side
768 Fifth Avenue at Central Park South (entrance on 58th St.)
(212) 759-3000

While most New Yorkers know the Plaza for the Oak Room, there is little doubt that, for the sake of this guide, the Oyster Bar is the place to be. Surrounded by beautiful murals by John Tarzian depicting scenes of happy Englishmen and women eating and drinking, it is possible to forget that you are in twenty-first-century New York. Even setting foot into the Plaza and walking through the halls that Eloise once roamed (a character based on Liza Minnelli) makes you feel as if time stands still within its walls. Founded in 1969, the Oyster Bar helped reintroduce oyster culture to New York City after years of the bivalve's decline due to overfishing. Today, the Oyster Bar is as dedicated to the environment as it is to serving good food, ensuring that the same dilemma will not happen again. Under the wise guidance of Food and Beverage Director Tom Norberg, the Oyster Bar is a trendsetter in promoting eco-gastronomy, and has dedicated a significant amount of time and energy to implementing real change for the better. Look for numerous Slow Food Ark products on the menu, such as the Delaware Bay oyster, which is in desperate need of support since most of the families who farm it are at risk of going out of business. The fish and chips are great too! What makes the Plaza so special is that it has managed to stay vibrant and alive even after all these years, tastefully paying attention to modern-day issues, rather than indulging in an epicurean bid to save a few outdated notions of what makes for good food.

Pravda
Soho
281 Lafayette Street, between Houston and Prince Sts.
(212) 226-4944

Opened six years ago by Keith McNally of the famed restaurants Balthazar and Pastis, Pravda specializes in Vodka, Vodka, Vodka. At Pravda, you will find examples of this distilled grain from Russia, Sweden, Estonia, Slovenia, and also Poland, Italy, the U.S., and Canada. You will also find a series of "Pravda's Own Infusions," vodka drinks flavored with raspberry, ginger, blackcurrant, pineapple, coconut, cherry, fig, cranberry, and even chile with horseradish.

The bar is a ten-step walk down from street level—you feel as if you are walking down a fire escape—with luxurious leather armchairs and bar stools inside. The lights are low, but because of many lamps (with Russian writing on them) and candles on the tables, the bar remains a light and happy place. When you are there, you feel like you are in a Russian speakeasy. The designers will tell you the design is a romantic vision of Russian Constructivism. As with other McNally enclaves, bottles set on shelves behind a bar with mirrored walls adds depth to the room and makes it beautiful to look at. A second floor also features a small bar, which is open from Wednesday to Saturday. While Pravda serves good food, it is the drinks, atmosphere, and cool crowd that make it special for a stop after work or late at night.

NOTABLE

Bohemian Hall and Park
Astoria, Queens
29-19 24th Avenue, between 29th and 31st Sts.
(718) 728-9776
Subway: N, W to Astoria Blvd.

The name doesn't refer to artsy types or latter-day beatniks, but to the medieval Kingdom of Bohemia, once a part of the Holy Roman Empire. Bohemian Hall is the last remaining beer garden in New York City, which was once home to many such places. Here you can commune with nature in an open-air setting, surrounded by sturdy brick walls, and enjoy inexpensive German and Czech beers served in steins.

The Burp Castle
East Village
41 East 7th Street, between Second and Third Aves.
(212) 982-4576

Here you will find 12 Belgian beers on draft, including Chimay, which ain't easy to find on draft anywhere else. Serving 300 bottled beers in the summer and 700 in winter, you won't have any trouble finding your favorite brew here. Classical music and very cool wall paintings (featuring drunk monks in the ocean being eaten by sharks, women getting drunk in heaven, and crusaders fighting dragons in hell) makes the Burp Castle a place worth a visit.

Decibel Sake Bar
East Village
240 East 9th Street, between Second and Third Aves.
(212) 979-2733

Down the stairs and into the recesses of an East Village basement, a cavernous lair devoted to sake, sake, and more sake, with an assortment of Japanese appetizers that complement this bar's choice drink.

Hogs & Heifers
West Village
859 Washington Street at 13th St.
(212) 929-0655

With slabs of beef perfuming the surrounding streets of the Meatpacking District by day, and motorcycles filling them by night (a sign outside asks bikers to arrive and leave quietly to respect the neighbors), Hogs & Heifers is not the place you want to bring your teenage daughter. The bar is filled with bras of guests who get down and dirty dancing on the bar. One drinker explains that "the place was founded in 1992 for anyone who rides a bike: man, woman, transvestite, gay, or straight." So if you own a Harley (or wish you did), Hogs & Heifers might be the place for you.

Holiday Cocktail Lounge
East Village
75 St Marks Place, between First and Second Aves.
(212) 777-9637

Here you will find a Ukrainian bartender who often as the night goes on will break into song as he reaches for bottles to mix your drink. A real joint, long home to musicians and East Village artists—or at least the few that are left—because of the cheap drinks.

Hudson Bar at the Hudson Hotel
Clinton
356 West 58th Street at Ninth Ave.
(212) 554-6000

While impresarios Ian Shrager and Philippe Starck have already made their mark on international bar and hotel culture, they have not lost any momentum in their own empire-building. The Hudson Hotel is the latest and freshest addition, and the Hudson Bar is decked out in a design fusion of gel cushions, Louis XV chairs, and original cocktails lit up by a glowing floor that reflects a specially commissioned Francesco Clemente mural on the low-slung ceiling.

Marie's Crisis
West Village
59 Grove Street, between Bleeker St. and Seventh Ave. South
212-243-9323

This great piano bar in the West Village is an institution, where for no cover charge and a measly one-drink minimum you can go and sing along with dozens of theater-lovers. Bring your best Broadway belting voice, for this is truly a sing along around the piano, with no karaoke microphones to assist you. Marie's Crisis is a communal good time for all, with show-stopping performances dropped in from time to time either by the theatrical waiters or a particularly talented or enthusiastic patron. The songs are usually pretty mainstream, so don't get discouraged if the first few songs are foreign to you. Hang around and pretty soonthe familiar strains of *West Side Story* or *Chicago* are bound come along, and it'll be your turn to shine!

Ñ
Soho
33 Crosby Street, between Broome and Grand Sts.
(212) 219-8856

Pronounced "enya," this *tapas* bar is a small, lively place for an after-work drink and a light bite before dinner, with a nice selection of *tapas* and two dozen sherries, in addition to the ubiquitous sangria.

Paddy Reilly's
Gramercy Park/Flatiron District
519 Second Avenue at 29th St.
(212) 686-1210

Great live Irish music makes this bar special seven nights a week. The music is so good that patrons are immediately put into a happy mood, facilitating great mingling and conviviality! Open from 11:00 A.M. to 4:00 A.M., Paddy Reilly's doesn't serve food, but you are allowed to bring it in.

Pete's Tavern
Gramercy Park/Flatiron District
129 East 18th Street at Irving Pl.
(212) 473-7676

Pete's is the oldest continuously operating bar and restaurant in New York, dating back to 1864 and filled with tradition, as you'd expect. It's said that O. Henry (the writer H. H. Munro) penned his most famous short story, "The Gift of the Magi," here. The food isn't as inspired as the bar's long history, but that's clearly not the drawing card.

Sakagura
Midtown East

211 East 43rd Street, between Second and Third Aves.
(212) 953-7253

Obscurely located in the basement of a Midtown office building, Sakagura boasts what is probably the greatest selection of sakes in New York City, with more than 200 in stock.

St. Nick's Pub
Hamilton Heights/Sugar Hill

773 St Nicholas Avenue at 149th St.
(212) 283-9728

St. Nick's has live music six nights a week with comedy on Tuesdays. A big picture of Miles Davis provides the background for a number of talented artists who perform here. The bar is small and cozy, making the music the centerpiece: If you feel like talking, St. Nick's might not be the right spot.

Top of the Tower Bar
Midtown East

Beekman Tower
3 Mitchell Place (49th St. and First Ave.)
(212) 355-7300

Located at the top of Beekman Hill, just blocks away from the United Nations, the Beekman Tower, designed by architect John Mead Howells, is one of New York's great Art Deco skyscrapers, renowned for its dramatic volumetric massing and bold verticality. The twenty-sixth-story view at the Top of the Tower Bar (the rest of the building is a hotel) is spectacular and takes in Queens and Brooklyn to the east and the pocket of historic Midtown skyscrapers to the west. A piano bar makes for nice background music, but it's the view that takes center stage.

Barney Greengrass
Upper West Side
541 Amsterdam Avenue, between 86th and 87th Sts.
(212) 724-4707
Closed Monday
$$ (Cash only)

Barney Greengrass, a family-run Jewish "appetizing" shop and restaurant that has been around for nearly a century (and in its current location since 1929), is both a carrier of old food traditions and a lively participant in the contemporary restaurant world. Like other venerable New York institutions, the tradition of smoked fish lends historical gravitas (or is that gravlax?) to the long display cases glistening with myriad slabs of fish and other goodies such as chopped liver, whitefish salad, and caviar. The formica-and-leatherette coffee shop bustles with efficient waiters and noshing customers, among whom you're likely to spot Upper West Siders from Philip Roth to Jerry Seinfeld. The restaurant does a serious brunch business, anchored by an exhaustive menu of irresistible dishes, including smoked fish platters in countless combinations (smoked salmon, sturgeon, sable, whitefish, pickled herring), scrambled eggs and onions and Nova (a signature dish), chopped chicken liver, borscht, tender cheese blintzes, and fresh bagels and bialys brought in from the Lower East Side. You won't need to eat for the rest of the day after brunch at Barney Greengrass, but this is probably a good thing since it will take a while to work off the cholesterol-heavy menu.

City Bakery
Gramercy Park/Flatiron District
3 West 18th Street, between Fifth and Sixth Aves.
(212) 366-1414
$$

Cake plates piled high with chewy, pancake-sized cookies and fluffy muffins can deceive a newcomer into thinking City Bakery restricts itself to the boundaries of its name. But move past the pastry island that is the centerpiece of this airy, cavernous space, and that presumption is swiftly killed by the salad bar. It's more like a salad wing, with 25 to 30 warm and cold items that change daily and can include sautéed bitter melon with egg, cornbread-coated catfish, and roasted Alita squash from the Greenmarket. Early in the day, if you're still in the light breakfast mode, you can opt for a virtuous but satisfying and delicious helping of yogurt and granola. But you can also order from an assortment of hot and cold plates. Among the choices are a Niman Ranch BLT, caramelized Thai shrimp, and a corn dog served with peanuts and a pretzel. The falafel—three fried chickpea patties as moist and crumbly as a birthday cake and coated with sesame seeds—is arrayed on a striking bed of field greens, cucumber, cherry tomatoes, and sweet red pepper. Owner Maury Rubin's staff uses a vintage Hamilton-Beach blender to transform homemade ice cream into milkshakes so rich that one twelve-year-old boy stunned his father by proclaiming himself too full to finish. (He did ask for a to-go cup.)

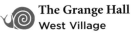

The Grange Hall
West Village

50 Commerce Street at Barrow St.
(212) 294-5246
$$

Situated in a tiny crevice of the West Village, the Grange Hall is an outpost of local and organic foods cooked with a delicate, cheeky flair. Though it can get crowded before and after shows at the neighboring Cherry Lane Theatre, it offers a relaxed and comfortable atmosphere for a drink or a bite to eat.

The restaurant opened in 1902 in the space of the old Blue Mill Tavern. The mahogany booths, soaring columns, winged bar, terrazzo floor, and etched glass partitions all date back to the 1940s. Ninety fortunate patrons can dine on a menu of updated Midwestern classics. Chicken salad has become Nitrite-Free Smoked Chicken and Strawberry Salad. Hoping for a burger and fries? Try the very lean quarter-pounder, a great beef hamburger on a brioche roll with lemon-peppered Idaho fried potatoes; skeptics might shy away, but the fries are really tangy and crisp. The menu gets an overhaul four times every year, and specials change daily, depending on availability at the Greenmarket.

The Grange Hall offers lots of vegetarian options, including a delicious nod to nostalgia: the organic peanut butter and raspberry preserves double-decker sandwich. The restaurant is committed to seeking out local and organic food, paying frequent visits to the farmers' market every week.

With a neighborhood atmosphere that belies its city locale, the Grange Hall is a nurturing choice for a meal in the West Village.

Pastis
West Village

9 Ninth Avenue at Little West 12th St.
(212) 929-4844
$$

Founded in 1999, Pastis is one of the more pleasant places in New York to eat brunch. Most restaurants that boast outdoor seating have little more to offer then car-exhaust fumes, questionable characters walking by, and dirty sidewalks, but at Pastis you are protected from the street by colorful flowerbeds. The streets also see little traffic, which makes for a quieter experience. For a view over the flowerbeds you have the lovely little cobblestone square off Little West 12th Street. Inside, you get a country bistro feel with family-style seating, a sleek long bar, and mirrors on the walls.

The brunch food is tasty and features items such as Eggs Bamboches, Eggs à la Basquaise, and Brioche French Toast. The crowd is always beautiful—an episode of *Sex and the City* was filmed here during the show's first season. Daily newspapers from around the world decorate the entrance, providing content for those eating alone. When you eat as Pastis, you feel as if you are in the French countryside, a much-needed relief for those seeking a respite from the hustle and bustle of New York life.

Pink Tea Cup
West Village
42 Grove Street, between Bleecker and Bedford Sts.
(212) 807-6755
$$ (Cash only)

The Pink Tea Cup is a soul food institution, serving the West Village since 1954 with large portions of stick-to-your-ribs home cooking. The decor is dominated by the pink-painted walls and the celebrity photos on one wall (the other is devoted to Dr. Martin Luther King). If you go for lunch or dinner, you can get incredible smothered pork chops, steak, and chicken, as well as chitterlings, ham hocks, and barbecued pigs' feet.

Yet PTC also serves one of the best brunches in the city. It isn't that the food is exotic or creative. No, the beauty is in its very unpretentious simplicity—everything is exquisitely prepared, and tastes exactly the way it's supposed to. Scrambled eggs are perfect, the orange juice is fresh, and the coffee tastes great. I was so impressed that I asked the waiter what kind it was. "Chock Full O'Nuts," he told me, "but we do add an extra scoop." It might not be a super-premium brand, but like everything else at PTC, it's good because it's made with care.

If you've never had grits before, or hated them, try them here. These are the Platonic ideal of grits—perfectly cooked, creamy, and buttery. The only suggestion we'd make is to offer some real maple syrup for pouring over the enormous pecan pancakes. Maple syrup is Yankee soul food, after all, and corn syrup just doesn't cut it.

Prune
East Village
54 East 1st Street, between First and Second Aves.
(212) 677-6221
Brunch Saturday–Sunday 10:00–3:30; dinner daily
$$

Prunes have lately been re-imaged as "dried plums," but the restaurant Prune has managed to retain its name (which is the owner's nickname). This is a small, lively restaurant for people truly interested in food. The decor is virtually nonexistent—just a few mirrors on the wall—and the tiny, open kitchen sits at the rear of the room. The lighting is well done—bright enough to read menus without flashlights and low enough for intimacy.

The brunch menu is delightful here, with old standards such as eggs Benedict and a smoked fish platter from Russ and Daughters (see p. 289), but also including Dutch pancakes and more creative selections such as ricotta with raspberries and figs.

Almost every dish on the dinner menu is unique and distinctive, even the small bar menu. Each appetizer is an individual creation: grilled veal hearts marinated in *gremolata;* Arctic char in oxtail broth under deep-fried herbs; roasted marrow bones with parsley salad; pastrami duck breast with small rye omelet; and braised tongue and octopus in parsley sauce. Main dishes include roast suckling pig with pickled tomatoes, black-eyed peas, and aioli; and ruby-red shrimp boil with sausage, potatoes, and smoked paprika butter.

This restaurant prides itself on its use of fresh seasonal vegetables, including baby beets with their greens in aioli, sugar snap peas in mint sauce, and grilled *cippolita* onions. Desserts include passionfruit pudding cake, and pistachio *pithivier* with buttermilk ice cream and blackberries.

Prune also has a "hidden jewel"—a small intimate room downstairs, seating 6 to 8 people around a piano-shaped table. Reserve early and show up promptly, or you might lose your table at this justifiably popular restaurant.

Sarge's
Murray Hill
548 Third Avenue, between 36th and 37th Sts.
(212) 679-0442
Open 24 hours
$$

Founded in 1965, Sarge's serves only one kind of pancake (plain) and only two types of ice cream (vanilla and chocolate). The coffee is huge, and if you order a Diet Coke the waiter will ask if you like a lemon wedge inside (rather than simply putting a huge slab of unwashed rind into your drink). The menu has something for everyone and features regular deli fare such as sandwiches, burgers, and breakfast food. If you like home fries, they burn them just right. The waiters, the other guests, and the atmosphere (which includes colorful Belle Époque lamps hanging from the ceiling) make you feel that it is 1974 and that Richard Nixon will be on the cover of your morning paper. But when you wake up from your reverie and discover that it is 2003, you will be relieved to know that there still are some places that have not changed to meet the latest fad.

Tom's Restaurant
Prospect Heights, Brooklyn
782 Washington Avenue, between St. John's and Sterling Pls.
(718) 636-9738
Subway: 2, 3 to Eastern Pkwy.–Brooklyn Museum
Open Monday–Saturday 6:00 A.M.–4:00 P.M.; closed Sunday
$ (Cash only)

If a visitor from another planet ever asks you what the term "neighborhood restaurant" means, take him, her, or it to breakfast at Tom's. Established in 1936, the present owner Gus Vlahavas and his staff make everyone feel like a regular, even on your first visit. On any given morning, you'll see local cops taking a coffee break and young mothers with strollers coming in for a late breakfast (Tom's serves it all day, until they close, at 4:00 P.M.). Settle down at a table and you'll be plied with little amenities: an orange wedge, a moist towelette, and maybe a ginger cookie to help finish off your coffee.

For breakfast, try one of the pancake specials (lemon ricotta, pumpkin walnut), served with seasonal fresh fruit. Lunch features similarly hearty and well-prepared diner fare: homemade soups du jour, sandwiches, and several daily specials. Be sure to order an egg cream or a cherry-lime rickey from the old-fashioned soda fountain up front. The food, the atmosphere, and the prices will definitely start your day off right.

Veselka
East Village
144 Second Avenue at 9th Street
(212) 228-9682
Open 24 hours
$

While known as a great late-night hangout, it would be a gross injustice not to consider the merits of Veselka as one of the finest diners in the city.

Of Ukrainian origin, Veselka boasts wonderful specialties from all over Eastern Europe, including homemade borscht (utilizing fresh beets), fantastic pierogies, Hungarian beef stew, and blintzes that are oftentimes described like delicate crêpes.

For nearly fifty years, Veselka has been an East Village landmark. Ideal for kicking back with the morning paper or for a midafternoon meeting, the 24-hour kitchen keeps busy throughout the day. If you are looking for great eggs or buttermilk pancakes, Veselka doesn't disappoint—you can even get real maple syrup!

Veselka is much more than a neighborhood coffee shop; it's a hub of neighborhood activity—and the great food and friendly service are the reason why.

NOTABLE

Aquavit
See Fish & Seafood, p. 184.

Balthazar
See French, p. 57.

Casa
See Latin American, p. 109.

Danal
East Village
90 East 10th Street, between Third and Fourth Aves.
(212) 982-6930
$$$

With its hodge-podge antiques, patchwork quilts, flowerpots, and fireplaces, Danal feels just like a country home. It serves rustic French food, high tea on the weekends, and a great Sunday brunch. Comfort food in a cozy space.

Great Jones Café
See Bars, Pubs & Taverns, p. 164 and Soul Food, p. 133.

Jing Fong
See Chinese, p. 45.

Kitchenette
Financial District
80 West Broadway at Warren St.
(212) 267-6740
$$

Serving all-day breakfast or brunch on weekends, Kitchenette brings comfort food to New Yorkers pining for the country. Berry pancakes, French toast, omelets, cheese grits, and turkey sausage are just a few of the filling options, and there are cakes, cookies, and other baked goods too.

Other Location
Kitchenette Uptown, 1272 Amsterdam Avenue, between 122nd and 123rd Sts.; (212) 531-7600. Open to 11 P.M. for dinner; BYOB.

La Flor Bakery and Café
Woodside, Queens
53-02 Roosevelt Ave. at 53rd St.
(718) 426-8023
Subway: 7 to 52nd St.–Lincoln Ave.
$ (Cash only)

On a gray New York morning, the kind where you can't see the tops of the buildings through the fog, I know exactly where I want to go. The Puebla Breakfast at La Flor is sunshine on a plate, tortillas radiating from a steaming mound of scrambled eggs mixed with spicy sausage, potatoes, and squash. The pastry basket is loaded with scones and muffins, split and toasted to stay or to go—just the way to start the day. Try one of Viko Ortega's superlative sticky buns with some coffee, or perhaps an order of *heuvos rancheros* or bourbon-vanilla French toast.

M&G Soul Food Diner
See Soul Food, p. 134.

Sarabeth's Kitchen
Upper West Side
423 Amsterdam Avenue at 80th St.
(212) 496-6280
$$

Sarabeth's Kitchen is a much-loved institution for its classy American cooking, including a famously indulgent brunch menu, but it's also one of the finest producers of preserves in the city, with Sarabeth's jams and other fruit spreads widely available in retail shops, in addition to occupying center stage in its three restaurants and bakery.

Other Locations

1295 Madison Avenue at 92nd St., (212) 410-7335
945 Madison Avenue at 75th St., (212) 570-3670
75 Ninth Avenue at 15th St., (212) 989-2424

Tea & Sympathy

See Coffee and Tea, p. 247.

PATRICK MARTINS

DELIS

Carnegie Deli
Theater District
854 Seventh Avenue at 55th St.
(212) 757-2245
$$ (Cash only)

Located in the heart of the Theater District, there are more stars hanging on the wall than in the sky at this New York institution. As you are waiting in line to get tickets to see David Letterman, or as you stumble home after a night of debauchery, Carnegie Deli is always sure to fill you up. Everyone from Mr. T to James Carville has flocked here to order menu items under categories such as Egg-Stravaganzas and Forshpeis. As with all delis, the best thing to order is a Dr. Brown's Cel-Ray tonic (produced and bottled in Queens from the original 1869 recipe) and a corned beef or pastrami sandwich lathered in mustard. If you can't decide, you can always have the Woody Allen ("lotsa corned beef plus lotsa pastrami"). The pastrami is smoked and the corned beef is cured by Carnegie Deli, and they make all of their own desserts.

Katz's Delicatessen
Lower East Side
205 East Houston Street at Ludlow St.
(212) 254-2246
$

Katz's Deli on the Lower East Side is a New York institution that has been glamorized and made famous by the media and canonized by Billy Crystal and Meg Ryan in the film *When Harry Met Sally*. But Katz's is much more than a hip spot to see and be seen; it's an authentic deli-catessen, the real thing. Rare, even in a city like New York. What I love about Katz's are its salted and cured meats, a tradition that comes straight from Eastern Europe and is totally foreign to most Americans today. At Katz's, they spend thirty days curing their corned beef—no tricks or rush-ing technique. The result is sweet and salty, fatty and delicious.

Their food preparation has not changed in seventy-five years, and that's why Katz's pastrami expresses more about New York City and its deep ties to Eastern European culture, and the poverty and the tenacity by which it can be distinguished, than any history book on the shelf. The Katz's of today—busy, bright, bustling, a little worn around the edges, and jam-packed with people—is a tribute to the Eastern European immi-grants who brought their food culture to New York, a testament to food done the traditional way. A Katz's pastrami sandwich with mustard on rye is poetry to my ears after traveling away from home for any length of time. It is as New York as the Yankees, and as immigrant as anyone named on Ellis Island.

Second Avenue Deli
East Village
156 Second Avenue at 10th St.
(212) 677-0606
$$

The neon lights flicker on lower Second Avenue. The burned-out bulbs leave enough to clearly spell out the name of one of the few remaining kosher delis in all of North America. The original marquis of the Second Avenue Deli remains today, in stark contrast to a new facade that was erected in honor of the deli's founder, Abe Lebewohl. Patrons can enjoy numerous Old World specialties, from matzoh ball or mushroom-barley soup to boiled *flanken* or blintzes. The deli's stalwarts remain their corned beef and tongue, still house-cured, that evoke gastronomic pleasure at mere sight. In addition to the ultimate deli foods, Second Avenue is a living relic, an homage to the history of the neighborhood and to a culture. The sidewalk in front of the restaurant has been made into a shrine, The Yiddish Theatre Walk of Fame. In the entrance, an original Automat, long passed its working days, serves as a reminder of a time when a few nickels could get you a pastrami sandwich or a plate of latkes. While minimum order requirements can be hassle, you'll never walk away hungry.

Stage Deli
Theater District
834 Seventh Avenue, between 53rd and 54th Sts.
(212) 245-7850
$$

With a long, fabled history full of famous names and dramatic turns between old and new owners, the Stage Delicatessen is the epitome of New York excess. Whether you opt for a celebrity-monikered combo sandwich—from Joe DiMaggio's corned beef, pastrami, chopped liver, and Bermuda onion to James Brown's pastrami, turkey, and Swiss cheese—or just a regular sandwich ("if you can call them regular," the menu cautions), you'll run the risk of dislocating your jaw just trying to get your mouth around these towers of glistening sliced meat enclosed parenthetically with humble slices of rye bread. While tourists and local show biz folk alike tuck into "novie" smoked salmon, matzoh ball soup, chopped chicken liver, cheese blintzes, slabs of strawberry cheesecake, and other deli favorites, the true calling card of the Stage Deli will always be their overstuffed sandwich (like the overstuffed patron that totters out afterward).

NOTABLE

David's Brisket House
Crown Heights, Brooklyn
533 Nostrand Avenue, between Fulton St. and Atlantic Ave.
(718) 783-6109
Subway: A, C to Nostrand Ave.
Closed Sunday
$

Completely out of place in this Carribean neighborhood, David's serves what is perhaps the moistest, most tender brisket sandwich in the city. It is run by a Puerto Rican guy who learned to ply his trade in Jewish delis in Manhattan. Most of the patrons seem to treat the narrow space as a diner, ordering more conventional fare, but don't be fooled—this is the real deal.

Russ & Daughters
See Markets, p. 289.

Sarge's
See Brunch, p. 174.

ELIZABETH LITTLES

FISH & SEAFOOD

Aquavit
Theater District
13 West 54th Street, between Fifth and Sixth Aves.
(212) 307-7311
$$$$ (prix fixe)

In business since 1987, Aquavit occupies a nineteenth-century townhouse that for years belonged to the Rockefellers, a historic building designed by J. Henry Hardenburg, whose other buildings include the Dakota and the Plaza Hotel. Inside, the space is broken into an informal café and bar on the entry level and a main dining room that transitions from cozy booths on one side to a soaring, six-story-high, glass-ceilinged atrium space, complete with an 18-foot waterfall.

Like the building itself, the cuisine here is rooted in tradition, yet full of modern appointments. Chef Marcus Samuelsson, who was born in Ethiopia but raised in Sweden, uses an artistic flair in combining the essential elements of Scandinavian cuisine, especially fish, with changing seasonal ingredients. The three-course lunch or dinner prix fixe menu includes, among other options, a crispy salmon served with roasted beets and asparagus in a Meyer lemon sauce. For dessert try the black pepper cheesecake served with pineapple terrine and lime sorbet, or the fennel *panna cotta.*

The café is a good place to sample some traditional Scandinavian specialties such as the gravlax or the house-smoked salmon, or a plate with four different kinds of herring (a shot of ice-cold aquavit and a Carlsberg beer are almost mandatory accompaniments to this dish). The restaurant serves a Sunday *smorgasbord* brunch that even my Danish grandmother would approve of, with old familiar standards such as Jansson's Temptation (Swedish scalloped potatoes, with onions, anchovies, and capers).

Aquavit also operates AQ Café in the lobby of the Scandinavia House, where they serve sandwiches, soups, and salads as well as weekly specials, at very attractive prices.

Other Location
AQ Café, 58 Park Avenue, between 37th and 38th Sts.; (212) 847-9745; closed Sunday

Chip Shop
Park Slope, Brooklyn
383 Fifth Avenue at 6th St.
(718) 832-7701
Subway: F, M, N, R to Fourth Ave.–9th St.
$ (Cash only)

The chip shop is a steadfastly British institution, but like many other culinary imports, it fits right in with the New York foodscape. This Chip Shop in particular, in the heart of Park Slope, is the rare theme restaurant that serves up very fresh and expertly fried fish, from cod and haddock to shrimp, scallops, and fishcakes, plus a variety of other—you guessed it—fried foods, such as chicken fingers, croquettes, and battered sausage, all accompanied by the ubiquitous and excellent "chips" (French fries). There are numerous non-fish choices, particularly on the "English Restaurant" section on the menu, from a Ploughman's Lunch to Shepherd's Pie, although those not engaged in physical labor for a living might opt out of these calorie bombs (which is not to say that the fish and chips is diet food!).

Just in case you weren't convinced of the fry-or-perish mission of the Chip Shop, the dessert section includes six variations on that bizarre emblem of British tastes, the deep-fried Mars bar—one extreme of which is the fried Twinkie. To complete the trans-Atlantic experience, the walls are covered with all sorts of pop iconography, from an early newspaper review of a Beatles concert to portraits of Charles and Di and racy James Bond posters. Don't be distracted too much by the Anglophilia, though—the tasty fish by itself is reason enough to come.

Esca
Theater District

402 West 43rd Street at Ninth Ave.
(212) 564-7272
Closed for lunch Sunday
$$$

Here the specialty is regional Italian seafood in the style of the Amalfi Coast. *Crudo* is the most original menu option: raw fish prepared in olive oil and salt instead of soy and wasabi. Chef-owner Dave Pasternak is dedicated to sustaining local fisherman much in the spirit of any true Italian chef specializing in food that swims. Besides sourcing locally, Esca also supports humane fishing techniques that keep in mind the delicate ecological balance of our waters. Pasternak is active in the New York food community as a spokesperson for responsible fish service, and he edified readers of the *New York Times* on the subject when he authored the Chef Column for eight weeks in the fall of 2002.

Esca's seafood pastas are also very good: spaghetti with sea urchin or *bucatini* with spicy octopus sauce. Excellent homemade gelati by Pastry chef Meredith Kurtzman are a nice way to conclude a night of fish. Be advised: Esca only serves fish—there is no red meat on the menu (and only one chicken dish). Dave Pasternak, we sea-lute you!

Grand Central Oyster Bar & Restaurant
Midtown East

Grand Central Terminal, Lower Level
42nd Street, between Vanderbilt and Lexington Aves.
(212) 490-6650
Closed Sunday
$$$

Woody Allen once joked about a philosopher who firmly believed that nothing existed outside of his own mind, except the Oyster Bar at Grand Central Station. Located in the very heart of Grand Central Terminal, between the Upper and Lower Concourses, it's easy to picture the bar as a nexus of activity. But though lunchtime can be noisy and chaotic inside the cavernous space, things calm down considerably once the evening rush hour is over.

The Oyster Bar has been operating since 1913; it's as old as Grand Central itself, and its famous tiled, vaulted ceiling was recently restored after a fire in 1997. This distinctive brand of "timbrel vaulting" was designed by an architect named Rafael Guastavino, who emigrated to New York from Barcelona in 1881, bringing with him this classic Catalonian style. The earth tones above your head, and the white vinyl chairs at the counter, popping up like so many toadstools, lend a kind of funky, Middle-Earthish atmosphere to the space.

But it's the seafood that really stands out at this venerable landmark. On a typical day, the staff will shuck roughly 4,000 oysters, serving them on the half shell with two lemon wedges and little containers of seafood sauce and red wine vinegar with onions. The sauce and vinegar are completely superfluous—it's almost a sacrilege to use them with the clean, pure, utterly fresh oysters.

If you've tried, and hated typical raw oysters, you simply must try them here. You may still not be sold on them, but at least you'll know that you're rejecting the very best. And the variety is breathtaking: It's not unusual to see 30 different types of oysters listed on the daily raw bar board. Most are from Long Island, New England, or the Canadian Maritimes, but there are also a few types flown in from the West Coast, and even one (the Coromandel) from New Zealand.

How different do these oysters taste? There's a tremendous variation: A Duck Island oyster from Long Island has a strong, briny taste up front that fades to a full, meaty flavor; the Kumamoto from California, with its beautiful gnarled shell, has meat with a silky-smooth texture and a rich flavor, more reminiscent of an oyster mushroom than an oyster. The first time I tried a Kumamoto, the knowledgeable counterman put them down in front of me, beautifully presented on a bed of shaved ice.

"These," he said reverentially, "are the best oysters in the world." And I'm inclined to agree.

The best way to eat an oyster is to gently loosen it from the shell with your small fork, then lift the shell to your lips and slurp it down. The act is decadent, yet elegant—picture Cole Porter drinking champagne from a beautiful woman's shoe. The price is also decadent, averaging a bit over $2 per oyster. But I once made a meal of sixteen perfect oysters and a glass of sparkling wine for a reasonable price. It was one of the best and most memorable dinners in my life.

Beyond the raw offerings, the Oyster Bar serves a wide variety of fish and seafood dishes, including less-than-reliable versions of classics such as *bouillabaisse, coquille St. Jacques,* oysters Rockefeller, and crab cakes. Stick to the simple stews and panroasts made with oysters, clams, shrimp, lobster, scallops, or a combination. The wine list is large and for obvious reasons inclines toward the white end of the spectrum.

After the renovations made to Grand Central a few years ago, it's become a kind of destination of its own, with markets, stores, and lots of great food. And the Oyster Bar is tucked away like a pearl inside the shell of the great building. Long may its luster continue.

Le Bernardin
Theater District

155 West 51st Street, between Sixth and Seventh Aves.
(212) 554-1515
Closed Sunday
$$$$ (prix fixe)

Awarded four stars shortly after its doors opened more than fifteen years ago, Maguy LeCoze maintains the highest standard of excellence in food, presentation, and gracious service that she and her brother Gilbert created for Le Bernardin. Chef Eric Ripert's beautiful ways with fish are legendary, with every wonderful thing imaginable from the ocean appearing on the menu. The presentation shines here, and the signature dishes, which change every night, include the yellowfin tuna appetizer, broiled shrimp topping the Bernardin pizza, and beautiful poached halibut served on a sweetbread purée with a black truffle sauce. Scallops are sautéed and served with a wonderful Parmesan polenta and an interesting wild mushroom consommé. The combination of flavors that Chef Ripert presents are both delicate and powerful. New and exciting combinations are the latest thing, with a roasted lobster in a black pepper–brandy butter or the just-cooked salmon infused with Earl Grey tea. Choose a simple dessert with a coffee to finish your wonderful meal.

Mary's Fish Camp
West Village

64 Charles Street at West 4th St.
(646) 486-2185
Closed Sunday
$$

There is a reason why the menu and quality of ingredients at Mary's Fish Camp seem familiar: the Mary referred to in the restaurant's name was an original owner of Pearl Oyster Bar before she split off to start her own fish shack. And the fish shack is not exactly a metaphor; Mary's Fish Camp is styled, in typical West Village gentrified fashion, as a humble, wood-hewn restaurant impersonating a Florida fish camp. But despite the rustic overtones, the atmosphere is sophisticated, uncluttered, and modern; with painted benches, a long curved bar, and two walls of windows that flood the airy space with tons of light during the day.

Accordingly, the food is carefully executed and very fresh. The lobster roll figures prominently, and fresh shellfish of all kinds have a starring role—from steamers, cockles, and oysters to lobster knuckles and salt-fried shrimp—but the rest of the menu is also filled out with fresh seasonal vegetables, whether eaten raw in a salad or *gazpacho,* or grilled to accompany the fish of the day.

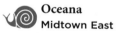

Oceana
Midtown East

55 East 54th Street, between Park and Madison Aves.
(212) 759-5941
$$$$

When you are craving fish of the highest quality, you won't go wrong if you reserve a table at Oceana. Opened in 1992 by the Livanos family, Oceana quickly earned a reputation as one of the top seafood restaurants in New York. In a playful nod to its Greek roots, the restaurant's interior was designed to resemble an ocean liner, and many of Chef Cornelius Gallagher's dishes are assembled with all the multitiered theatricality expected of a luxury cruise. And the fish is so fresh it tastes as if it had just been reeled in from the deck. Oceana places great emphasis on using fish in season and features local products such as American caviars and oysters from the East and West Coasts. All are expertly combined with ingredients from around the world, many of them unusual: Asian pears, crystallized seaweed, lovage, tamarind, fresh pea leaves, and quince purée come to mind. The incredible feat pulled off by Chef Gallagher is that all these combinations really work. And don't forget to sample Chef David Carmichael's equally fantastic desserts.

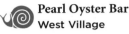

Pearl Oyster Bar
West Village
18 Cornelia Street, between Bleecker and West 4th Sts.
(212) 691-8211
Closed Sunday
$$$

On a narrow, quiet, and sweetly named street in the West Village, Pearl Oyster Bar has for several years now raised the bar for simple yet outstanding seafood in New York City. A succinct and succulent menu features the catch of the day and seasonal specialties such as steamers, along with house specialties, including the lobster roll and must-haves like raw or fried oysters. A lobster roll, when done well, can become the cornerstone of a seafood restaurant's reputation, and Pearl's rendition is nearly flawless, with large, tender chunks of lobster meat in a light mayonnaise and celery dressing bursting from the flanks of a toasted and buttered hot dog roll. Perhaps the only awkward part of the lobster roll is the accompanying pile of vermicelli-thin fries that defy the best forking attempts, forcing you to either work a pinchful of errant fries past the corners of your mouth, or be patient with one fry at a time (it's like trying to eat rice with chopsticks one grain at a time).

No reservations means that getting into Pearl necessitates a strategy: When the place opens for service, show up promptly, even early, for the first seating, or about 90 minutes after that for the second seating, and so on. With the exception of one four-top in the window, all seats are stools at the long marble slab bar or along a narrow shelf on the opposite wall, so Pearl is best experienced by couples or lone diners—and patient ones at that.

RM
East Side
33 East 60th Street, between Park and Madison Aves.
(212) 319-3800
Closed Sunday
$$$$

Chef Rick Moonen's passion for quality and his unique culinary touch are as evident as ever. Attention to freshness and sourcing of ingredients

SHEEPSHEAD BAY RESTAURANTS

Sheepshead Bay, an inlet formed by the eastern end of Coney Island in southeastern Brooklyn, has long been known for its fishing excursions—boats taking eager recreational fishers on six-hour tours to seek out striped bass, fluke, tuna, and bluefish. It was also a neighborhood dominated for decades by Lundy Bros., a fish restaurant extraordinaire, which opened in a Spanish-style edifice in 1934 that in its heyday was supposedly the largest restaurant in the U.S., with seating for 2,800 diners.

Those days are gone, but the ocean breezes are still refreshing in the heat of a New York summer, and the boats still compete for customers, now alongside a floating dance hall. After closing in 1979, Lundy's reopened just a few years ago in a fraction of its former space, renting out the rest to a dentist's office and tattoo parlor, among other tenants. Along with Randazzo's Clam Bar, which is lit like a 24-hour coffee shop but has fresh steamers and fried calamari (plus a signature red sauce that finds its way onto most of the menu), these two fish restaurants are saved by their fresh clams—whether raw, steamed, in chowder, deep-fried, or sautéed with garlic as a topping for linguine—and these fine specimens of molluskhood seem to distill the salty air right onto your plate.

While Sheepshead Bay may be too far to go just for some local seafood, a platter of littlenecks on the half shell washed down with a cold one could be the perfect way to end a long day out hunting for tuna and other elusive prizes.

Lundy Bros.
Sheepshead Bay, Brooklyn
1901 Emmons Avenue at Ocean Ave.
(718) 743-0022
Subway: Q to Sheepshead Bay
$$

Other Location
Lundy Bros., 205 West 50th Street at Broadway; (212) 586-0022

Randazzo's Clam Bar
Sheepshead Bay, Brooklyn
2017 Emmons Avenue, between East 21 St. and Ocean Ave.
(718) 615-0010
Subway: Q to Sheepshead Bay
$$

are equally significant. For years, the chef has been committed to promoting ocean conservation and he has put his name and reputation at the forefront of the seafood conservation movement. Moonen was one of the first chefs to remove Caspian caviar from his menu (after it was discovered that beluga are in such decline that their very survival is at risk), and he was the international spokesman for the "Give Swordfish a Break" campaign. Causes and concerns are important, to be sure, but it all boils down (or simmers or steams) to the food at RM. Stunning seafood creations have become Rick Moonen's calling card throughout his career. A three- or six-course prix fixe menu is available in the stylishly decorated dining room, replete with photographs of gently rolling waves. An à la carte menu is also available at the bar and in the second-floor lounge.

Union Pacific
Gramercy Park/Flatiron District
111 East 22nd Street, between Lexington and Park Aves.
(212) 995-8500
Closed Sunday
$$$$ (prix fixe)

Chef Rocco DiSpirito helms a sophisticated, Asian-influenced restaurant in the Flatiron District that echoes both the flavors of local, seasonal ingredients and the exoticism of Asian flavors and preparations. Fish is a prominent, but by no means dominant, theme on the menu, which also includes all the usual proteins, from duck to lamb. Yet fish is a highlight, with first courses such as tuna tartare and other sashimi and creative main course selections such as halibut with chard.

A finely calibrated approach to isolating the flavors of individual vegetables, such as corn and eggplant, is sometimes obscured by an overly sweet hand in what should be the most savory of dishes. But the last course offers sublime relief, with a fine cheese list and excellent "hand-turned" ice creams and sorbets (which change daily but have included cherry and litchi), whose bracing fruit essences serve as the final palate cleanser.

NOTABLE

Gage & Tollner
Downtown Brooklyn
372 Fulton Street, between Jay and Smith Sts.
(718) 875-5181

Subway: A, C, F to Jay St.–Borough Hall
$$$

Any restaurant that has survived in the same location since 1879 clearly has something going for it, and Gage & Tollner—an Italianate Brooklyn landmark—has been restored for another generation of diners to enjoy. The dining room's vaulted ceiling, mirrored walls, and brass chandeliers epitomize old-school elegance, and the food ranges from classics such as crab cakes and lobster Newburg to lighter, more contemporary preparations. The service, too, is old-school in the best sense of the word—attentive and professional.

Johnny's Famous Reef
City Island, Bronx
2 City Island Avenue
(718) 885-2086
6 train to Pelham Bay Park, 29 bus to end of City Island
Open March–November
$$ (Cash only)

Frequently busy, noisy, and raucous, this enormous cafeteria-like restaurant serves some of the best fried seafood in the city: shrimp, clams, squid, oysters, lobster tails, frogs' legs—you name it. Grab a picnic table on the huge outdoor patio, with its great view of Long Island Sound.

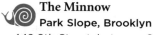

The Minnow
Park Slope, Brooklyn
442 9th Street, between Sixth and Seventh Aves.
(718) 832-5500
Subway: F to 7th Ave.
Closed Tuesday
$$

In 2001, Park Slopers lucked out when the Minnow opened thanks to Aaron and Vicki Bashy. This seafood-filled menu allows guests the option to eat delicious fish any way they like it.

Ping's Seafood
See Chinese, p. 46.

HAMBURGERS

Corner Bistro
West Village
331 West 4th Street at Jane St.
(212) 242-9502
$ (Cash only)

Louie Rubio has been working the tight confines of the Corner Bistro kitchen for twenty years. Originally from Equador, Rubio says the secret to their delicious burger is that the meat has very little fat in it and it arrives fresh each day so that it is never frozen. The burger is broiled and never fried, which according to Rubio is a must. The menu at Corner Bistro is simple and offers only eight items ranging from the Bistro Burger (with bacon, lettuce, and tomato) to the grilled chicken sandwich, chile, and French fries. Open from 11:30 A.M. to 4: 00 A.M., the Bistro has two rooms, which are getting harder and harder to find seats in as its popularity grows. Dark wood tables and curmudgeonly bartenders make you feel as if you are in an old-time New York bar. The Bistro attracts a mellow crowd including the occasional movie star who can't resist the sweet taste of the burgers. Often you get the sensation that many of your fellow customers have traveled long distances on a pilgrimage to eat here. The burgers are certainly worth it.

db bistro moderne
Theater District
55 West 44th Street, between Fifth and Sixth Aves.
(212) 391-2400
$$$

For $28 you can have a burger fit for a prince. Listed as "a sirloin burger filled with braised short ribs, foie gras, and black truffle served on a Parmesan bun," every true burger lover must try a Daniel Boulud burger at least once in his or her life. It is not as heavy as one would think, and the French fries that accompany it are some of the best in New York. As with the rest of the db's menu—which features Greenmarket and other quality local and seasonal products—the burger is not only tasty, but superior to standard fare from an eco-gastronomic standpoint. The bistro itself is elegant but cool, and the service is great.

Island Burgers and Shakes
Clinton
766 Ninth Avenue, between 51st and 52nd Sts.
(212) 307-7934
$ (Cash only)

Hell's Kitchen has produced a hell of a good burger. Island Burgers lists 63 kinds of burgers on their menu, ranging from the "Basic" to the "Frog" (boursin, bacon, onions), to the "Julius" (Caesar salad, pita bread), to the "Hippo" (curried sour cream, bacon, cheddar, onion, scallion, sour-dough), to "It's A Mad, Mad World" (pesto, salsa, Swiss cheese, pickle relish, pita). Yet with each selection, the toppings never overwhelm the taste of the burger itself. Founded in 1998 by William Brown, Island Burgers also makes perfectly grilled *churascos*, a.k.a. Grilled Chicken Breast Sandwich. Sadly, you will not find French fries on the menu. The reasons for this include not having access to enough electricity or gas and a lack of space (the restaurant is very small). Also, if you like beer or wine with your burger you'll have to bring it yourself. Unlike most burger joints, it is worth a trip out of your way to reach this Island oasis.

Jackson Hole
East Side
232 East 64th Street, between Second and Third Ave.
(212) 371-7187
$

There are seven other Jackson Holes in New York, but only the 64th Street location makes our list of hamburger greatness. Part of the reason for this is the atmosphere. Set five steps below the city sidewalk, the Hole has low ceilings, low lights, and cramped tables, but manages to be warm and convivial nonetheless. Founded in 1972, the diner boasts a 7-ounce burger that is bigger than the bun itself, forcing eaters to take a few bites around the circumference before getting to the bread. The burger is so big that it often breaks as you eat it, but it tastes so good that this is a minor inconvenience. The simpler the better at Jackson Hole, with cheese and bacon being the best possible toppings.

'21' Club
Theater District
21 West 52nd Street, between Fifth and Sixth Aves.
(212) 582-7200
Closed Sunday; closed Saturday June–August
$$$

'21' began its life in 1920 as a speakeasy thanks to two college students, Jack Kriendler and Charlie Berns. The speakeasy moved three times (once because of the construction of Rockefeller Center) before finding a permanent home on New Year's Eve of 1929 where it is today. The place is worthy of a visit for two reasons: the fantastic burgers (at around $29 they should be!) and the historic memorabilia hanging from the ceiling. The burgers include a blend of herbs and spices, onions, and duck fat, served on a sourdough roll. In 2001, 7,930 of them were ordered. Then, too, there are the thousands of trinkets on display here, including one of John McEnroe's tennis rackets and a replica of PT109, a gift from John F. Kennedy Jr. CEOs of various corporations have also donated toys to the ceiling (if you go, you will probably encounter a number of CEOs, so dress nicely). If you have the time (and if they allow you) visit the underground wine cellar, where people like Elizabeth Taylor, the Nixon daughters, and Chelsea Clinton store bottles of wine.

NOTABLE

P.J. Clarke's
Midtown East
915 Third Avenue at 55th St.
(212) 759-1650
$$

Located in the heart of midtown, a small, two-story brick building in a neighborhood dominated by high-rises like the Citicorp Building and the Lipstick Building, P.J. Clarkes has been serving great burgers and reasonably priced beer since 1890. After its recent makeover and change in ownership, we hope it doesn't change too much.

Knickerbocker Bar & Grill
Greenwich Village
33 University Place, between 8th and 9th Sts.
(212) 228-8490
$$$

Thick, tender, perfectly cooked, and garnished simply with fries, the burgers at the Knickerbocker are sensational and worth every penny. T-bone steak has a following here, too, along with the handy bartenders and live jazz.

Peter Luger
See Steak Houses, p. 213.

J.G. Melon
Lenox Hill
1291 Third Avenue at 74th St.

(212) 650-1310
$ (Cash only)

This Upper East Side saloon, established in 1972, serves an unadorned purist's hamburger, with no offerings of guacamole or pineapple slices or other nonsense to get in the way of the flavor. Plus, the cottage fries are hard to beat.

Relish
Williamsburg, Brooklyn
225 Wythe Avenue, between Metropolitan Ave. and North 3rd St.
(718) 963-4546
Subway: L to Bedford Ave.
$$

This neighborhood spot is located in trendy Williamsburg and makes a mean grilled sirloin burger served on a roll with French fries or buttermilk onion rings. The atmosphere is mellow and casual and offers three choices as to where to eat: the diner, the patio, or the lounge in the back.

Smith & Wollensky
See Steak Houses, p. 215.

Soup Burg
Lenox Hill
922 Madison Avenue at 71st St.
(212) 734-6964
$

If you find yourself somewhere near the Meadow in Central Park, head over to Soup Burg for a visit. When you first walk in, it does not seem unlike hundreds of other coffee shops around New York. But as soon you bite into one of their outstanding burgers you'll be happy you came.

LATE NIGHT

 **Blue Ribbon**
Soho
97 Sullivan Street, between Prince and Spring Sts.
(212) 274-0404
Open daily until 4:00 A.M.; closed Monday
$$

Long a sanctuary for employees of NYC's restaurant world, Blue Ribbon has expanded into a mini-empire of late-night hot spots. Things just start to heat up at around midnight when cooks and waiters emerge from the early-to-bed restaurants, having spent long shifts on their feet and in front of hot stoves or hot-headed customers. This clientele knows their stuff, and what they demand is really quite simple: soul-satisfying food and damn good wine. Blue Ribbon successfully delivers both. The menu varies from dishes such as fried chicken and mashed potatoes to fresh, fried, or grilled sardines to steak tartare, oysters, and even crawfish. The wine list has well-priced offerings from all over the globe.

The best way to start a night at Blue Ribbon is at the raw bar with, of course, a glass of bubbly. Invariably, there is a wait (though well worth it), as reservations are only accepted for parties of five or more. The crowd is always exciting, filled with the frenzied restaurant crew just letting loose while most folks are winding down, as well as food aficionados of all types. Often you'll find celebrities popping by to enjoy the food and the scene (one late night we sat next to the Red Hot Chili Peppers because, really, where else would you eat after a gig?).

The word is that the newest Blue Ribbon in Brooklyn's Park Slope neighborhood is serving a delicious brunch. Perfect for those late mornings that spill into the afternoon after a long night of eating out at late-night restaurants!

Other Locations
Blue Ribbon Brooklyn; 280 Fifth Avenue, between Garfield and
    1st Sts, Park Slope, Brooklyn; (718) 840-0404; Subway: M, N, R
    to Union St.; open Tues.–Sun. 6:00 P.M.–4:00 A.M.
Blue Ribbon Bakery; 33 Downing Street at Bedford St, West
    Village; (212) 337-0404; open daily 12:00 P.M.–2:00 A.M.

Double Happiness
Chinatown/Little Italy
173 Mott Street, between Broome and Grand Sts.
(212) 941-1282
Open Friday–Saturday 6:00 P.M.–4:00 A.M.
$$

Located on a dark, gloomy chunk of street at the frontier of Little Italy and Chinatown, this stylish basement lounge hides a somber past: A speakeasy during Prohibition, it became a Mafia-run bar and was eventually the scene of a bloody gang murder. Renamed after a Chinese ideogram representing good luck in marriage (in this case, the union of Chinese and Italian influences), Double Happiness mixes original Chinese details (such as a giant abacus, an ancient calculator made of wood marbles), and a dim, clandestine, mob-inspired atmosphere. There are many nooks and crannies where you can withdraw and savor some exotic house cocktails, such as the Green Tea Martini (citrus vodka, Cointreau, green tea extract, and lemon juice) or the Pear Ginger Martini (lemon vodka, Cointreau, pear cognac, and fresh gingerroot juice) along with a plate of flavorful delicacies, such as the crispy red snapper and arugula tacos or the spicy barbecued duck confit *empanadas*.

Florent
West Village
69 Gansevoort Street, between Greenwich and Washington Sts.
(212) 989-5779
Open to 5:00 A.M.; Saturday open 24 hours
$$ (Cash only)

For almost twenty years, Florent has been serving hungry diners into the wee hours of the morning, and judging from how crowded the place is even at 4:00 A.M., it doesn't look like it will stop doing so anytime soon. Florent boasts many menus, but for the sake of this guide we will speak only of the "Supper or Breakfast" menu. Offering items such as skirt steak, burgers, and salads, as well as a full selection of eggs, French toast, and omelettes, Florent gives every customer the hypercaloric meal they need after a hard night's work or play.

Florent used to be the sole bastion of light late at night in the seedy underbelly of New York's Meatpacking District. Today it is one of many businesses there. Founder Florent Morellet says he is the dinosaur of the neighborhood but claims that he opened there in 1985 because he liked it the way it was and not because he wanted to change it. "Don't get me wrong," he explains, "I like the way the area has changed; I just don't want credit for it." When it first opened, the immediate area around Gansevoort Street was filled with bars like the Anvil, Mineshaft, Alex and Wonderland, J's, and Mother's. In the 1980s, Club Mars opened there.

Designed in a 1940s diner style with bright lights, Florent is simple and clean. The walls are decorated with maps from around the world, including three hand-painted by Florent himself. Florent also started a Bastille Day street fair, featuring hay on the sidewalk to soak up the "blood" from the "guillotines," a tradition since 1989.

NOTABLE

Angel's Share
See Bars, Pubs & Taverns p. 159.

Bukhara
See Indian & Pakistani, p. 79.

Carnegie Deli
See Delis, p. 181.

Gam Mee Ok
See Korean, p. 106.

Han Bat
See Korean, p. 107.

Joe's Pizza
West Village
233 Bleecker Street at Carmine St.
(212) 366-1182
Open daily 9:00 A.M.–5:00 A.M.
$

The best late-night pizza in the city—available by the slice until the sun comes up—comes out of the oven fresh and fragrant, which is more than can be said for some of Joe's after-hours clientele, who have partied a bit too hard.

Other Location
7 Carmine Street at 6th Avenue; (212) 255-3946

Kang Suh
See Korean, p. 104.

Kum Gang San
See Korean, p. 107.

Lucky Strike
Soho
59 Grand Street, between Wooster St. and West Broadway
(212) 941-0479; (212) 941-0772 (reservations)
Open to 2:00 A.M.; Friday–Saturday to 4:00 A.M.
$$

The success of this bistro—Keith McNally's first—has been constant for nearly two decades. Nothing surprising there, since the decor is lovely, the service efficient, the food always reliable (great appetizers, salads, and steak frites) and everything on the menu is available until late!

Mamoun's Falafel
Greenwich Village
119 MacDougal Street, between Bleecker and West 3rd Sts.
(212) 674-8685
Open to 5:00 A.M.
$ (Cash only)

The best way to absorb a night of drinking is to finish with fried chickpea fritters in a falafel-filled pita from Mamoun's.

New York Noodle Town
See Chinese, p. 49.

Odeon
Tribeca
145 West Broadway, between Duane and Thomas Sts.
(212) 233-0507
Open to 2:00 A.M.; to 3:00 A.M. Friday–Saturday
$$

This Franco-American bistro continues to be hip, especially late at night, when the *artistes manque* and celebrities come out to play. But focus on the food; it's probably the least pretentious thing here, and at its best is simple and well prepared.

Sarge's
See Brunch, p. 176.

Veselka
East Village
144 Second Avenue at 9th St.
(212) 228-9682

Open 24 hours
$

You really get a sense of the diversity of the East Village community if you hit Veselka late at night. Takeout business is brisk, and students, hipsters, and old-timers alike appreciate the affordable and filling fare. The menu is strong on Eastern European comfort food such as borscht and blintzes, but extends to "American" and even vegetarian choices. Veselka also serves a leisurely brunch on weekends.

ELIZABETH LITTLES

PIZZA

Di Fara Pizza
Midwood, Brooklyn
1424 Avenue J at East 15th St.
(718) 258-1367
Subway: Q to Ave. J
$$ (Cash only)

There are plenty of pizzerias that claim to make the best slices in the city, and I am certain every single New Yorker has an opinion as to where to find the best slice or pie. The phrase "the best slice" has become as watered down as "the original Ray's" or "gourmet deli." Perhaps what Slow Food can offer is a new alternative to these stale phrases and overused exclamations by creating a new phrase to define excellence, "Made with love and care." If I had to nominate only one place for the "Made with love and care" category, it would be Pizzeria Di Fara. The owner, Domenico DeMarco, a native of Sorrento, has been making pizzas, one by one, in this small corner store for forty years. He makes two kinds of pizza, round and square, and as pizza-lovers watch Domenico work his magic, salivary glands are called into action and stomachs rumble.

For the square pizza, the dough is kneaded, pulled, and stretched over the back of a rectangular pan, then fitted into the pan and adorned carefully with homemade tomato sauce and a little salt and extra-virgin olive oil. It is then placed in the oven for approximately 10 minutes. When removed, a mixture of imported *mozzarella di bufala* and fresh Brooklyn mozzarella is placed on the par-baked crust, and then an additional ladleful of sauce is spread carefully around the edges of the pie to ensure a moist, chewy, saucy crust. The pie is then put back in the oven, to shortly reappear bubbling and delicious. But the fun doesn't stop there: Fresh basil and oregano plants are available for customers who want to pick the leaves and dress their own slices. Parmigiano Reggiano is freshly grated every half hour or so, to prevent it from drying out. Undeniably, this is pizza "made with love and care."

Grimaldi's
Brooklyn Heights, Brooklyn
19 Old Fulton Street, between Front and Water Sts.
(718) 858-4300
Subway: A, C to High St; 2, 3 to Clark St.
$$ (Cash only); no deliveries

From 1990 until 1996, this preeminent pizzeria—located near the Brooklyn Bridge and the old Fulton Ferry Pier—was named Patsy's or Patsy Grimaldi's, after its founder. This Patsy started working at the original East Harlem Patsy's in 1941, which was owned by his uncle, Pasquale Lancieri. When the original Patsy's was sold in the early nineties, the name was licensed to another company, legal battles ensued, and (confused yet?) the long and short of it is that this pizzeria is now named Grimaldi's.

Fortunately the pizza hasn't changed a bit. The toppings are still excellent, with house-roasted red bell peppers and a brightly flavored sausage, redolent with fennel, made at the Corona Heights Pork Store in Queens. Grimaldi's crust, compared to other places, is a bit stiff (you can hold it at the back, between your thumb and middle finger, and it won't droop) and unexceptional. But the mozzarella and mild tomato sauce are very fresh and good, and on most nights the coal-fired brick oven churns out your pizza after only a 10-minute wait. In fact the operation is so fast and efficient that an artist friend of mine from Park Slope once said that he actually double-parked his car outside Grimaldi's on a busy night, and the waiter gave him to-go curb service. Only in New York.

The atmosphere is straight out of Italian central casting: red-and-white-checked tablecloths, a jukebox pumping out songs from the likes of Dion and the Belmonts—well, you get the picture.

Grimaldi's pizza consistently receives high praise. While it's certainly not my favorite, probably because of the crust, the excellence of the toppings alone ensures it a strong A- grade. And the historic neighborhood (not to mention its proximity to both Brooklyn Ice Cream Factory and Jacques Torres Chocolates) makes Grimaldi's a great place to visit, especially via the new water taxi service that stops a Fulton Ferry Pier, only a few steps away.

John's Pizza
West Village
278 Bleecker Street at Jones St.
(212) 243-1680
$$ (Cash only); no deliveries

Another perennial contender for the title of New York's best pizza, John's has been on Bleecker Street since 1929 (probably the most positive development to hit the city in the year of the stock market crash), and they're still turning out one of the best pies you will find anywhere, at the incredibly reasonable price of $11.50 for a large pizza—a few dollars less than most of the other big-name pizza places.

The restaurant has two separate dining areas served by two coal-fired brick ovens. The wooden booths are carved with initials from patrons past and present, and there are bizarre but typical Venetian canal scenes on the wall, plus the usual reviews and memorabilia, including one of

Pete Rose's baseball jerseys. The queue for tables typically stretches out the door, but trust us, it's worth waiting for a seat.

John's may well have the best crust in the city: thin yet sinewy, firm yet pliable, scorched and surprisingly flatbreadlike. Unlike other top-notch pizzerias, the mozzarella here is shredded instead of thinly sliced; the sauce is typical of New York pizza, that is, not very spicy or assertive. But the ratio of sauce to cheese is perfect, and the toppings are flavorful.

You can also order calzones and pasta dishes. John's definitely deserves its famous reputation and its place in the pantheon of the best New York pizza parlors.

La Pizza Fresca
Gramercy Park/Flatiron District
31 East 20th Street, between Broadway and Park Ave. South
(212) 598-0141
$$

La Pizza Fresca is one of only a handful of American restaurants to be awarded an *attesta* (certificate of authenticity) from the Naples-based Associazione Vera Pizza Napoletana, or AVPN. To qualify as "true Neapolitan pizza," the dough must be hand-pressed and made with Italian flour and a precise amount of water; Italian-style tomatoes (such as San Marzano) must be used, as well as *mozzarella di bufala,* from the milk of water buffalo raised in the region near Naples; the pizza must be small, between 9 and 10 inches in diameter; and you must be able to fold a slice twice, into quarters, without breaking the crust, which is crispy outside, chewy inside.

That's a lot of authenticity to live up to, but La Pizza Fresca's *pizzaiolo,* Alessandro Rivas, does it artfully, firing the pies in a wood-burning brick oven. Opened in 1996 by Massimo Vitiano, the LPF management trained at Ciro Santo Brigida in Naples, the restaurant owned by Antonia Pace, the AVPN president. The attention to detail really shows in the lovely pies that come to your table, everything from the minimalist Marinara and Margherita to the Quattro Formaggi and the Quattro Staggioni (with prosciutto, mushrooms, and artichokes). The eponymous La Pizza Fresca is made with tomato sauce, fresh *mozzarella di bufala,* cherry tomatoes, black olives, Parmigiano Reggiano, and fresh basil. All of the ingredients, from the extra-virgin olive oil to the *prosciutto di Parma,* are of the highest quality.

But there's more than just pizza at La Pizza Fresca. Appetizers include a plate of grilled vegetables drizzled with balsamic vinegar, served over greens with a side of *schiacciata* (a focaccia-style bread). There are pasta dishes (such as the *fettuccine ai carciofi,* with artichoke hearts and cherry tomatoes), as well as daily meat and fish specials. The wine list offers some interesting Italian varietal choices, and the espresso here is very good as well.

La Pizza Fresca's dining area is long and low ceilinged, and it can get noisy when things get busy. It's not a place you'd go every week—and the modest-sized pies aren't very filling for the price—but for a special, high-end, and absolutely traditional Italian pizza experience, it's the best place of its kind.

Lombardi's
Chinatown/Little Italy
32 Spring Street, between Mott and Mulberry Sts.
(212) 941-7994
$$ (Cash only)

Established way back in 1905, Lombardi's lays claim to being not only the first pizzeria in New York, but the first one in America. For that alone it deserves recognition.

Consistently rated the best pizza in Manhattan by Zagat, one year the survey dubbed Lombardi's pies The Best on the Planet. And while there's absolutely no doubt that these are primo New York–style coal-oven pizzas, are they really the city's (much less the *world's*) best? The fact is, once you've hit the uppermost echelon of pizzerias (say, the top three to five places in the city), the term "best" goes beyond mere technical merit and enters the realm of personal preference. On certain days I would give Lombardi's the blue ribbon; on other days, Totonno's or John's or even Patsy's might get the nod. All I can say, faced with this quandary, is try it for yourself, and *vive la difference.* You certainly will not be disappointed at Lombardi's.

Be prepared to wait on most nights for a table in the narrow dining room with its high tin ceilings and walls adorned with old photographs and paintings of gods and goddesses. The anticipation, as any pizza lover knows, is part of the overall experience.

Lombardi's house salad is better than at most similar places, studded with fresh arugula. And the pizzas are stellar, made with excellent mozzarella and a good, typically mild San Marzano tomato sauce. The lightly singed crust folds well, but is a bit saltier than at other pizzerias. The pizzas are garnished with fresh basil, and the ingredients (such as the oven-roasted peppers, beefsteak tomatoes, and sweet Italian sausage from Esposito's) in general are great, but if anything *too* plentiful; the crust is a bit overloaded and unbalanced—something no one but a pizza purist would object to.

The signature pies at Lombardi's are their White Pizza (with mozzarella, ricotta, and Romano cheese, but no tomato sauce) and the Fresh

Clam Pie, which features hand-shucked clams, oregano, fresh garlic, Romano cheese, and extra-virgin olive oil. It's astoundingly good, on a par, if not slightly better (forgive me, Mother Yale!) than the *bianca* clam pies at the famous Pepe's and Sally's in New Haven, Connecticut.

Patsy's Pizzeria
East Harlem
2287-91 First Avenue, between 117th and 118th Sts.
(212) 534-9783
$-$$ (Cash only); no deliveries

Pizza heretics may claim that a slice is just a slice. If that's the case, how does one explain the legions of loyal Patsy's supporters who make the trek up to East Harlem just to get a single serving—or two, or three—of some of the best coal-oven pizza in the city?

A Patsy's slice is pizza stripped to its barest essentials: cheese, sauce, and crust. This is elemental pizza; additional toppings would only distract from the transcendent experience. The only acceptable additions are the grated Parmesan and the dried red pepper flakes that you can shake on yourself—they, too, are completely unnecessary. Simply fold the pizza in half lengthwise and bring it to your mouth. You'll find that the sauce is more flavorful and less wimpy than the typical New York sweet and mild version.

Aside from the hulking masonry pizza oven, there's nothing in the dingy little space devoted to slices but a couple of stand-up counters and a soft drink machine. You won't be tempted to linger, which is the point, but people come here to focus on serious pizza, not ambience. Next door there's a sit-down area with table service, where you can order an excellent pie with all the familiar toppings, fresh and hot from the oven, or order it to go and join the procession of double-parked cars on First Avenue whose owners had the same idea. Patsy's has been around for almost a century, and it's always worth the trip uptown. The other places named Patsy's sprinkled throughout the city have merely licensed the name, and are not under the same ownership. As is usually the case with famous pizza joints, stick with the original.

Totonno Pizzeria Napoletano
Coney Island, Brooklyn
1524 Neptune Avenue, between West 15th and West 16th Sts.
(718) 372-8606
Subway: W to Stillwell Ave.–Coney Island
Open to 8:30 P.M.; closed Monday–Tuesday
$$ (Cash only); no deliveries

Totonno's opened in 1924, when Coney Island was in its prime—the playground of the working class—and looked very different than it does today. The Stillwell Avenue train station is currently getting a major $250 million overhaul, which hopefully will help breathe new life into the neighborhood. Meanwhile, the ocean is still here, and the salt air, and the boardwalk—as nice as ever for strolling. The old Parachute Jump is still standing, though other amusement park attractions are only a memory. The modern midway huddles near the old wooden Cyclone roller coaster, which provides a brief but thrilling ride. And the Brooklyn Cyclones, a minor-league affiliate of the Mets, play right next to the boardwalk, providing yet another reason to take the train down to Coney Island.

Who ever heard of a pizza joint that closes at 8:30 P.M.? Well, when you see the neighborhood where Totonno's is located, three longish blocks away from the boardwalk, you realize that there's not much nightlife on Neptune Avenue. Across the street from the pizzeria you'll find an auto parts, auto glass, auto alarm, and auto body shop.

Inside the pizzeria is a bit rundown, with pressed tin walls and ceilings, a couple of booths, and seven tables. The photos on the walls make you feel as though you've entered a time warp: a 2-cent special edition of the old *New York Daily Mirror* bears the headline, "Truman Announces: War Over"; and there's a framed photo of the 1955 Brooklyn Dodgers, the year "Dem Bums" finally beat their nemesis, the Yankees, in the World Series. After your long pilgrimage to get here, Totonno's feels almost like a shrine to all things Brooklyn.

Coal-fire brick oven pizza has got to be the fastest Slow Food there is, and the pie arrives on your table literally steaming, topped with molten fresh mozzarella, and it remains too hot to handle for a few minutes—the longest wait you will ever have. Biting into a slice, the crust is thin, pliant, and full of flavor—better in my opinion than Grimaldi's or Lombardi's, and on a par with John's. The list of toppings isn't extensive (no ham and pineapple, thank God), and your menu choices are pizza, large or small, and calzone. Period. As my pizza maven friend Norman says, "Clearly, they do not suffer from 'mission creep'!"

On one of our recent visits, the *pizzaiolo*, who had just finished showing off his Totonno's tattoo for a visiting camera crew, told us that a neighborhood rabbi often drops in for pizza with his family. He doesn't order the meat toppings, of course, which aren't kosher, but he cuts himself a little slack regarding the mozzarella. As he reportedly said, "A lot of my congregation do bad things every day. I'm only eating pizza."

NOTABLE

Bella Blu
Lenox Hill
967 Lexington Avenue, between 70th and 71st Sts.
(212) 988-4624
$$–$$$

The pizzas that issue from the mosaic-tiled masonry oven are excellent, but they're only the tip of the iceberg at this Northern Italian restaurant that serves up satisfying, well-prepared dishes to a young, hip clientele.

Dani's House of Pizza
Kew Gardens, Queens
81-28 Lefferts Boulevard at Greenfell St.
(718) 846-2849
Subway: E, F to Kew Gardens–Union Tpke.
$$

Along with Nick's, Dani's makes some of the best pizza in Queens, with a strong emphasis on the fundamentals: excellent crust and tomato sauce.

Denino's Pizzeria & Tavern
Staten Island
524 Port Richmond Ave., between Hooker Pl. and Walker St.
(718) 442-9401
Staten Island Ferry, then S44 bus to Hooker Pl.
$ (Cash only)

Denino's is widely considered to be the best pizza on Staten Island (no idle boast, since Lee's Tavern and Nunzio's are worthy competitors), and it's worth the occasional trek to remind yourself how good it can get. The 1930s-vintage neighborhood tavern where it's made is nothing fancy: just a bar, a pool table, and a few tables in the back. But the pies are very good, with a thin, crispy crust and a mellow red sauce. Many toppings are available, but Denino's makes a darn good *bianca* (white) pizza with lots of mozzarella and onions. What's not to like?

Full Moon Pizza
Belmont, Bronx
600-02 East 187th Street at Arthur Ave.
(718) 584-3451
Subway: B, D to Fordham Rd.
$$ (Cash only)

Full Moon is a great place to start or end a shopping trip on Arthur Avenue. Try their broccoli rabe calzone; it's warm, crispy, chewy, cheesy, and full of peppery greens. Word must be out because they often run out before the lunch rush is over. The pizza is also great, thin and tasty.

Joe's Pizza
West Village
232 Bleecker Street, at Carmine St.
(212) 366-1182
Open daily 9:00 A.M.–5:00 A.M.
$–$$

This stand-up or takeout place in the Village is popular for its cheese and pepperoni slices. They're very tasty, available fresh and hot almost anytime, day or night. Some people swear by Joe's slices, though purists might find them a bit too cheesy. And for those who simply can't wait for a free table at John's, just up the street, Joe's Pizza offers instant gratification.

Other Location
7 Carmine Street at Sixth Ave.; (212) 255-3946

Louie & Ernie's
Pelham Bay, Bronx
1300 Crosby Avenue at Waterbury Ave.
(718) 829-6230
Subway: 6 to Buhre Ave.
$$

Louie and Ernie Ottuso have been serving up slices ever since the late 1940s back in East Harlem. In 1959 they moved the business to its current location in the Bronx, and their thin-crust pizza made with full-cream mozzarella still holds pride of place in the neighborhood. They also uphold another old-time pizzeria tradition that we admire: As soon as the day's supply of dough is used up, the place shuts down. It may not make sense to an MBA student, but it's undeniably a Slow way of looking at life. It also makes a statement: Get here early, before the good stuff is gone.

Mimi's Pizza and Family Restaurant
Upper East Side
1248 Lexington Avenue at 84th St.
(212) 861-3363
$

This family-run pizza joint has been serving up excellent slices for years. You couldn't tell that from walking by, but ex-Upper East Side residents actually make pilgrimages to have another taste. During the 1980s, Mimi's survived the opening of a Cosmos across the street—longevity is what happens when you make great food!

Nick's Pizza
Forest Hills, Queens
108-26 Ascan Avenue, near Austin St.
(718) 263-1126
Subway: E, F, G, R, V to Forest Hills–71st Ave.
$$ (Cash only); no deliveries

In general, the better a pizzeria's decor, the more mediocre its pizza will be. Patsy's, John's, and Totonno's interiors certainly won't be featured in *House Beautiful*. So Nick's comes as a pleasant surprise: It's an inviting place, with wood floors, tin ceilings and walls, and good lighting that also has terrific brick oven pizza. Nick's buys its mozzarella and sausage from nearby Corona Heights Pork Store, and the freshness and quality of all their ingredients is evident. Also, unlike the minimalist pizza joints, the salads are worth ordering here, as are the calzones and even the cannoli, if you can find room for one at the end of the meal.

Nunzio's
Staten Island
2155 Hyland Boulevard at Midland Ave.
(718) 667-9647
Staten Island Ferry, then S51 bus to Grant City
$$

Nunzio Trivoluzzo opened his original pizzeria on Staten Island way back in 1943, and sixty years later his successors are maintaining a tradition of excellence. Nunzio's slices are among the best in New York, with a nice pliant crust and a flavorful sauce that's made from San Marzano tomatoes, punctuated with fresh basil and a bit of black pepper.

Picasso Café
Gramercy Park/Flatiron District
43 East 29th Street, between Madison and Park Ave. South
(212) 696-4488
Closed Sunday
$$

A long, low-ceilinged room means that Picasso gets noisy when it's busy, but the sturdy wooden furniture, and the attractive wood-fired brick oven add a lot to the atmosphere at this café owned by Andrew Chapman. Picasso's pizzas have an crispy, cracker-thin crust that comes out nicely charred and tastes a bit sweet. But the high-quality toppings are the real stars of the show: excellent mozzarella, along with fresh arugula, bresaola, pancetta, artichoke hearts, and more. Salads, antipasti, focaccia sandwiches, pastas, and char-grilled meats are all worth ordering, as is the baked calzone filled with mushrooms and prosciutto.

Slice of Harlem
Harlem
308 Malcolm X Blvd. (Lenox Ave.), between 125th and 126th Sts.
(212) 426-7400
$$

Excellent thin-crust pizza and slices, plus heroes and pasta dishes to go.

Other Location
2527 Frederick Douglass Boulevard (Eighth Ave.) at 135th St.;
  (212) 862-4089

Two Boots Restaurant
East Village
37 Avenue A, between 2nd and 3rd Sts.
(212) 505-2276
$$

Pizza purists may scoff at the overloaded slices and the cornmeal crust, but Two Boots is so popular *because* owners Phil Hartman and Doris Cornish have gone beyond New York pizza tradition. Their love of Cajun food is evident in both the red sauce, which is much spicier than the typically mild, sweet New York standard, and in the creative toppings, such as andouille sausage and barbecued shrimp.

Other Locations
42 Avenue A at 3rd St.; (212) 254-1919
Grand Central Terminal, Lower Concourse, 42nd St. and
  Lexington Ave.; (212) 557-7992
30 Rockefeller Center, between 49th and 50th Sts.; (212) 332-
  8800
514 2nd Street, between Seventh and Eighth Aves., Park Slope,
  Brooklyn; (718) 499-3253
74 Bleecker Street, between Broadway and Lafayette St.; (212)
  777-1033
201 West 11th Street at Seventh Ave. South; (212) 633-9096

STEAK HOUSES

Peter Luger
Williamsburg, Brooklyn
178 Broadway at Driggs Ave.
(718) 387-7400
Subway: J, M, Z to Marcy Ave.
$$$$ (Cash only)

"For how many? Medium Rare or Rare?" And that is the extent of most interactions between waiter and customer at Peter Luger Steak House. In business since 1887, Peter Luger is the best steak house in New York. In fact, the quality and taste far exceeds the steak you will find at other New York restaurants.

A few years after the death of Peter Luger, the family put the restaurant up for auction. Saul Foreman, who manufactured metalware across the street, was the only bidder, and the restaurant became his in 1950. Saul did make a few changes to the menu, including adding shrimp cocktail, hash brown potatoes, cream of spinach, and desserts, but his biggest contribution to Luger's was his dedication to quality. Saul and his family decided that with relaxed government standards for the grading of meat, they could not rely on middlemen to choose it for them. Only family members could be relied upon to ensure the quality of each piece. Led by Saul's wife, Marsha, and their daughter Marilyn Spiera, Luger's has been selecting and serving the best meat in New York for years. (Zagat has rated it the #1 steak house every year practically since the inception of their guide.) Today, Marilyn, her sister Amy Rubenstein, and Marilyn's daughter Jody carry on the family tradition. The color of all meat must be pink, with an even conformation of fat dispersed throughout. While there are almost no secrets at Luger's, there is one: the amount of time they dry-age their meat.

The meat is broiled at very high heat and burned on the outside to perfection (if you are wary of ordering your meat rare, this is the place to do it). It melts in your mouth. I would go so far as to say you should ask for an extra order of steak (which is served presliced) just to have enough. The bacon is also among the best you will ever taste. If you go for lunch, delicious burgers only cost $5.95 (served only at lunch, and only on weekdays). If you like bread before your meal or if you order the tomato and onion appetizer, try the Peter Luger sauce. While Slow Food doesn't readily encourage drowning food in bottled sauces, this one is sweet and delicious. Invented by a waiter named Willie many years ago, it is sometimes referred to as Willie-sauce by the staff. Willie is not the only waiter to have contributed to the Luger legacy. Most of the staff has been serving customers for years (Wolfgang Zweiner has been there since 1964), and the regular faces add to the feeling of tradition.

The restaurant has a typical steak house atmosphere. Don't expect great wine (though they do serve great beer from the neighboring Brooklyn Brewery) or to be treated as good as the meat tastes. Luger's only accepts one credit card—their own. Peter Luger serves superior steak, and that is why one should go. As one of the owners explains, Peter Luger is different because, "We kept to our high standard—we did not change even when new trends came along. No fat-free, no fusion, no nouvelle cuisine. We stuck to what we knew—we narrowed in and became specialists." Indeed they did!

NOTABLE

Christos Hasapo-Taverna (Christos the Hellenic Steak House)
Astoria, Queens
41-08 23rd Avenue, between 41st and 42nd Sts.
(718) 726-5195
Subway: N, W to to Astoria-Ditmars Blvd.
$$

A retail butcher by day and restaurant by night, Christos defines itself as a Greek steak house because they cook steak the Greek way: with virgin olive oil and Greek spices. Greek appetizers and fresh whole fish are also served. Established in 1994, some people say it has one of the best price/quality ratios for steak and lamb in New York.

Gallagher's Steak House
Theater District
228 West 52nd Street, between Broadway and Eighth Ave.
(212) 245-5336
$$$$

Founded way back in 1927 as a speakeasy and restaurant by dancer/comedienne Helen Gallagher, this venerable steak house still boasts its large circular bar, red-and-white-checked tablecloths, and wood-paneled walls festooned with celebrity photos and memorabilia. There's a lot of tradition here, and the dry-aged steaks (which you can see from the street, curing in their glass-walled meat locker) are grilled over hickory-wood charcoal, including the porterhouse and the gargantuan "king loin" sirloin.

Keens Steakhouse
Garment District/Koreatown
72 West 36th Street, between Fifth and Sixth Aves.
(212) 947-3636
$$$$

This may not be the best steak house in New York, but it may be the one that best preserves the steak house tradition. The ceiling is lined with the long-stemmed clay pipes that were for years given to members (men only, of course) as they arrived. Daniel Webster's pipe is on display here, as is Douglas MacArthur's.

The menu is equally venerable: steaks and chops, introduced by iceberg lettuce and backed up by a choice of potato and creamed spinach. Try Keen's signature dish, the double mutton chop.

MarkJoseph Steakhouse
Financial District
261 Water Street, off Peak Slip
(212) 277-0020
Closed Sunday
$$$$

Only a few years old, this upstart steak house is building a reputation as "Peter Luger without the attitude." As at Luger, you can order a porterhouse for two, three, or four people, and you'll get presliced meat that's been dry-aged and salt-cured to perfection. The bar here is also a good place to hang out and have a single-malt Scotch or other libation before or after dinner.

Post House
East Side
Lowell Hotel
28 East 63rd Street, between Madison and Park Aves.
(212) 935-2888
$$$$

Part of the Lowell Hotel, the Post House has been around for more than twenty years. The American decor is beautiful, featuring an eclectic collection of odd objects on the walls including a canoe, eagles carved of wood, a Botticelli-esque painting, and modern art. The meat, which is broiled, is dry-aged on the premises by Executive Chef Andres Tzul.

Smith & Wollensky
Midtown East
797 Third Avenue at 49th St.
(212) 753-1530
$$$$

The excellent steak au poivre and the world-class hash brown potatoes are reason enough to come to Smith & Wollensky, but since 1977 they've also served all manner of steaks and chops, as you'd expect. And Wollensky's Grill, their sibling restaurant down the block at 48th Street, makes a mean burger. Fantastic cheap burgers too!

Sparks
Midtown East
210 East 46th Street, between Second and Third Aves.
(212) 687-4855
Closed Sunday
$$$$

The steaks at Sparks are juicy, tender, and delicious—the beef tender from more than a month of aging. Sparks doesn't dry-age their meat, as other steak houses do, but wraps it tightly during the aging process.

The wine list (more than 500 entries) is exhaustive, with a few good values. Save room for some coffee after dinner and a slice of Eileen's Cheesecake, which is dry and elegant, not creamy and messy. Enjoy, indulge, and listen to your arteries hardening. Well, nobody lives forever.

WINE BARS

Craftbar
Gramercy Park/Flatiron District
47 East 19th Street, between Broadway and Park Ave. South
(212) 780-0880

The staff at Craftbar fits skillful and polished professionalism into a package that befits its name and offers experienced consumers a thrilling balance between innovation and control. Certainly a restaurant that almost any discriminating palate can enjoy, the ambitious wine list and engaging menu best serve the seeker.

Wines are available by the glass, half-glass (a brilliant idea that more places should adopt!), or bottle. You'll discover a number of interesting wines, including a Swiss Chasselas, a 1991 Carema, an oaked Austrian Sauvignon Blanc and an intense Washington State Merlot. All of the wines were offered by knowledgeable recommendation and were poured in good condition. A number of intriguing selections join more common bottlings on a list where glasses start at $7.00.

An open kitchen dominates the back of the long, narrow space and turns out the kind of creative, fully realized, and well-prepared food that has given Craft, Craftbar's larger and more expensive sibling, a reputation as a necessary destination for the restaurant-obsessed.

D.O.C. Wine Bar
Williamsburg, Brooklyn
83 North 7th Street at Wythe Ave.
(718) 963-1925
Subway: L to Bedford Ave.

On the western edge of Williamsburg's resurgent and trendy Northside you will find a comfortable corner room that will very likely transport you to your own Sardinia, given enough time and a few glasses of that island's excellent wine. Done up like a village café with rough-hewn tables, D.O.C. Wine Bar successfully imports the feeling of conviviality that so many travelers to Italy yearn for upon their return to these often unforgiving shores. The owners, Claudio and Rossana, are Sardi and they have stocked their well-priced list with a number of the island's selections, as well as other interesting bottles from the lesser-known Southern Italian regions: Puglia, Campania, Sicily, and Calabria. More commonly available wines such as Chianti and Montepulciano d'Abruzzo are also available.

D.O.C's menu offers an interesting selection of cured meats and cheeses, as well as a number of light dishes that make fine use of several types of fresh ingredients, plus well-made bread. Slow Food members who have been paying attention to the ever-expanding Ark of Taste will be pleased to find the Sardinian version of *bottarga* (cured mullet roe) on the menu.

Enoteca I Trulli
Gramercy Park/Flatiron District
124 East 27th Street, between Lexington and Park Ave. South
(212) 481-7372
Closed Sunday

Enoteca is the wine bar attached to the well-regarded restaurant I Trulli. An elegant space with a broad bar and a row of small tables, Enoteca is a civilized place with a decidedly upscale feel. The wine list is Italian-only and, if I Trulli's list is requested, one of the deepest in the city. It's also one of the fairest, with glasses starting at $5.00 and bottles at $18.00. Wines are offered in three-glass flights, generally organized by region or grape variety, or simply by the glass or bottle. Because the restaurant focuses on Italy's southern regions (the owner hails from Puglia), a number of interesting southern wines are available, most of them representing the best values on the list. If you have the good fortune to visit when wine director Charles Scicolone is pouring, do not hesitate to engage him in conversation, as he has stories relating to virtually every wine in the place, and he likes to tell them. Enoteca has its own menu of cured meats, cheeses, olives, and a well-priced three-course prix fixe, as well as complete access to I Trulli's more expensive full lunch and dinner menus.

For those on a really tight budget, Vino, an affiliated all-Italian wine store across the street, holds free, themed wine tastings every Friday evening and Saturday afternoon.

'ino
West Village
21 Bedford Street, between Sixth Ave. and Downing St.
(212) 989-5769
Cash only

The tiny 'ino, shoehorned into a storefront on charming Bedford Street in the West Village, was one of the first wave of panini-and-wine joints to open around the city several years ago. It remains among the best. The efficient floor staff pours interesting selections from a fairly priced all-Italian list, while the cooks manning the sandwich presses in the small open kitchen are sure-handed and swift. The idea behind the pressed sandwich-and-wine bar is simple: serve appealing food and honest, unpretentious wines at a low enough overhead to allow prices that rarely exceed those of a diner, and attract happy customers. The idea works for those wine lovers who have grown weary of the uninspired selections on many lists that try to keep most bottles under $30.00. Trading in an average, inexpensive California Merlot for a more interesting but equally priced Aglianico or Dolcetto is a good way to keep the active palate exercised without having to sell the farm.

As if this weren't enough reason to visit 'ino, they also open early, at 9:00 A.M. (11:00 A.M. on weekends), serving good coffee and a terrific breakfast.

Otto Enoteca Pizzeria
Greenwich Village
1 Fifth Avenue at 8th St.
(212) 995-9559
$$$

From the masterminds behind the New Italian institutions of Babbo, Lupa, and 'ino comes this rollicking pizza and wine bar. Right from the street, you feel the energy of a bustling Roman train station: a large open area, scattered with communal stand-up tables, holds the scores of hungry diners clutching their *biglietti* (Otto's kitschy way of assigning tables to waiting patrons: When the city on your "train ticket" appears on the blackboard, it's time to eat!). Although touted for its "griddled" pizza, it's the *antipasti,* daily *bruschetta,* and *fritto* specials that are the clear standouts. The *antipasti* are divided into categories: meat, vegetables, fish, and cheese. Don't miss the addictive fried chickpeas topped with *bottarga,* diced red onion, and fresh lemon; or the meaty anchovies with chunky croutons and scallions. Even the cheeses distinguish themselves: with each order, the waiter approaches your table toting oversized Mason jars full of unique condiments. Fresh, creamy ricotta, pecorino, and Coach Farm goat cheese are paired with a black truffle honey, sour cherries in syrup, and a spicy Seville orange chutney. Pizzas, as deftly explained by the waiter, are either "Otto Pizzas" (prepared with less traditional ingredients, such as *lardo,* thin strips of pork fatback) or more recognizable versions, such as the classic *Margherita.* They are individually sized, with a thin, griddled crust (not unlike a good pita bread), and they are good, but not great. The all-Italian wine list takes its cue from the appetizer menu: It's interesting, affordable, and there is a lot to choose from. Save room for the excellent house-made gelatos that offer classic flavors (chocolate, hazelnut with chocolate chips), as well as outstanding surprise specials (olive oil gelato with blood orange segments). Otto's appeal is universal: baby seats, large groups, and couples will all feel at home.

Paradou
West Village
8 Little West 12th Street at Ninth Ave.
(212) 463-8345

Paradou is a modest, well-lighted room and a serene rear garden located in what is a fascinating neighborhood for those food lovers who fancy themselves amateur urban historians or food-minded sociologists. The Meatpacking District, situated on and just south of the far western end of 14th Street in Manhattan, is declining as a commercial ghetto of meat processors and rising as a commercial and residential ghetto of moneyed hipsters. Known more properly as the Gansevoort Market, the twenty-block area has been a vital part of New York's food distribution system since 1884, and remains one of the last industrial landscapes in Manhattan that was designed in that interest. The newcomers cater to and are frequented by like-minded folks who find a vague reflection of Europe in the cobblestone streets and the chic boutiques that are sprinkled among the loading docks and corrugated-iron awnings. Bustling cafés are open to sidewalks that still stink of rancid fat and rotting flesh. The district and its attractions, Paradou being a fine example, are most worthy of a visit.

The restaurant maintains an all-French list that is broken down by color and region. The list is not inexpensive—nothing comes in under $30.00 for a full bottle—but it does touch on the major regions without forgoing the very appealing wines of Provence, the Languedoc, Corsica, and the southwest. Most wines are available in three sizes, a 250 ml carafe, a 500 ml carafe, or a standard 750 ml bottle. The glassware is modest by most current New York standards—thick tumblers that recall the utilitarian standards that many European wines are judged by in their home cafés.

The food at Paradou is fresh and flavorful, mostly lighter fare with a selection of salads, grilled sandwiches, crêpes, and a variety of plates featuring pâtés, terrines, charcuterie, and cheeses.

Veritas
Gramercy Park/Flatiron District
43 East 20th Street, between Broadway and Park Ave. South
(212) 353-3700

The wine bar section of this book poses a difficult problem if an impressively large wine list with depth in desirable vintages is held as a factor in an institution's inclusion. After all, many of New York's most comprehensive wine selections are housed in restaurants that are covered in other parts of the guide, or are simply too expensive to merit a recommendation to the wine enthusiast who is simply looking for an interesting selection at an everyday price. The merits of Veritas allow for a middle ground.

Veritas is an unusual restaurant. Its modular-office décor, austere bar, and by-the-book, new-American menu might well have passed into Park Avenue South oblivion several years ago were it not for the restaurant's exhaustive wine list and the impressive attention it receives from an obviously devoted staff. The list is actually a book, handed out with a casualness that suggests Veritas has made sure contact with a knowledgeable and appreciative audience. Divided into four sections (by-the-glass, market, reserve, and dessert) the list has been designed to highlight different things for different people. The by-the-glass and dessert sections generally hew to the larger emphasis on noble European varieties and historically important regions, while the market section takes liberties and throws in a few otherwise obscure wines from places such as Portugal, Austria, and South America. The reserve selection is firmly rooted in Burgundy and Bordeaux, with additional strength in collectable wines from California, Piedmont, Tuscany, Germany, Alsace, Champagne, the Loire, and Australia. The prices are good, often surprisingly so.

Anything offered at table is available at the modest but comfortable bar. The menu has à la carte and prix fixe options.

NOTABLE

The Bar @ Etats-Unis
Upper East Side
247 East 81st Street, between Second and Third Aves.
(212) 396-9928

Located across the street from the New American restaurant Etats-Unis (see p. 19), this small bar has an extensive selection of wines from around the world. You can order off the parent restaurant's menu here as well.

Bar Veloce
East Village
175 Second Avenue, between 11th and 12th Sts.
(212) 260-3200

A sleek, East Village take on the wine-and-panini theme, with an intelligent and even adventurous list of fairly priced Italian wines. The menu follows suit with carefully tended antipasti, delicate *tramezzini,* and robust panini.

Savoia
Carroll Gardens, Brooklyn
277 Smith Street, between Degraw and Sackett Sts.
(718) 797-2727
Subway: F to Carroll St.

The pizza-makers at this newcomer to Brooklyn's Smith Street restaurant eruption are mindful of what their Neapolitan cousins might think, so they roll the dough thin and cook it carefully in a hot oven. Equal care goes into a thoughtful pan-Italian wine list that holds a few surprises and is always easy on the wallet.

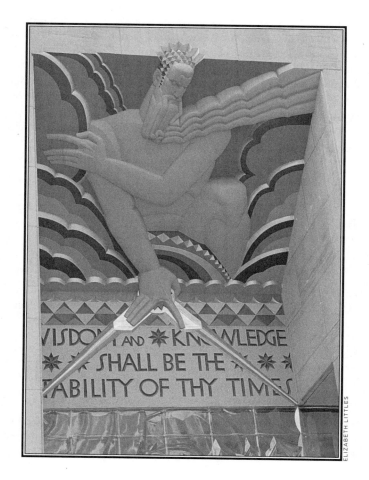

PART III

FOOD SHOPS, MARKETS & PRODUCERS

BAGELS, BIALYS & KNISHES

Absolute Bagels
Upper West Side
2788 Broadway, between 107th and 108th Sts.
(212) 932-2052

The youngest in the trio of Upper West Side bagel titans, Absolute opened its doors to the public in 1990. Samak, the owner and bagel maker, emigrated from Thailand and plied his trade at Ess-A-Bagel before embarking on his own pursuit to create the definitive bagel. His hand-rolled bagels are baked fresh seven days a week and serve an ever-expanding clientele of Upper West Siders, as well as those who are willing to travel the expanse of Manhattan for a top-notch nosh. In a plain café-style setting, Absolute holds one advantage over its local bagel competitors in that it offers plenty of seating. Bagels can be consumed at their absolute peak of freshness, right on the spot! Samak's bagels are medium in size, tender and chewy, with a mellow sweetness that can only come from using barley malt in the blending process rather than cheaper, overly sweet sugar.

Columbia Bagels
Upper West Side
2836 Broadway at 110th St.
(212) 222-3200
Open 24 hours

Sure, the name may not be original, but the bagels here are some of the finest in the city. Hand-rolled, "kettled," then baked, Columbia produces a bagel with a perfect old-style crust with a crisp firmness that yields to a chewy, somewhat cakey interior. Established in 1986, Columbia makes and serves their bagels to neighborhood students and throngs of local regulars. The long, narrow storefront can barely accommodate the bustle of customers in the morning, but devotees are rewarded for their patience with fresh, aromatic bagels to start the day. The Plain bagels are perhaps their best variety, followed closely by the Raisin, which has a delicate sweetness that marries the barley malt of the bagel mixture with the natural sugars of the raisins. As a testament to their quality and consistency, Columbia (as well as H&H) supplies the bagels sold at Zabar's.

Ess-A-Bagel
Gramercy Park/Flatiron District
359 First Avenue at 21st St.
(212) 260-2252

Eclectic crowds file into the cramped flagship store, and the line often winds its way right out the door. Since 1976, Ess-A-Bagel (literally, "Eat a

Bagel" in Yiddish) has staked out a secure reputation as the premier baker of the "oversized" bagel. Through the lines customers can catch a glimpse of the kettle where the hand-rolled bagels are gently boiled before being baked to a crisp finish. The steam rises in such a steady stream that the ambience is more construction zone than café. The decor doesn't appear to have changed much since the seventies and, in part, provides a certain appeal to the store. The rest of the "charm" comes from often less-than-patient counter help that works hard to keep the line feeding through the storefront at an even pace. Though the oversized bagel is ideal for sandwiches (and Ess-A-Bagel serves everything from smoked fish to sliced turkey), the first bite of a plain bagel with cream cheese has the wonderful crunch of a fresh baguette. It is no surprise that the best bagels are those that come warm right out of the hopper, and, if you're not in a hurry, they can be enjoyed right in the store as the rest of the world rushes by on First Avenue (or stands in line deciding which bagel to order).

Other Location
831 Third Avenue, between 50th and 51st Sts.; (212) 980-1010

H & H Bagels
Upper West Side
2239 Broadway at 80th St.
(212) 595-8003

A conundrum ensues with lofty H&H. Long the crown jewel of New York bagelries, H&H pumps out millions of bagels a year for retail and wholesale consumption. A separate West Side plant has even been built to handle a worldwide shipping business. There is no denying that they produce some of the finest-tasting bagels in the world, using only the finest ingredients. The spacious Upper West Side storefront often can't contain the long lines of bagel worshipers who snake through the store and often out onto Broadway (particularly on the weekends). H&H bagels consistently have a wonderful texture, from the hardened exterior crust to the soft, never-too-doughy interior. Furthermore, the slightly sweet flavor lingers in aroma and taste. While H&H bagels are not hand-rolled, they are "kettled" and baked using traditional ingredients and methods. In addition, they are certified kosher, and the store offers other kosher products for sale as well.

As marvelous as the bagels are, the conundrum deepens when considering that H&H only sells bagels to go, unsliced. You can purchase bagels and packaged cream cheese separately, but not a bagel with cream cheese to enjoy as you hit the street. H&H loyalists have grown accustomed to this minor detail, as well as the stratospheric price of 95 cents per bagel.

Other Location
639 West 46th Street at Twelfth Ave.; (212) 595-8000

Kossar's Bialys
Lower East Side
367 Grand Street, between Essex and Norfolk Sts.
(212) 473-4810; (877) 424-2597
Closed Saturday until 11:00 P.M.

Bialystock, Poland, may be a long way from New York City, but great bialys can still be found on the Lower East Side! A longtime New York landmark, Kossar's is the oldest bialy bakery in the country, having been established in 1936. Each bialy is hand-rolled using the finest ingredients, including high-gluten flour and freshly ground onions. Whitey, the bialy baker at Kossar's for the past twenty-five years, creates a floury bialy that is not as dense or heavy as a bagel.

The small storefront is dedicated entirely to production. In addition to Whitey's prep station and brick oven, the store is filled with old-world speed racks with wooden shelves lined with fresh bialys. The aroma is at once engaging and hunger inducing. Kossar's bialys (as well as their other products, including bagels) are certified kosher. Furthermore, the store remains open until Friday afternoon and opens again late Saturday night, long after the Sabbath has ended, to begin baking for Sunday, the busiest day of the week.

While once a mainstay only for local Jewish customers, Kossar's does a brisk business catering to tourists and others seeking to enjoy and preserve this ethnic food tradition.

Mrs. Stahl's Knishes
Brighton Beach, Brooklyn
1001 Brighton Beach Avenue at Coney Island Ave.
(718) 640-0210
Subway: Q to Brighton Beach

Just under the elevated Q train, as it makes a sharp right turn to head to Coney Island, sits Mrs. Stahl's Knishes, a Brighton Beach institution since 1935. The entire history of Mrs. Stahl's is unclear, but the tradition of baked knishes—a tradition that has few havens left—has been passed on and is thriving in this neighborhood of new Russian immigrants. The store itself has turned into something of a fast-food joint serving burgers, kosher hot dogs, chicken, and fries in addition to traditional knishes (which have kosher certification through the New York State Department of Agriculture). The truth of the matter is that, as the neighborhood has changed, the traditional knish customers have either moved or passed away. To compete, Mrs. Stahl's has been forced to expand their menu to appeal to a broader audience. Still, the knishes are made on premises by hand and have a wonderful flavor and delicate moistness that is rare. Old-timers and kids alike who have just come off the beach enjoy this Old World delicacy that could easily serve as a hearty lunch. Like much of Brighton Beach, the store is somewhat rundown. The best bet is to take a knish or two to the beach for a postswim snack.

Murray's Bagels
Greenwich Village
500 Sixth Avenue, between 12th and 13th Sts.
(212) 462-2830

The quintessential neighborhood bagelry, Murray's lies in an ideal location to serve Greenwich Village, as well as the West Village. The small, cozy storefront provides a comfortable haven for fans of old-fashioned bagels. Hand-rolled every day, kettle-boiled, and then baked, the silky-sweet smell of fresh bagels carries out onto Sixth Avenue before you even walk through the door. The subtle sweetness of the bagels is common among the best bagels in the city and indicates the use of the highest-quality ingredients, particularly barley malt. While the Plain bagel always seems to be the most popular, special attention should be paid to Murray's Multi-Grain, perhaps the best of its kind in New York. Try the salty, assertive belly lox or another type of cured fish on a Murray's bagel sandwich to go, with tomato and red onion—a New York feast for brunch or lunch. For some reason, it always amuses us to hear the counterman at Murray's say, "Belly up!" as he passes our sandwich to the cashier.

Other Location
242 Eighth Avenue, between 22nd and 23rd Sts.; (646) 638-1335

Yonah Schimmel Knishery
Lower East Side
137 East Houston Street, between Forsythe and Eldridge Sts.
(212) 477-2858
Closed Saturday

In what was once an enclave for Jewish immigrants from Eastern Europe, this famous city landmark stands as a link to the past. Since 1910, when Yonah Schimmel, a young rabbi, started baking knishes to supplement his income, this historic storefront has seen a remarkable overhaul of the neighborhood. With the recent gentrification of the historic Lower East Side nearly complete, the knishery has survived to serve a whole new generation of customers who flock here for a hearty knish and a cream soda. Dense with filling, knishes are still prepared by hand in the basement, baked, and brought up to street level by a dumbwaiter in the center of the restaurant. The period storefront remains intact despite the transformation of other neighborhood businesses. Framed black-and-white photos of the Lower East Side as well as old reviews and press clippings line the walls. Old registers and other equipment scattered about contribute to the general Old World ambience. Even a photo of Yonah Schimmel himself still hangs in the storefront window, linking past generations to the present and future. Truth be told, these are boon times for the knishery. So much so that waiter service has even returned to the modest seating area. Next we'll see tablecloths and linen napkins!

NOTABLE

Knish Nosh's Potato Knishes
Rego Park, Queens
101-02 Queens Boulevard at 67th Rd.
(718) 897-5557
Subway G, R, V to 67th Ave.

Delicate, crisp pastry casings surround the prototypical fillings of knishery: potato, spinach, and kasha (buckwheat groats).

New York Bagels
West Side
164 Amsterdam Avenue, between 67th and 68th Sts.
(212) 799-0700

Hand-rolled, high-quality bagels are sweetened with malt and have an excellent flavor and texture.

Other Location
1228 Second Ave., between 64th and 65th Sts.; (212) 327-0333

BREAD BAKERIES

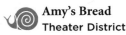 **Amy's Bread**
Theater District
672 Ninth Avenue, between 46th and 47th Sts.
(212) 977-2670

As the smell of freshly baked bread and sweets drifts onto Ninth Avenue, locals and tourists alike line up outside of Amy's Hell's Kitchen location to sample one of the many treats for sale. An oasis in the heart of Midtown, Amy's Bread is a cross between a Parisian *boulangerie* and a cozy Midwestern kitchen. Everyone feels at home here.

Baker Amy Scherber worked in the kitchens of Bouley and Mondrian before opening her own place back in 1992, which today not only sells retail, but also wholesales breads and baked goods around the city, including at another retail location in Chelsea Market.

Try Amy's signature Semolina with Golden Raisin and Fennel, the beautiful Green Olive Picholine, or just a simple (but outstanding) French baguette. Many of Amy's breads are made with organic ingredients.

Theoretically, you could eat three meals a day here (the original store seats 12) and have snacks in between, and quite a few of Amy's regulars are known to do just that! At Amy's one can enjoy the grilled sandwiches, sticky buns, old-fashioned double layer cakes, and decadent brownies, just to name a few goodies. The staff provides consistent, friendly service.

Other Locations
75 Ninth Avenue (at Chelsea Market); (212) 462-4338
972 Lexington Avenue (Upper East Side); (212) 537-0270

Balthazar Boulangerie
Soho
80 Spring Street, between Broadway and Crosby St.
(212) 965-1785

While Balthazar has moved its baking operations out of the cramped Spring Street facility where it began, the bread has suffered little from being transplanted. An assortment of pastries and sharply crusted breads is available at the bake store, and the breads are also served in the restaurant. You may think the darkest of their breads is burned, just by looking at the crust, but you should never judge a loaf by its cover. Go ahead and taste it: This is bread as it should be.

E.A.T.
Upper East Side
1064 Madison Avenue, between 80th and 81st Sts.
(212) 772-0022

Eli's Manhattan
Upper East Side
1411 Third Avenue at 80th St.
(212) 717-8100

The Vinegar Factory
Upper East Side
405 East 91st Street, between York and First Aves.
(212) 987-0885

It would be easy to say that Eli Zabar is not a "real" artisan baker, because of the volume of bread that issues forth each day from the two production bakeries located next to the Vinegar Factory on East 91st Street, which supply both Eli's Manhattan and the Vinegar Factory, as well as Zabar's pricey takeout restaurant, E.A.T. But despite the presence of a flour bin that holds 70,000 pounds of flour, Eli's breads all benefit from a fair bit of handwork. At the main bakery some of the shaping is automated, and there's a huge tunnel oven where all of the high-volume breads are baked. At the smaller bakery across the street, however, all of the work is done by hand, with small mixers and deck ovens. All of the formulas are developed in-house, with firm ties to their European roots. For example, Eli's bakes a Poilane-like loaf that is supremely fresh and has a great texture to boot!

Pastries come from a third bakery, made with butter and fresh fruits obtained from Eli's own stock; once again, nothing is "farmed out" to other vendors, and the quality is uniformly high.

Breads may be purchased at any of the locations mentioned above, or at many other stores in New York. Don't let the ubiquity fool you: Eli's bread really is Slow.

Orwasher's Bakery
Lenox Hill
308 East 78th Street, between First and Second Aves.
(212) 288-6569

Abram Orwasher continues the fine baking tradition that his grandfather started in 1916, producing a variety of Eastern European and classic Jewish rye breads. In fact, his rye sourdough starter has been fed continuously since his grandfather developed it when the bakery first opened. When you eat it, you're eating history.

All the products are kosher, preservative-free, and handmade. Some of the breads are still mixed and baked using the original equipment. In fact, the ovens date from the original construction of the building, forming part of the back wall of the bakery. Three large brick hearth ovens carry the load; oil-fired today, they were heated originally with wood, and then with coal. If anything goes wrong with these venerable ovens Orwasher's has to blend magic with mechanics to revive them! In true Slow fashion, Mr. Orwasher manages to maintain tradition while producing breads and pastries of the highest quality. From a man whose motto is, "Only bad bread needs butter," Orwasher's bread is sure to please. Try the cinnamon-raisin loaf—so good it's practically transcendental.

Sullivan Street Bakery
Soho
73 Sullivan Street, between Broome and Spring Sts.
(212) 334-9435

CRUST. That's what it's all about at Sullivan Street Bakery. Outstanding rustic Italian breads are the specialty. From double-crusted Filone to their Integrale, to the rustic Pugliese loaf, the sesame semolina, and varied focaccias, owner and baker Jim Lahey is consistently producing high-quality breads. He's got a Slow approach to breadmaking, baking in small batches and cutting and shaping by hand.

Lahey picked up his baking secrets in Italy, and he seeks to re-create the traditional neighborhood bakery, by sustainably serving the local community and restaurants.

Sullivan Street Bakery supplies breads for markets and restaurants throughout the city. You can taste his breads at the bakery before choosing a loaf to take home. Or try one of Sullivan Street's pizzas, with the thin and crispy crust typical of wood-fired brick-oven pies.

Other Location
533 West 47th Street, between Tenth and Eleventh Aves.; (212) 265-5580

Uzbekistan Tandoori Bread
Kew Gardens, Queens
120–35 83rd Avenue, between Leffert and Metropolitan Aves.
(718) 850-3426
Subway: E, F to Kew Gardens–Union Tpke.
Closed Saturday

When was the last time you tried fresh Uzbeki bread? Probably never, but this spot is well worth the trip out to Queens. Owner and baker Isak Barayev tends to his imported *tandoor* ovens while the restaurant serves up kosher Central Asian fare. He makes only one bread. It's a large bialy-shaped loaf made with white flour and sprinkled with sesame and black onion seed. It's always warm and fresh. You can sit in the restaurant and wait for the next batch to come out while listening to Persian music and sipping tea.

Barayev has been written up before and seems comfortable with his newfound notoriety. He still produces 40 breads an hour from morning till evening every day except for the Sabbath. You can even hear live music most nights during the week; call ahead to make sure.

NOTABLE

Le Pain Quotidien
Upper East Side
1131 Madison Avenue, between 84th and 85th Sts.
(212) 327-4900

The *baguette à l'ancienne* probably never was so good in ancient times. This version is made simply, from unbleached flour, salt, yeast, and water. Le Pain claims they slowly ferment the dough in small batches and bake five times a day. It has a substantive full flavor without being grainy or heavy. Other interesting products available here include the peanut rye and the walnut *boule*.

Other Locations
100 Grand Street at Mercer St.; (212) 625-9009
1336 First Avenue at 72nd St.; (212) 717-4800
833 Lexington Avenue, between 63rd and 64th Sts.; (212) 755-5810
50 West 72nd Street, between Central Park West and Columbus Ave.; (212) 712-9700

Moishe's Kosher Bake Shop
Lower East Side
504 Grand Street, between Columbia and Willett Sts.
(212) 673-5832
Closed Friday at sundown to Sunday morning

It is hard to beat the prices at this kosher baker of challah and rye bread. The *babka* is also unbelievable, as is the *rugelach*.

Other Location
115 Second Avenue, between 6th and 7th Sts.; (212) 505-8555

Napoli Bakery
Williamsburg, Brooklyn
616 Metropolitan Avenue, between Lorimer and Leonard Sts.
(718) 384-6945
Subway: L to Lorimer St.; G to Metropolitan Ave.

Napoli Bakery is a tiny, flourescent-lit storefront on busy Metropolitan Avenue, in Williamsburg's Italian neighborhood. You'll only find bread for sale here, no pastry. At only $2.50 for a large loaf, the bread is a great value, with a crunchy outer crust and soft, spongy interior.

Parisi Bakery
Chinatown/Little Italy
198 Mott Street, between Kenmare and Spring Sts.
(212) 226-6378
Cash only

Parisi has been baking bread in a brick oven since 1910, and they make great seeded Sicilian rolls, which you can also find in many markets in Little Italy.

Other Location
290 Elizabeth Street at Houston St.; (212) 460-8750

Settepani Bakery
Williamsburg, Brooklyn
602 Lorimer Street, between Conselyea and Skillman Sts.
(718) 349-6524

Biaggio Settepani turns out incredible Italian breads from his coal-fired brick oven, such as his *ciabattini* and the golden, fragrant *pandoro*, which is baked specially around the Christmas holidays. Making *pandoro* involves Slow baking in the extreme; it's a time-consuming labor of love, but the results are heavenly. Try Settepani's delicious baked goods, too, including the traditional biscotti and the sophisticated bittersweet chocolate *pannetone*.

Other Location
196 Lenox Avenue at 120th St., Manhattan; (917) 492-4806

Silver Moon Bakery
Upper West Side
2740 Broadway at 105th St.
(212) 866-4717

Silver Moon bakes many different kinds of artisan bread, including some seasonal specialties such as Cider Bread. But what really stands out is their incredible Fig and Peppercorn Bread: Soft and warm, fruity and savory, it's great with cheese and wine, if you can get it home before tearing into it.

Terranova Bakery
Belmont, Bronx
691 East 187th Street, between Beaumont and Cambreleng Aves.
   (2 blocks northeast of Arthur Ave.)
(718) 367-6985
Subway: B, D, to 182nd–183rd Sts.

Bread that is fragrant and often still warm from the oven, like no other. It is crusty, unpretentious, wholesome. This is the kind of bread that you cut a slice off, sprinkle with sea salt and oregano, drizzle with a bit of good olive oil, and enter another dimension.

A. Zito and Sons Bakery
West Village
259 Bleecker Street, between Sixth and Seventh Aves.
(212) 929-6139
Cash only

One unusual specialty at Zito's is their lard bread (made with prosciutto, lard, and provolone), but you can find many other worthy specimens as well at this historic and beloved bakery in the heart of the West Village.

ELIZABETH LITTLES

CHOCOLATE & CANDY

Black Hound
East Village
170 Second Avenue, between 10th and 11th Sts.
(212) 979-9505

Black Hound is a sweet tooth's dream. Walk inside this tiny shop and you feel a bit like Charlie in Willy Wonka's wonderful chocolate factory. Cakes, cookies, and candies of extraordinary taste are very artfully presented. There are tall tins and Shaker boxes filled with beautiful, colorful treats for yourself and your loved ones. The myriad flavor combinations include ginger, lemon, raspberry, apricot—just about anything you might dream of exists here. Butter cookies come in many shapes and sizes, with tiny chocolate butterflies being my personal favorite.

Easter cookies, Passover cookies, sweetheart baskets—Black Hound covers every holiday in the tastiest and most elegant way. But shopping here only for holidays would be a mistake; buy something just for dessert, or take home a springtime assortment to break the monotony of a gray drizzly day.

The candy counter with its exquisite chocolate baskets will make your heart beat faster. Black Hound's superlative chocolate truffle sauce is made with or without liqueur. Big Georgia pecans are lightly coated with a sweet and spicy mixture; finely chopped on top of vanilla ice cream with the truffle sauce, they make a chocolate sundae to die for.

Join the Black Hound Club online and they will not only prepare and deliver all of your corporate gifts, they will remind you of your personal favorites as well—as if this were really necessary.

Garrison Confections Inc.
Chelsea
The Chocolate Loft
119 West 23rd Street, between Sixth and Seventh Aves., Suite
    1003
(212) 929-2545
Closed Saturday–Sunday

Andrew Shotts once worked as a pastry chef at La Côte Basque and the Russian Tea Room, and in late 2001 he launched his first line of artisanal chocolate bonbons, all of which combine high-quality Guittard chocolate with rich ganaches and other fillings to make some of the finest confections in the city. Shott works in small batches, using traditional techniques. *USA Today* recently named him one of the top ten artisanal chocolatiers in the country.

Garrison Confections introduces a new line every season, and the choices are keyed to a seasonal theme. A recent Autumnal Equinox line featured chocolates flavored with caramel apple, spiced pumpkin truffle, muscadine, and forest fruit.

The Chocolate Loft is really Garrison's production facility, not a retail location; it's located on the top floor of an industrial building in Chelsea not far from the St. Vincent de Paul church. However, you can call in advance and arrange to pick up your order during regular weekday business hours, or purchase them over the Internet at www.thechocolateloft.com. You can also find selected flavors of Garrison's chocolates for sale at the Chocolate Bar (see p. 240) for the same price you'd pay at the "factory." These little chocolates don't come cheap ($14 for an assorted box of 12, $28 for 24 pieces), but they are meant to be savored, or presented as an extra-special gift.

Jacques Torres Chocolate
D.U.M.B.O., Brooklyn
66 Water Street, between Dock and Main Sts.
(718) 875-9772
Subway: A, C to High St.
Closed Sunday

If you're up and about very early in the morning, you might catch a glimpse of Jacques Torres peddling his mountain bike from his apartment in Manhattan over the Brooklyn Bridge to his chocolate shop. Even better, if you show up just after 8:00 A.M. at his store in the D.U.M.B.O. neighborhood (an acronym for Down Under the Manhattan Bridge Overpass), on a street where old warehouses are being transformed into cafés and performance art spaces, you may get one of his flaky croissants, still warm from the oven, or a *pain au chocolate* to have with your morning coffee at one of the few tables in the front of the shop. On Saturday mornings, there's even more of a variety of pastries to choose from.

Torres, a former executive pastry chef at Le Cirque and the Dean of Pastry Studies at the French Culinary Institute, started his own chocolate factory here in Brooklyn in 2000. You can actually see the chocolates being made through the large plate-glass windows that show off the whole operation. All of the fillings for the bonbons are made from scratch starting with raw ingredients, and Torres never uses any additives or preservatives. Instead he has a machine that mixes everything quickly and without incorporating a lot of air (which can lead to rapid oxidation and a brief shelf life).

The chocolates are anything but cheap (they run $10 for a dozen assorted bonbons, but they are so intensely flavored, fresh, and satisfying that this seems like a bargain. The two dozen or so flavors typically available include cinnamon praline (milk chocolate with a cinnamon ganache and ground hazelnut filling); Earl Grey tea (infused in a dark creamy center), and Bandol Breeze (named after Torres's hometown in Provence, it contains apricot pâté de fruit and almond marzipan).

Torres distributes his chocolates to several of the city's premier hotels, and supplies restaurants such as Pico (p. 147) and retail shops such as Lunettes et Chocolat and the Chocolate Bar.

La Maison du Chocolate
Lenox Hill
1018 Madison Avenue, between 78th and 79th Sts.
(212) 744-7117; (800) 988-5632

If you have spent a long time searching for the temple of the cacao bean, you will find it at La Maison du Chocolate. Founded in the late seventies by the wonderful French chocolatier Robert Linxe, it came to the United States in 1994. This charming little store is almost identical to its Parisian twin, and the exactitude of the hundred tiny rows of tiny morsels is a wonder to behold, even if you don't care that much for chocolate.

The French-style macaroons are truly delicious, with a crisp shell and chewy sweet filling inside. Other classics include silky cognac truffles, beautifully squared and sugared fruit jellies, and candied chestnuts, which are available all winter long.

The Arribes is wafer thin with a creamy, intensely chocolate filling. The Flamenco is another house speciality, a milk and dark chocolate ganache that is subtly infused with rosemary, basil, and jasmine. For a more unusual taste, try the Pavé du Fauborg with its delicate herbal ganache. Trinidads are thin and dark and have a distinctive snap that pleases every time. Cocoa powder packed in tins and praline and dark chocolate almonds are great and perfectly wrapped for giving.

Flown in twice every week from France to both the Madison Avenue and Rockefeller Center locations, the product is impeccably fresh and tasty. You can also enjoy a cup of tea or Caracas hot chocolate in the tiny salon and relax while you survey the crowds or just admire the symmetry of the elegant boxes with their lovely dark brown ribbons. Or perhaps you should just press your nose against the window and daydream about Paris!

Other Location
30 Rockefeller Center, 49th St. between Fifth and Sixth Aves.;
(212) 265-9404

Li-Lac Chocolates
West Village
120 Christopher Street, between Bedford and Bleecker Sts.
(212) 242-7374

Li-Lac Chocolates has the best caramels in town: creamy, sweet, and made since 1923, they have been a longtime favorite of generations of New Yorkers. Everything has always been made right here at the Christopher Street location, including Li-Lac's delicious chocolate and maple walnut fudge. They use an American chocolate for making and enrobing their confections that is smooth and creamy with a lovely flavor; they also use it to fill the 1,000 specialty molds that form their novelty chocolates. Almost anything you can imagine can be molded in chocolate, and Martha Bond, Li-Lac's longtime owner, has been doing so for many years.

Chocolates filled with old-fashioned butter cream and raspberry centers are among the most popular at Li-Lac, though the truffles (made with amaretto, champagne, and a few other liqueurs) are always in demand as well. The caramel and nut chews with pecans or cashews or the caramel bars, with or without nuts, make great gifts for friends.

The wonderful old candy cases and lilac-colored walls in the West Village store give you a calm and familiar feeling as soon as you walk in. Li-Lac has had only two family owners in its eighty years, and their winning product line has been keeping customers interested and happy day after day. They will gladly sell you a single piece of anything, a policy that is probably in place thanks to the children who stop in at the shop on their way home from school.

Other Location
The Market at Grand Central Terminal, Lexington Ave. at 43rd St.

Mondel's Homemade Chocolates
Morningside Heights
2913 Broadway at 114th St.
(212) 864-2111

Family-owned since its founding in 1944, Mondel's Chocolates is a real neighborhood treasure. Started by Carl Mondel, who was born in Transylvania in 1893, the business struggled for twenty years to establish itself. All the hard work and patience ultimately paid off; in 1966, a review in *The New Yorker* put Mondel's on the map, and helped bring in a steady stream of sweets-lovers. Today, Carl's daughter Florence still presides over the store and hand-pours the candies with a dutiful, caring attention to detail.

Mondel's is a real old-fashioned neighborhood candy store that barely accommodates ten people at a time, and Columbia students have crowded into it for many, many years. Chocolate-covered ginger, nut barks, tiny mint-chocolate cups, and my personal favorites, the turtles, are always available. The caramels are simple, but they always satisfy. Everything is made on the premises in the back, and if you are lucky enough to walk by when the door is open you will catch a whiff of the most heavenly scents.

Lots of varieties make choosing a challenge. The trays here are constantly filled with a dizzying assortment of the most delectable treats. Courteous, pleasant service adds to the sweet experience.

Florence Mondel continues to delight in the wonderful diversity of the neighborhood where, as she says, "you can speak with any kind of accent and people accept it as normal." I guess the old saying is true: Some good things never do change.

NOTABLE

The Chocolate Bar
West Village
487 Eighth Avenue, between Horatio and Jane Sts.
(212) 366-1541

This little coffee and sweet shop opened in 2002. There isn't a huge selection, but you can find high-quality truffles from local chocolatiers Jacques Torres and Andrew Shotts at the same price you'd pay at the source; best of all, you can mix and match flavors. The tasty baked goods are from Balthazar Boulangerie, and there are coffees, teas, and New York products for sale, such as the delicious Rosemary-Caramel Dessert Sauce made in Manhattan by Lunchbox Food Co.

Eggers Ice Cream Parlor
See Ice Cream, p. 262.

Fauchon
East Side
442 Park Avenue at 56th St.
(212) 308-5919

For a Parisian experience in the middle of Manhattan, head to Fauchon. This place is famous for its delicious gourmet treats, including preserves, teas, macaroons, fruit confits, and chocolates. The gelati, which are only available at the 77th Street location, come in classic, premium flavors such as vanilla, chocolate, pistachio, and banana—all made with top-quality ingredients.

Other Location
1000 Madison Avenue at 77th St.; (212) 570-2211

Hinsch's Confectionery
See Ice Cream, p. 258.

Payard Patisserie & Bistro
See Pastries & Baked Goods, p. 304

The Sweet Life
Lower East Side
63 Hester Street at Ludlow St.
(212) 598-0092

A tiny shop crammed with goodies, Sweet Life has a great selection of dried fruits and nuts as well as imported and hand-dipped chocolates and the best malted milk balls and licorice in the city. Their helpful staff make this a must stop in the neighborhood.

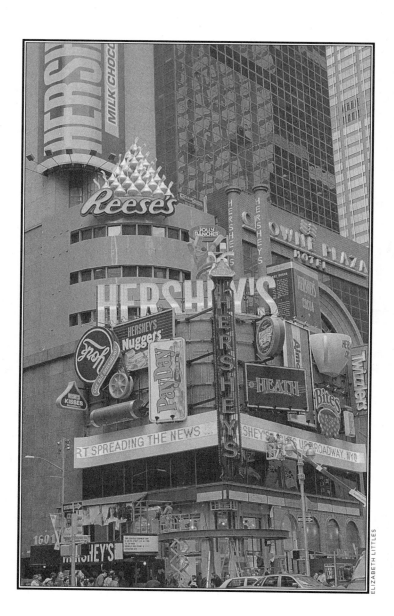

COFFEE & TEA

Caffè Reggio *(Coffee House/Restaurant)*
Greenwich Village
119 MacDougal Street, between Bleecker and West 3rd Sts.
(212) 475-9557
$ (Cash only)

Still in business after more than seventy-five years, Caffè Reggio is the grandaddy of Greenwich Village coffee houses. The awning out front proudly declares "Original Cappuccino," and the story is that Reggio's original owner, Domenico Parisi, indeed introduced cappuccino to America in the 1920s, a few years after the coffee drink became popular in Italy.

The focus of the café is the gleaming, chrome and bronze espresso machine. Any café worth frequenting has one of these behemoths, but how many places can say that their machine was made in 1902, and was the first of its kind? The rest of the decor is almost as impressive, featuring reproductions of Italian artwork dating back to the Renaissance (including a sixteenth-century work by Caravaggio), and an antique bench that bears the Medici coat-of-arms.

Caffè Reggio is located only a short distance from Washington Square Park, and in nice weather it's great to sit outdoors at the sidewalk tables. Try the double espresso Romano, finished with amaretto or Sambuca liqueur. And sample one of the Italian pastries or desserts, such as the *sfogliatella,* a crisp pastry with ricotta. You can also order all kinds of inexpensive light dishes throughout the day, from breakfast staples to pastas, panini, salads, and soups.

Ito En *(Tea Retail Store)*
Lenox Hill
822 Madison Avenue at 69th St.
(212) 988-7111
Closed Sunday

A newcomer to New York (and the U.S.), Ito En, the largest green tea producer in Japan, has planted itself firmly on upper Madison Avenue. The name simply means Ito's Estate (Ito being a Japanese name that's as common as Smith in America). Tea estate, that is. In a townhouse setting of natural wood colors and graceful art, 75 teas are available for retail sale. Among the wonderful imports are fine teas, mainly from Japan and China, as well as artisan teapots and cups. Furthermore, the store stocks limited tea blends designed for each season of the year. The teas can all be "nosed" from specially designed flasks that are purposefully displayed for customer interaction, and the staff is well versed in the subtle and not so subtle nuances of tea production, selection, and brewing. In addition to loose teas, Ito En also produces the most refreshing blends of all-natural chilled teas (which are sold at other stores, too) such as Green Jasmine and Oolong. The ingredients are simple: water and tea.

On the second floor, the store operates KAI (literally "meeting" or "gathering"), a restaurant that serves lunch, afternoon tea, and dinner. The sleek decor is the perfect setting to take a break after a stroll down Museum Mile.

Mud Truck *(Coffee Takeout)*
Greenwich Village
Astor Place (Lafayette and 8th Sts.)
(212) 529-8766
Monday–Friday 7:00 A.M.–2:00 P.M. (open until 5:00 P.M. in
fall/winter)

A bright orange beacon sits parked in the middle of Astor Place each weekday morning, greeting patrons on their way to work by foot or by subway. The Mud Truck—a refitted Consolidated Edison utility truck designed to brew and serve coffee—is a unique idea for a coffee shop, especially since this neighborhood has been overrun with Starbucks: in fact, The Mud Truck lies nestled right between two Starbucks stores that are within eyesight of each other.

As you ascend the stairs from the Uptown 6 train, groovy tunes blare from the truck, hand-selected by owner/brewmaster/DJ Greg Northrop. The Mud Truck has its own blend of coffee that is roasted locally, and Northrop anticipates opening other gourmet coffee trucks in the future.

In addition to coffee and other specialty drinks, the Mud Truck sells great muffins, tarts, and other morning snacks. The bottom line is that the Mud Truck's brand of gourmet street coffee is damn good, rich In aroma and flavor, and (best of all) a regular-size cup only costs a buck!

Other Location
Corner of Broadway and 14th Street

Oren's Daily Roast *(Coffee Takeout/Retail Store)*
Midtown East
The Market at Grand Central Terminal, Lexington Ave. and 43rd St.
(212) 338-0014

With nine locations around Manhattan (including two in Grand Central Station alone), Oren's has truly become New York City's neighborhood coffee shop. The small chain of stores was founded by Oren Bloostein in 1986 and has steadily grown since the days when the original store housed the roaster, to today's network of stores, which are supplied from Oren's own roasting facility in New Jersey. Beans are carefully selected from premium coffee buyers around the world and roasted daily to ensure that each store serves the freshest coffee available. On any given day, Oren's stores pour approximately seven different kinds of coffee, ranging in flavor from light and mild to darker, rich blends. Oren's seems to have trained its staff well (particularly at Grand Central Market), and employees are well versed in the blends available on any given day. In addition, Oren's sells their blends of whole bean and ground coffee for home use, as well coffee accessories and a modest selection of teas. As great as Oren's coffee is, one question remains. When might we see an Oren's in the Outer Boroughs?

Other Locations

985 Lexington Avenue at 71st St.; (212) 717-3907

1144 Lexington Avenue, between 79th and 80th Sts.; (212) 472-6830

1574 First Avenue, between 81st and 82nd Sts.; (212) 732-2690

33 East 58th Street, between Madison and Park Aves.; (212) 838-3345

Grand Central Café at Grand Central Station; (212) 953-1028 (open Sunday)

Penn Station (34th St.) at LIRR Concourse; (212) 279-6291

434 Third Avenue, between 30th and 31st Sts.; (212) 779-1241

31 Waverly Place, between University Pl. and Greene St.; (212) 420-5958

The Pembroke Room at the Lowell Hotel   (*Tea Room*)
East Side

28 East 63rd Street, between Madison and Park Aves.

(212) 838-1400

Open daily 3:00–6:00 P.M.

$$$

On the second floor of the stately and rather proper Lowell Hotel, the Pembroke Room offers traditional tea service with a flair and service that excels. With winged chairs, baubled sconces, and an artful decor, the opulent yet cozy tea room is ideal for the most authentic (and formal) English tea experience in the city. From the relaxing Van Cliburn-esque recordings to the selection of the finest ingredients for food preparation, each exacting detail is chosen conscientiously and with great care. Hot water (slightly "underboiled") is changed with precision every 15 minutes to ensure that tea does not oversteep to the point of bitterness.

The Pembroke Room offers "full tea" as opposed to "high tea," a subtle distinction that means it does not include typically heavier foods such as meats. Instead, the full tea, slightly lighter in style, is highlighted by the service of traditional scones, seasonal berries with cream, assorted sandwiches, cheeses, tarts, and butter cookies. An efficient selection of the highest-quality loose teas and herbal infusions are steeped by the pot and served individually. Afternoon tea is $28 ($35 with champagne), but it's a singular experience that continues to preserve a vaunted English tradition. Reservations are essential.

Porto Rico Importing Co. *(Coffee & Tea Retail Store)*
Greenwich Village
201 Bleecker Street, between MacDougal St. and Sixth Ave.
(212) 477-5421

For downtown devotees of great coffee, Porto Rico Importing Co. has become an indispensable resource. The flagship store on Bleecker Street first opened in 1907, and three generations of the Longo family have distributed the finest coffees of the world ever since. The collection of rich aromas of nutty caramel and chocolate hit you before you even walk through the door. The coffees are neatly arranged in open sacks (don't touch the beans, please!) and categorized by color-coded labels; Yellow for Regular Caffeinated, Blue for Decaf, Red for Flavored Coffees, and Green for Organic. Porto Rico also features Fair Trade coffees, products that have been designated as such based on standardized requirements for workers' wages and earth-conscience practices regarding the use of chemicals and pesticides. The store also sells assorted teas as well as every imaginable tea accessory, from hard-to-find filters to brushes designed especially to clean your home bean grinder. Of course, you can also get a cup of coffee as well.

Other Locations
40½ St. Marks Place, between First and Second Aves.; (212) 533-1982
107 Thompson Street, between Prince and Spring Sts.; (212) 966-5758

Tamarind Tea Room *(Tea Room/Restaurant)*
Gramercy Park/Flatiron District
41-43 East 22nd Street, between Park Ave. and Broadway
(212) 674-7400
$$

With only 11 seats, the intimate and charming Tamarind Tea Room is a delightful place for an afternoon respite or a satisfying meal. Adjacent to the well-known Indian restaurant, Tamarind, patrons can order from either menu to accompany a selection of 14 teas, all supplied by the Williamsburg, Brooklyn, distributor In Pursuit of Tea. The collection of authentic loose teas are brewed and served individually. The Tea Room menu provides recommendations to pair with a delectable selection of traditional ethnic sandwiches such as tandoori salmon or chicken with mushrooms, as well as modern Indian wraps. Dessert recommendations are also provided, such as mango cheesecake or chocolate mousse. The comfortable atmosphere of the Tea Room is accented with artful representations of Shiva, the Hindu Lord of Dance. The space can be reserved for private functions and is also a very popular destination for patrons of other restaurants for dessert.

Tea & Sympathy   *(Tea Room)*
West Village
108-110 Greenwich Avenue at Jane St.
(212) 807-8329
$

Choose a dreary, chilly, overcast day to get cozy at Tea & Sympathy, and you might just feel that you have snuggled up in the comfy living room of an English granny. Be advised, though: The tiny place is always packed for lunch and brunch, and the wait outside, in the rain or snow, can last several hours on the weekend. Once inside, you might even be moved around to accommodate other customers. It is much more pleasant on weekday afternoons, when one can linger as long as desired, sleepily listening to the waitresses's Cockney accents, over a steaming pot of tea (choose from among an impressive list), bangers and mash, Welsh rarebit, Scotch egg, shepherd's pie, or the classic high tea fare—a selection of little sandwiches or scrumptious scones with cream and homemade jams. Before you leave, pop next door to Carry On Tea & Sympathy, to pick up flavorful pork sausages, shortbreads, funny teapots, and other British specialties.

Via Quadronno   *(Coffee House/Café)*
Lenox Hill
25 East 73rd Street, between Madison and Fifth Aves.
(212) 650-9880
$$$

Oddly enough, it's not easy as you might think to find a great cup of espresso in New York City. Maybe it is the nature of the city's water ("soft" and low in calcium) or perhaps it's the fault of the espresso machines, the inexperience of most *baristas*—even the climate has been held responsible. Whatever the reason, Via Quadronno makes what many people (including *New York Times* food writer William Grimes) consider one of the best espressos in the city—if not *the* best, especially since the closing of Espresso Madison in 1999. Part of Via Quadronno's success might be the blend of coffee they import from Trieste. The rest, though, comes from sheer attention to detail and correct brewing procedure, which in the end is probably the most important factor in making a great cup of espresso. The atmosphere at Via Quadronno makes you feel like you're in a café in Northern Italy instead of near Museum Mile in Manhattan: Patrons typically stand at the counter and drink their morning cup of espresso. The food is worth coming in for as well: The panini, soups, and salads are all rather pricey, but very good.

Wild Lily Tea Market   *(Tea Retail Store/Tea Room)*
East Village
545 East 12th Street, between Aves. A and B
(212) 598-9097
Closed Monday
$$

Deep in the heart of the East Village, across from a charming community park and garden, lies Wild Lily, a serene retail teashop. In addition to the retail store, four tables and a bar cluttered with hand-crafted cookies provide limited seating to sample and indulge in a calming pot of tea. The traditional teas, mainly from China and Japan and many organic, are categorized by steeping time ("only one minute," "two minutes," and "three to five minutes") and are available alongside a light fare of snacks and sweets. Loose teas, with wonderful names such as Iron Goddess and Buddha's Finger, are sold to go by the ounce. A takeout menu offers detailed descriptions and suggestions as to when specific teas are most useful (Buddha's Finger is "suitable after yoga class"). The shop also sells traditional and more contemporary designs of teapots and accessories. This tiny tea store and its "Umbrellas of Cherbourg meets tea garden" motif is the companion of Wild Lily Tea Room, a sister restaurant in Chelsea that offers a broad menu as well as an array of public exhibits and musical presentations.

Other Location
Wild Lily Tea Room, 511-A West 22nd Street, between Tenth and
    Eleventh Aves.; (212) 691-2258

NOTABLE

'ino
See Wine Bars, p. 218.

Le Pain Quotidien
See Bread Bakeries, p. 233.

McNulty's Tea & Coffee Co. *(Coffee Retail Store)*
West Village
109 Christopher Street, between Bleecker and Hudson Sts.
(212) 242-5351

A century-old purveyor of coffees from around the world, featuring a wide selection.

T Salon T Emporium *(Tea Retail Store/Tea Room)*
Gramercy Park/Flatiron District
11 East 20th Street, between Broadway and Fifth Ave.
(212) 358-0506
$$

Upstairs you'll find an impressive selection of loose teas and special blends, while on the ground floor there's a tea room serving light fare and baked goods to enjoy with your cuppa.

Ten Ren Tea and Ginseng Company *(Tea Retail Store/Tea Room)*
Chinatown/Little Italy
75 Mott Street, between Bayard and Canal Sts.
(212) 349-2286

A charming, civilized shop with a nice selection of teas and tea paraphernalia. Ten Ren owns their own tea plantation in Taiwan, and they are knowledgeable and helpful about the types they sell, which you can sample, fresh-brewed, before you buy.

Other Location
135-18 Roosevelt Avenue, between Main and Prince Sts., Flushing, Queens; (718) 461-9305; Subway: 7 to Flushing Main St.

Whole Foods Market *(Tea Retailer)*
Chelsea
250 Seventh Avenue at 24th St.
(212) 924-5969

Among other brands of tea they sell, Whole Foods carries a broad selection from two local distributors, In Pursuit of Tea and Rishi.

DAIRY

Alleva Dairy
Chinatown/Little Italy
188 Grand Street at Mulberry St.
(212) 226-7990

Opened in 1892, Alleva Dairy is the oldest dairy in the country. From the cozy storefront on Grand Street, Bobby Alleva, the fourth generation to oversee the operation, continues his family's tradition by making fresh ricotta cheese and mozzarella every day. The store has grown in its diversity of products over the years, and today includes other specialty cheeses, cured meats, extra-virgin olive oils, and vinegars, as well as other gourmet products. Though the landscape of Little Italy has changed drastically, Alleva's still caters to regular customers who grew up with the dairy as a focal point of everyday life in the neighborhood. Even those who have moved too far away to patronize the store in person can still enjoy the rich traditions of Alleva's by mail order.

Artisanal
Murray Hill
2 Park Avenue at 32nd St.
(212) 532-4033

It is telling that of the three designations the owners have given Artisanal: Fromagerie, Bistro, Wine Bar, Fromagerie comes first. Chef Terrance Brennan, who first gained acclaim for his passion for craft cheese at Picholine, has created a marvelous retail cheese space within his all-encompassing restaurant. Nearly 250 cheeses are available not only to patrons of the bistro but to retail customers as well. While the heavy hitters (as well as the lesser-known cheeses) of Western Europe are well represented, Brennan's *fromager* has made a concerted effort to highlight the finest cheeses of North America. Stalwarts such as Bonne-Bouche from Vermont and Bingham Blue from Colorado are balanced by an extraordinary collection of cheeses from Canada, especially Quebec. With the restaurant's modern-age cheese cave filled to capacity, plans are underway to complete a Midtown facility for aging cheese as well as for importing and distributing cheese through mail order under the guidance of cheese expert Daphne Zepp. The hardest part of utilizing Artisanal only as a retail shop is resisting the urge to sit down for a good drink and a cheese plate at the bar or in the bistro itself. Then again, why fight it?

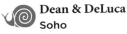

Dean & DeLuca
Soho
560 Broadway at Prince St.
(212) 431-1691

This is where New York's second revolution of serious cheese all began, and we are still reaping the rewards today. Back in the late seventies when craft cheese was more commonly spelled with a "K," Steve Jenkins *was* the revolution when he went to work for Joel Dean and Giorgio DeLuca and began importing great cheeses from Europe. At that time, the best artisanal cheeses in New York could be found at the few remaining traditional Italian dairies that catered to an immigrant clientele familiar with the real thing. Americans had up until that point enjoyed international cheeses only when they traveled abroad to Europe.

Today, Dean & DeLuca's cheese counter remains an integral part of New York's cheese culture. The scent of cheese wafts through the store, and the counter has grown to include wonderful selections from around the United States as well. Towers and columns of cheese are stacked in an artful display and practically hide the *fromager* from sight.

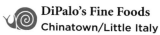

DiPalo's Fine Foods
Chinatown/Little Italy
200 Grand Street at Mott St.
(212) 226-1033

From a storefront the size of a modest studio apartment, the DiPalo family has been preserving and celebrating their cultural heritage for four generations. Opened in 1910 (and in its current location since 1925), the store is packed to the brim with the highest-quality Italian cheeses and gourmet products. The dairy continues to be a hub of activity for local patrons as well as regulars from outside the neighborhood, whose parents and grandparents frequented the Little Italy landmark.

Today, Louie DiPalo holds court and the entire family is involved in the day-to-day operation of the store, including Louie's sister, mother, and even the kids, who help out on weekends. The store offers a broad selection of D.O.P. cheeses (a designation that attests to a traditional product's region of origin and authenticity in how it was produced), as well as imported cured meats. Though they have been importing cheese from Italy since the 1930s, DiPalo's remains one of the oldest *latteria* (dairies) in the country. Using domestic whole cow's milk, wonderfully rich mozzarella (lightly salted or smoked) and ricotta cheese are made fresh every day. The familial atmosphere of DiPalo's cannot be understated.

Whether you're a regular or a first-timer, great care and attention is paid to each customer as well as to the extraordinary array of artisan products.

Fairway
West Side
2127 Broadway at 74th St.
(212) 595-1888

Provided you can actually reach the cheese counter, you won't be disappointed at Fairway. Long acknowledged as one of the finest overall markets in the city, the cheese counter holds a mythical status among devotées of fine cheese—especially raw-milk cheeses. The "cheese cave" is located in such a cramped nook of the store that, while beautifully arranged, it is difficult to traverse when the store is busy (which is always!). The stunning cheese "exhibit" is worthy of any museum of gastronomy. The bottom line, though, is that Fairway offers one of the most comprehensive selections of cheeses from around the world. Developed and overseen by famed Master Cheesemonger Steve Jenkins (author of the definitive book, *The Cheese Primer*), the cheese cave is an oasis from the mad, uncivilized world of canned goods and boxed cereals in other parts of the store. Pause. Don't rush. Ask questions. A visit to Fairway is an experience that should not be wasted. There is always something new to try or a fine old product that has made its way back to the sales counter.

Other Location
2328 Twelfth Ave., between 132nd and 133rd Sts.; (212) 234-3883

Joe's Dairy
Soho
156 Sullivan Street, between Prince and Houston Sts.
(212) 677-8780
Closed Sunday–Monday
Cash only

Joe is long gone (the store was originally owned by Al when it was established in 1866), but the tradition of a fine-quality dairy lives on in the current owner, Anthony Campanelli. Five days a week Anthony oversees the production of fresh mozzarella. The whole cow's milk curd (from just across the river in Moonachee, New Jersey) is boiled and stirred before it is shaped into portions for retail and wholesale use. Some 1,400 pounds of curd a day are turned into luscious, creamy mozzarella. Natural variations in the curd require each step of the process to be performed by hand to ensure consistency.

Twenty-five years ago, 75 percent of the mozzarella was sold at the small Soho storefront. Today, retail sales account for only 50 percent of the total business. Over the years, the neighborhood has changed, but it has also created an opportunity for new ethnic groups to experience this wonderful product. Located across the street from St. Anthony's of Padua, the dairy used to serve parishioners after Mass, but the number of regular churchgoers has dwindled to such an extent that the store is now closed on Sundays.

Joe's sells a small number of other Italian cheeses, as well as a nice selection of gourmet food products, but the mozzarella, lightly salted or smoked, is the real deal!

Murray's Cheese Shop
West Village

257 Bleecker Street at Cornelia St.
(212) 243-3289

Founded in 1940 as a wholesale distributor of eggs and butter, Murray's still sits on the same oft-traveled street in Greenwich Village. Attracting passersby is not a problem for Murray's; the fabled shop and New York City institution can count itself as one of the few truly outstanding outlets for world-class cheese in the entire country. Somehow the small storefront manages to contain an extraordinary collection of raw-milk cheeses, as well as other gourmet specialties and charcuterie, while sparing modest room for a few customers.

Rob Kaufelt, Murray's charming owner, has guided the store to prominence by focusing his inventory on cheeses from small producers around the world who employ traditional techniques for authentic flavor and true texture. He has assembled a crack staff that is unabashedly opinionated, and who waste no time describing the nuances of one goat's milk cheese compared to the next, or the merits of a particular rind over another. Murray's also offers a wide array of cheeses from America's best artisan cheesemakers.

Other Location

The Market at Grand Central Terminal, Lexington Avenue and 43rd St.

Ronnybrook Farm Dairy
Chelsea

Chelsea Market
75 Ninth Avenue, between 15th and 16th Sts.
(212) 741-6455

Three generations have committed their professional lives to dairy farming in an era when dairy, long a cornerstone of New York State's agricultural identity, has deteriorated in scale and economic viability. Unique is the fact that every product from the Ronnybrook Farm Dairy is made from the milk of their own cows. Their milk is not your random store-bought milk that is a blended product made from the milk of a variety of dairies. Rather, it comes from their herd of award-winning Holsteins, which graze all summer on the farm's beautiful pastures in the Hudson Valley. The Dairy supplies their Chelsea store and Greenmarket stand with extraordinary ice creams (you must try maple vanilla!), yogurt, butter, *crème fraîche,* and, of course, milk. At the Union Square Greenmarket, dedicated customers line up to have their old-fashioned Ronnybrook milk bottles refilled and indulge in the variety of the dairy's other wonderful creations. Even with the business that Ronnybrook does at the Greenmarket and at Chelsea Market, numerous stores in Manhattan and Brooklyn also feature their products.

Other Locations
Union Square Greenmarket, East 17th St. and Broadway

NOTABLE

Agata & Valentina
Lenox Hill
1505 First Avenue at 79th Street
(212) 452-0690

A&V boasts one of the least-known but spectacular cheese selections in the city. It's worth a trip out of your way, since you can also take advantage of the rest of the store.

S. Calandra and Sons
Belmont, Bronx
2314 Arthur Avenue, between 187th and Crescent Sts.
(718) 365-7572
Subway: B, D to 182nd–183rd Sts.
Cash only

For fifty years, the Calandra family has been making cheese: mozzarella, provolone, and the freshest ricotta that you're likely to find. When you walk into the shop, you're enveloped by the smell of whey. Spread the ricotta over a slice of good bread, sprinkle on some sugar and cinnamon and, voila, you have breakfast.

Ideal Cheese Shop
Midtown East
942 First Avenue at 52nd St.

(212) 688-7579
Closed Sunday

An excellent, long-standing cheese shop on the East Side, with a nice selection and a knowledgeable staff.

Lamazou
370 Third Avenue at 27th St.
(212) 532-2009

A small but excellent selection of European cheeses. Aziz, the proprietor, sells cheeses in their seasons and only when they are perfectly ready to enjoy—never before or after.

PATRICK MARTINS

ICE CREAM

Brooklyn Ice Cream Factory
Brooklyn Heights, Brooklyn

Fulton Ferry Landing Pier
Old Fulton Street at Water St.
(718) 246-3963
Subway: A, C to High St.
Closed Monday
Cash only

Location, location, location. That's the old real estate mantra, and one of the reasons to visit Brooklyn Ice Cream Factory. Housed in a funky old 1920s fireboat house at the foot of Old Fulton Street, the "factory" boasts one of the most spectacular views of Lower Manhattan, and the Brooklyn Bridge looms practically overhead. With its pressed tin walls and ceiling, the place looks like it's been here forever, but in fact the business only started in September 2001, just after the New York skyline changed forever. But there's a lot more history than that to ponder as you stand on the wooden deck overlooking the East River. George Washington directed the Continental Army's retreat to Manhattan from this spot on the night of 29 August 1776, following the Battle of Long Island. And Walt Whitman's famous poem "Crossing Brooklyn Ferry" describes the scene in the years before the 1883 completion of the Brooklyn Bridge.

But the main reason to make the trek to Brooklyn Heights—by subway, water taxi, or on foot over the bridge—is to sample the tremendous ice cream that Mark Thompson makes on the premises. An engineer by training, Mark graduated from Fairleigh Dickinson College and first learned how to make ice cream in Easton, Pennsylvania. After coming to New York, he began working for restaurateur Michael "Buzzy" O'Keefe, who also owns the River café, located right across the pier from the Ice Cream Factory. In fact, the café's pastry chef, Ellen Sternau, creates all the toppings and sauces for her sister operation, right down to the hot fudge sauce she makes from an intense Michel Cluizel chocolate with a whopping 72 percent cacao content.

Purists rejoice! You won't be confronted with the impossible choice of "52 Varieties" at the Ice Cream Factory. They stick to the classics: vanilla, chocolate, vanilla–chocolate chunk, chocolate–chocolate chunk, peaches & cream, strawberry, butter pecan, and coffee. As an ice cream maker myself, I judge a place based on my homemade product, and very few measure up. But Brooklyn Ice Cream's strawberry, I confess, leaves mine in the dust. The vanilla is clean-tasting, the chocolate strong and full of cocoa, and the butter pecan is subtle, full, and creamy. A small cone or dish costs $3, but the junior cone at $1.50 is the perfect amount after you've polished off a pizza at Grimaldi's (see p. 202), located just a few doors up the street.

Want the perfect end to a romantic date? There's nothing better than sharing an ice cream cone while gazing your fill at the lights of Lower Manhattan.

Chinatown Ice Cream Factory
Chinatown/Little Italy
65 Bayard Street at Mott St.
(212) 608-4170
Cash only

The perfect end to any meal in Chinatown is a wonderful cone at Chinatown Ice Cream Factory. If you find yourself lost in the maze of winding streets below Canal Street, just keep your eye out for the grand yellow flag painted with a whimsical, if cartoonish, dragon. The small and narrow storefront is a hub of activity, particularly after dinner, as throngs flock for wonderful Red Bean, Green Tea, and Lychee ice cream. These "Regular" flavors are the most popular, but Chinatown Ice Cream Factory also offers "Exotic" flavors like vanilla and chocolate for the less adventuresome. The Red Bean is luscious and creamy, with enough sweetness to be a wonderful palate cleanser.

Ciao Bella Gelato
Upper East Side
27 East 92nd Street, between Fifth and Madison Aves.
(212) 831-5555
Cash only

If it's possible to find happiness in a mouthful of food, Ciao Bella's Valrhona Chocolate gelato is it. The intense, smoky flavor of the French chocolate with the signature creamy richness of the gelato is an euphoric combination. In their posh little location just off Madison Avenue, Ciao Bella serves up lots of other indulgent flavors, too, such as the nostalgic Malted Milk Ball, or the heavenly Fromage Blanc. The Hazelnut is smooth and silky and made from Italian *gianduca* paste. Only 12 percent butterfat content makes it seem almost calorie-free! Ciao Bella is also served at many fancy restaurants, but by far the freshest and best taste comes when you buy direct from one of their shops. The gelato is just the right texture, not too icy and not too soft.

If you aren't inclined toward the decadently sinful, you can also choose from a long list of delicate sorbets. A seasonal special, the Blood Orange sorbet, is a sweet, tangy, must-try flavor. Unusual choices such as Ginger-Lemon and Raspberry Mint Tea sorbet round out the menu.

Though Ciao Bella's ice creams are now available as far away as San Francisco, the whole operation began with the Mott Street location in

Little Italy. Recently the creamery has teamed up with neighborhood brunch favorite Sarabeth's to make gelato and sorbetto flavors with Sarabeth's famous jams.

At any of their locations, Ciao Bella is a great way to indulge your ice cream craving and beat the New York summer heat at the same time.

Other Locations
285 Mott Street, between Houston and Prince Sts.; (212) 431-3591
227 Sullivan Street, between Bleecker and West 4th Sts.; (212) 505-7100
356 Carmine Street, between Bedford and Bleecker Sts.; (646) 230-0558

Cones
West Village
272 Bleecker Street, between Jones and Morton Sts.
(212) 414-1795
Cash only

West Village, East Village, Uptown, or Downtown: All roads lead to Cones. Two brothers, Oscar and Raul D'Aloisio, came to America from Buenos Aires and have found themselves a good home in New York City. Their exquisite frozen delicacies fall somewhere in the middle of the spectrum between ice cream and gelato. However you want to classify it, the stuff is darn good. The ice cream is soft and smooth, with a silky consistency that's irresistible. Some unusual flavors include a fabulous *dulce de leche* (caramel), *tiramisu,* double chocolate, white pistachio, and (in summertime only) the extravagantly good Dom Perignon.

All of the ice cream is house-made, artisanally and in small batches. Believe it or not, 80 lemons are squeezed into every 2-gallon tray of their fresh lemon sorbet. Only the ripest fruit is used for the strawberry and melon and the dozen other varieties.

Custard Beach
Greenwich Village
33 East 8th Street, between University Pl. and Broadway
(212) 240-6039

It's been said that you can substitute one serving of frozen custard for one egg yolk every week and you will be even—my doctor doesn't agree, but frankly I don't care. Frozen custard is a New York tradition, and such a childhood favorite for so many of us Baby Boomers that when we find the real thing we jump for joy and feel like we're in the Mickey Mouse Club again.

Good frozen custard, such as that served at Custard Beach, is nothing at all like Mister Softee or any other soft-serve ice cream—no, this is the genuine article. It's true comfort food, and there are many creamy, intense flavors to choose from: apple pie, cherry vanilla, gingersnap, chocolate malted crunch, and the fabulous *dulce de leche* (caramel) rotate throughout the week. Only vanilla and chocolate are available every day. The custard is made one gallon at a time every three hours in special machines that are made in the city of New York.

The ingredients list is very straightforward: cream, milk, sugar, and egg yolks. Belgian chocolate and real vanilla. No artificial flavors or colorings are used. One important distinction between ice cream and frozen custard is that commercial ice cream is almost 50 percent air—while frozen custard is only around 25 percent. In my family, too much air in ice cream was a sin, and my father and uncle (the cream kings) would have taken this icy, sweet vanilla frozen custard, layered it with some A&W root beer, and created a masterpiece.

Other Location
Dining (Lower) Concourse, Grand Central Terminal, 42nd Street,
   between Vanderbilt and Lexington Aves.

Emack and Bolio's
West Side
389 Amsterdam Avenue, between 78th and 79th Sts.
(212) 362-2747
Cash only

The Boston Brahmin of ice creams has come to the Upper West Side, and are we ever glad to have them! Even though Boston is a great ice cream town, New York refuses to play second fiddle. With two freestanding locations, and another in Macy's department store, Emack and Bolio's Peter Korn is hoping to expand to six shops eventually. E&B is best known for their Oreo and Grasshopper flavors, but there are so many varieties to choose from that you will have to return time after time to taste your way through the entire list.

Although Moondog—the late, lamented West Village ice cream chain — is only a memory today, you can still recapture that sublime malted experience with E&B's truly distinctive "serious chocolate madness." Vanilla is still the most popular ice cream flavor in America, and Emack and Bolio's version demonstrates why. Icy, sweet, and with more flecks of bean than you could imagine, E&B's vanilla is among the best you'll find anywhere.

Other Locations
56 Seventh Avenue, between 13th and 14th Sts.; (212) 727-1198
Macy's, 151 West 34th Street, 4th Floor; (212) 494-5853

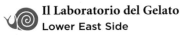
Il Laboratorio del Gelato
Lower East Side
95 Orchard Street, between Delancey and Broome Sts.
(212) 343-9922

Jon Snyder has ice cream in his genes. A Bronx native, his grandmother Antoinette Ceriale owned a Carvel Ice Cream franchise in Westchester County for thirty years. Then, when he was only nineteen, Jon left college and helped found the now-famous Ciao Bella Gelato company. Selling his interest after six years to pursue an M.B.A. degree at Columbia and trade equities on Wall Street, Snyder is once again back in the premium ice cream business with Il Laboratorio del Gelato, which opened in August of 2002 in a small storefront across the street from the Lower East Side Tenement Museum.

Snyder makes his ice cream right here in the back of the store, in small batches. Flavors change frequently. The first time we visited there were eight kinds of gelato and four varieties of sorbet in the case, and every one was a winner. The ginger ice cream was intensely flavored, as indeed were all of the others: dark chocolate, hazelnut, and coffee are particular standouts. The sorbets were also outstanding and equally delicious, consisting almost entirely of fresh fruit. We tried the lemon, orange, kiwi, and plum, made with plums Snyder had just bought (like many of his fresh ingredients) from the Union Square Greenmarket.

There's hardly any seating at the shop (Snyder intends to sell mainly wholesale to restaurants), so grab a gelato with Callebaut chocolate sprinkles, or an espresso shake, and take a stroll down historic Orchard Street. Between this excellent gelato and nearby Guss' Pickles (see Markets, p. 275), expectant mothers on the Lower East Side are fully covered whenever cravings strike.

NOTABLE

Eddie's Sweet Shop
Forest Hills, Queens
105-29 Metropolitan Avenue at 72nd Rd.
(718) 520-8514
Subway: E, F, V, G, R to Forest Hills–71st Ave.
Cash only

Eddie's looks like the quintessential ice cream parlor right down to the marble-topped mahogany counter and stained-glass windows. The malteds and sodas taste old-fashioned, too, ensuring the continued popularity of this longtime neighborhood soda fountain.

Eggers Ice Cream Parlor
Staten Island
2716 Hylan Boulevard, between Ebbitts St. and Tysens Ln.
(718) 980-6339
Staten Island Ferry, then 578 bus to Ebbitts St.

Founded in 1927, Eggers serves terrific sundaes, and also makes its own chocolates and sells a variety of old-fashioned candies.

Other Locations
1194 Forest Avenue, between Jewett Ave. and Manor Rd., Staten
    Island; (718) 981-2110
7437 Amboy Road at Yetman Ave., Staten Island; (718) 605-9335

Fauchon
See Chocolate and Candy, p. 240.

Hinsch's Confectionery
Bay Ridge, Brooklyn
8518 Fifth Avenue, between 85th and 86th Sts.
(718) 748-2854
Subway: R to 86th St.
Cash only

Hinsch's has been around for close to ninety years, and this old-fashioned diner/soda fountain is still going strong, making its own ice cream (try the peach in season) and milk shakes, as well as house-made chocolates.

Jahn's Ice Cream Parlor and Restaurant
Richmond Hill, Queens
117-03 Hillside Avenue at Myrtle Ave.
(718) 847-2800
Subway: J to 121st St.

Jahn's opened in 1928, but the decor looks even older, harking back to the Gay Nineties (1890s, that is). The ice cream sundaes and sodas are classic, and the burgers, waffles, and other diner food are pretty good, too.

Lemon Ice King of Corona
Corona, Queens
52-02 108th Street at Corona Ave.
(718) 699-5133
Subway: 7 to 103rd St.–Corona Plaza
Cash only

THE NEW YORK EGG CREAM

Truth be told, few foods seem to originate in New York. We tend to respectfully (or not so respectfully) borrow ideas from other cultures, oftentimes improve them, and make them our own. The exception, of course, is the egg cream, the legendary chocolate drink from Brooklyn that first became popular in New York during the 1920s and 1930s. Today, you can still occasionally find a legitimate egg cream at a delicatessen or old-fashioned lunch counter or soda fountain, but its origins remain a source of legend and mystery. Wonderfully, though the frothy head and rich chocolate flavor suggest otherwise, there are no eggs (or cream, for that matter) in an egg cream!

The exact origins of the name itself are not entirely clear. The assumption that the frothy-headed chocolate soda was once topped with whipped egg whites offers one possible explanation; an alternative theory is that the name "egg cream" somehow descended through heavy Eastern European accents from the grade of milk requested—"A-Grade"—to make the drink. This lack of certainty merely adds to the mystique.

The recipe itself is quite simple: a couple fingers of whole milk, a generous pour of Fox's U-Bet Chocolate Syrup (still manufactured by the fourth-generation family syrup-makers, H. Fox and Company on Thatford Avenue in Brooklyn, as it has been since 1900), and a steady stream of cold seltzer. Alternate ingredients should not be substituted. The drink should then be stirred vigorously with a long spoon—never blended or shaken. The result, success or failure, lies in the execution. Today, while some have taken the lazy avenue of using bottled seltzer water, the true egg cream can only be prepared with seltzer from a siphon. Traditional siphons can still be purchased on-line and in specialty stores, and newer home models work just as well. Without them, the egg cream becomes a muddy, lake-bottom mass, not worthy of the name.

While the egg cream's heyday has long since passed, it remains embedded in the recesses of Brooklyn lore, an ode to Old New York, the 1950s, the Dodgers, and to good clean fun.

—*Allen Katz*

Authentic ices that are light and satisfying, really fruity and sweet. Bring napkins and take the trip to Corona; it is absolutely worth it.

Piu Bello Gelato
Forest Hills, Queens
70-09 Austin Street at 70th St.

(718) 268-4400
Subway: E, F, R, V, G to Forest Hills–71st Ave.

An authentic *gelateria* that will take you to Italy with a song. Their gelato is creamy and rich, with many flavors to choose from, though *crema*, vanilla, and chocolate are still the biggest sellers.

Ralph's Famous Italian Ices
Staten Island
501 Port Richmond Avenue at Catherine St.
(718) 273-3675; 718-448-0853
Staten Island Ferry, then S44 bus to Port Richmond Ave. at
  Walker St.
Open April–October
Cash only

Ralph's is open during the spring and summer only and has a terrific variety, offering many kinds of ice cream and sherbet as well as Italian ices. The long lines will fade from your memory as soon as your lips get cold.

Other Locations
214-15 41st Avenue at Bell Blvd., Bayside, Queens; (718) 281-1749
73-04 Austin Street at Ascan Ave., Forest Hills, Queens; (718)
  263-8816

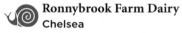

Ronnybrook Farm Dairy
Chelsea
Chelsea Market
75th Ninth Avenue, between 15th and 16th Sts.
(212) 741-6455
Cash only

This upstate dairy also sells their excellent ice cream at Dean & DeLuca and many other markets. Seasonal favorite flavors include Pumpkin Pie and Eggnog. Try the vanilla bean with a brownie from the Fat Witch Bakery, also conveniently located in Chelsea Market.

Serendipity 3
East Side
225 East 60th Street, between Second and Third Aves.
(212) 838-3531

As a born-and-raised New Yorker I can attest to how much fun it is as a child to go to Serendipity, an East Side favorite for more than forty-five years. From the foot-long hot dogs to the massive ice cream floats to the knickknacks sold at the front of the restaurant, this place is fun! Memories still run through my head of my childhood when I walk by! Try the Frozen Hot Chocolate—a New York classic.

Villabate Pasticceria & Bakery
See Pastries & Baked Goods, p. 300.

ELIZABETH LITTLES

MARKETS

If there is any task more difficult than assembling a list of the best (or at least the "slowest") restaurants in New York, it's trying to identify all of the worthy food shops and markets in the city's five boroughs. The number of great places is staggering, so we have relied on our instincts, personal knowledge, and investigative skills to identify at least what we feel is a good and representative sampling.

Have we left anyone out? Absolutely. The ebb and flow of the city's commercial life means that businesses are constantly going in and out of existence. Yet some of the places we've listed below (particularly in the **Butchers and Meat Markets** section) have been run for years—sometimes decades—by the same family, with succeeding generations continuing the old traditions in a way that is seldom seen anymore in America, where we seem to be constantly "reinventing" ourselves.

In the **"Super" Markets** section that follows, we list what we consider to be the best one-stop food stores in the city. In **Ethnic and Specialty Markets,** we have tried to cover selectively places that reflect not only some of the most interesting and worthwhile food shops, but also the broad spectrum of nationalities and cuisines that are found throughout this guide. This is essential information for home cooks who need a particular ingredient for that special ethnic dish. And, in the **Fish & Seafood Markets** section, we focus on stores that offer quality, service, and value, leaving aside for the moment the ethical dilemma of buying certain kinds of seafood in the face of shrinking global stocks.

Last, but certainly not least, we devote a section to a brief history of **New York City's Greenmarket,** and provide information on where you can find these stellar local farmers' markets around the city. With the ever-increasing demand for freshness and quality in food, and the desire for organic and sustainably grown produce, meats, and other items, we believe that Greenmarket has only scratched the surface of what is possible. It's an exciting and hopeful time for those of us who love good food.

"SUPER" MARKETS

Agata & Valentina
Lenox Hill
1505 First Avenue at 79th St.
(212) 452-0690

A&V is one of the best food shops in town. Here the focus is on Sicily. Owners Joe Musco, his wife, Agata, and Louis Balducci are so committed to the island that even the sloped stucco over the coffee bar and the floor tiles are made of materials brought over from Sicily. The cheese and olive counters are fabulous. Delicious sweets and pastas are made in-house. Great pizza is available for takeout. The vegetable and fruit departments are solid, although the meat and fish departments could use some work.

Chelsea Market
Chelsea
75 Ninth Avenue, between 15th and 16th Sts.
No phone

The first Oreo cookie was made at this former National Biscuit Company factory in 1912, so it seems appropriate to pass so many bakeries on a stroll down "Oreo Way." Fat Witch Bakery and Eleni's Cookies tempt passersby with brownie and cookie samples near the entrance, and the rolls and roll-makers at Amy's Breads are on display through the long glass wall. Buon Italia offers imported Agrimontana chestnuts in syrup, Sicilian tuna, and dried pasta in dozens of unusual shapes; they also prepare fresh gnocchi, ravioli, and other take-home dinners. Chelsea Wine Vault offers frequent free tastings. The deceptively named Manhattan Fruit Exchange is an excellent source for spices, beans, and nuts, as well as dried fruit and fresh produce. Some of the veggies are organic, but most are not local, though the "first of season" New Jersey tomatoes proudly occupy a center shelf. And what goes better with an Oreo than a cold swig of milk? Pick up a glass quart of creamy whole or chocolate milk from the "hopelessly out-of-date and proud of it" Ronnybrook Farms Dairy outlet, also home to unforgettable yogurt, butter, and ice cream—the perfect base for an Oreo sundae.

Citarella
Lenox Hill
2135 Broadway at 75th St.
(212) 874-0383

Known first and foremost as a fish market, Citarella sells a wide selection of fresh fish presented appealingly on large counters filled with ice. One day I decided to visit their meat department and quickly became a member of the growing masses who believe that Citarella has one of the better butcher counters in New York. The butchers are pleasant and knowledgeable and always ready to answer questions. Their produce departments are solid, and the 20-plus soups made in-house each day are sure to please.

Other Location
1313 Third Avenue at 75th St.; (212) 874-0383

Dean & DeLuca
Soho

560 Broadway at Prince St.
(212) 226-6800

To the eye, this is probably the most beautiful store in New York. If only for an espresso and sandwich at the bar, D&D is always worth a stop. The fruit counter is as pleasant to look at as it is expensive. The cheese counter is amazing (see Dairy, p. 251). The bread, coffee, and meat sections are very good and the price-to-quality ratio is reasonable. The back of the store boasts an array of useful kitchen tools and esoteric gadgets.

Eli's Manhattan
Upper East Side

1411 Third Avenue at 80th St.
(212) 717-8100

Folks on the Upper East Side can go to a pair of places for an often-bewildering array of goodies. Going to Eli's Manhattan or the Vinegar Factory is like going to a multinational food bazaar. At Eli's the layout is like a two-floor grocery, while the Vinegar Factory is more like wandering through the stalls at an old market. Cheeses and fresh meats, fish, vegetables, and baked goods are all available and uniformly excellent. (All the baked goods come from Eli's bakery on the same block as the Vinegar Factory.) Even items that are out of season can usually be found: Eli Zabar has several huge greenhouses on the roofs over 91st Street to grow everything from tomatoes to herbs. You'll also find prepared foods and a café/restaurant at both places.

Unfortunately, the prices are just what you might expect for this kind of quality and variety. Some say they are outrageous; most people simply gulp and head for the cash register.

Fairway
West Side

2127 Broadway at 74th St.
(212) 595-1888

Fairway is the trendsetter of a new breed of New York food markets: fully stocked with excellent specialty foods of all kinds (many imported directly by the market's intrepid buyers), and yet also competitively priced for everything from bread and olive oil to toilet paper and ketchup. The Harlem Fairway has parking and shorter lines, plus an entire refrigerated room (well-worn quilted monogrammed jackets are available for the underdressed) full of fresh meat and fish, dairy, and juice; but the Upper

West Side Fairway is just as impressive, with Steve Jenkins' cheese cave (a living example of his *Cheese Primer*) and a second floor dedicated to organic food plus a café run by Mitchel London. Fairway inspires Mecca-like pilgrimages, and it requires regular visits to keep on top of all the new products and humorous signage. If a store this big can have a personality, then Fairway is gruff yet jocular, brilliant, and well-fed.

Other Location
133 Twelfth Avenue at 132nd St.; (212) 234-3883

Grace's Marketplace
Upper East Side
1237 Third Ave at 71st St.
(212) 737-0600

Grace Balducci Doria and the Doria family have been selling upscale groceries and specialty foods to the Upper East Side since 1985 at Grace's Marketplace, a jam-packed neighborhood store that is just one of the results of the Balducci diaspora that has migrated across the city in recent generations. Especially strong in prepared foods (including cooking to order any fish or meat you choose), Grace's also carries a full selection of cheeses, cured meats, fresh seafood, and prime meats in addition to a wide variety of produce, dry goods, and pastries. Grace's Trattoria around the corner is a good place to stop for a light meal and rest after negotiating the aisles of the marketplace, and the welcoming sidewalk flower department is always selling fresh harbingers of warmer days.

The Vinegar Factory
Upper East Side
431 East 91st Street, between First and York Aves.
(212) 987-0885

Whole Foods Market
Chelsea
250 Seventh Avenue at 24th St.
(212) 924-5969

If it is true that you can find anything in New York City, it is also rare to find it all in one place. The challenge of being a true supermarket is to sell everything, from farmstead cheeses and sparkling fresh fish to flowers and toilet paper, without sacrificing quality or service. Happily, the Whole Foods Market in Chelsea is that market, a wide-aisled oasis that takes top-flight, one-stop shopping to the next level with a steadfast commitment to products, both food and otherwise, that are organic, sustainably grown, and ecologically friendly.

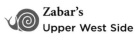

Zabar's
Upper West Side
2245 Broadway at 80th St.
(212) 787-2000

For more than sixty years Zabar's has anchored the New York gourmet food scene. The appetizer section, which features such delicacies as whitefish salad, herring, and chopped liver, has provided for more brunches than all the Jewish grandmothers east of the Mississippi. The fish counter (where New York institution Sam Cohen worked for decades before his death in 1999) is sacred. Be prepared to take a number here (some people have actually met and married thanks to the long lines). Rotisserie chicken, house-made knishes, and great bread round out the reasons to shop there. The cookware sold upstairs is inexpensive, and you can even grab breakfast next door at the Zabar's Café.

ETHNIC & SPECIALTY MARKETS

Abyssinia Ethiopian Grocery
Morningside Heights
225 West 116th Street, between Frederick Douglass and Adam
    Clayton Powell Blvds. (Eighth and Seventh Aves.)
(212) 663-0553

Supplies for Ethiopian cooking: spices, grains, and legumes, plus crafts and gifts.

Aji Ichiban
Chinatown/Little Italy
167 Hester Street, between Elizabeth and Mott Sts.
(212) 925-1133

This Hong Kong–based retail snack chain is the place to go for priced-by-the-pound dried spicy squid, mouth-puckering Taiwanese snowdrop plums, Hello Kitty chocolates, and *anything* gummy.

Other Locations
37 Mott Street, between Bayard and Pell Sts.; (212) 233-7650
188 Lafayette Street at Grand St.; (212) 219-0808
41-51 Main Street, between 40th Rd. and Sanford Ave., Queens;
    (718) 460-6663

A WALK DOWN ARTHUR AVENUE

Arthur Avenue Market
Belmont, Bronx
2344 Arthur Avenue, between Crescent Ave. and East 187th St.
Subway: B, D to 182nd–183rd Sts.
Closed Sunday

Established in 1940 by Mayor Fiorello La Guardia, the Arthur Avenue Retail Market is benefitting from a renewed interest among native New Yorkers and others who want to explore this old Italian neighborhood that's only a few blocks from Fordham University, the Bronx Zoo, and the New York Botanical Garden. The market itself stretches a full block to Hughes Avenue, and hosts a variety of sellers, with an emphasis on cured meats, cheese, and produce. There is an amazing array of specialty stores in the general neighborhood of Arthur Avenue, including the following:

- Addeo's Bakery, 2352 Arthur Ave., between 186th and 187th Sts.; (718) 367-8316. Traditional Italian breads.
- Artuso Pastry Shop, 670 East 187th St. at Cambreleng Ave.; (718) 367-2515
- Biancardi Meats, 2350 Arthur Ave., between Crescent Ave. and 187th St.; (718) 733-4058
- Borgatti's, 632 East 187th St., between Belmont and Hughes Aves.; (718) 367-3799. Family-owned since 1935. All pasta is made in-house.
- Calabria Pork Store, 2338 Arthur Ave., between 186th and 187th Sts.; (718) 367-5145. Fresh-made sausages and mozzarella, and imported Italian specialty items.
- S. Calandra & Sons, 2314 Arthur Ave.; (718) 365-7572. Fresh-made cheeses.
- Consenza's Fish Market, 2354 Arthur Ave. at 186th St.; (718) 364-8510
- Delillo Pastry Shop, 606 East 187th St., between Arthur and Hughes Aves.; (718) 367-8198. Family-owned for more than ninety years.
- Madonia Bakery, 2348 Arthur Ave. at 187th St.; (718) 295-5573. Family bakery established in 1918; artisan breads and baked goods.
- Mount Carmel Wine & Spirits, 613 East 187th St.; (718) 367-7833
- Randazzo's Seafood, 2327 Arthur Ave., between 187th and 188th Sts.; (718) 367-4139

- Teitel Brothers, 2372 Arthur Ave. at East 186th St.; (718) 733-9400. Italian specialty food store, in business since 1915.
- Terranova Bakery, 691 East 187th St., between Beaumont and Cambreleng Aves.; (718) 733-3827. See Bread Bakeries, p. 235.
- Vincent's Meat Market, 2374 Arthur Ave., between 186th and 187th Sts.; (718) 295-9048

Angelica's
East Village
147 First Avenue at 9th St.
(212) 677-1549

Large selection of herbs and spices, culinary and medicinal, plus organic whole grains and teas.

Aphrodisia
West Village
264 Bleecker Street, between Cornelia and Morton Sts.
(212) 989-6440

Every kind of spice and herb, and a wide selection of teas, all in bulk.

Ariana Afghan Halal Market
Flushing, Queens
42-49 Main Street, between Franklin and Blossom Aves.
(718) 445-4922

Halal butcher shop that also carries products such as dried fruit, nuts, spices, and specialty products from Afghanistan, Iran, and Pakistan.

Bangkok Center Market
Chinatown/Little Italy
104 Mosco Street, between Mott and Mulberry Sts.
(212) 349-1979

Thai specialty foods, including house-made curry pastes.

Bello Mexico
Jackson Heights, Queens
87-17 Roosevelt Avenue, between 87th and 88th Sts.
(718) 429-4300

Mexican and Peruvian food products.

Birlik Market
Sunset Park, Brooklyn
5919 Eighth Avenue at 60th St.
(718) 436-2785

Turkish market with good produce and breads.

Caputo's Fine Foods
Carroll Gardens, Brooklyn
460 Court Street at 3rd Pl.
(718) 855-8852

Salumi, fresh breads, homemade pasta, 20 types of sauces, and 7 different cheeses made fresh daily, plus tasty sandwiches and homemade soups.

Carniceria las Americas
Sunnyside, Queens
45-12 Greenpoint Avenue, between 45th and 46th Sts.
(718) 937-0553

Not just meats, but food supplies from all over Latin America.

Di Palo's Fine Foods
Chinatown/Little Italy
206 Grand Street at Mott St.
(212) 226-1033

Imported foods from Italy, plus fresh mozzarella and house-made ricotta. See Dairy, p. 252.

Dursos Pasta & Ravioli Co.
Flushing, Queens
189-01 Crocheron Avenue at Utopia Pkwy.
(718) 358-1311

Italian specialty and prepared foods; house-made sausages and pasta.

Eagle Provisions
Park Slope, Brooklyn
628 Fifth Avenue at 18th St.
(718) 499-0026

Polish meats and specialty foods.

El Tepeyac Mini-Market
Sunset Park, Brooklyn
3921 Fifth Avenue, between 39th and 40th Sts.

Ecuadorian and Mexican foods and imports, including *humitas* (Ecuadorian tamales).

First Avenue Pierogi and Deli Co.
East Village
130 First Avenue, between 7th St. and St. Marks Place
(212) 420-9690

Potato, cheese, and sauerkraut pierogies, plus other Polish and Ukrainian specialty items.

Fong Inn Too Inc.
Chinatown/Little Italy
46 Mott Street, between Bayard and Pell Sts.
(212) 962-5196
Cash only

Rice and soy products including soy milk and rice noodles are made on-site in this small shop.

Foods of India
Gramercy Park/Flatiron District
121 Lexington Avenue, between 28th and 29th Sts.
(212) 683-4419

Indian ingredients and hard-to-find spices.

Fung Wong Supermarket
Sunset Park, Brooklyn
5615 Eighth Avenue, between 56th and 57th Sts.
(718) 633-0788

Chinese groceries.

Gentile's Market
Lenox Hill
1041 Madison Avenue, between 79th and 80th Sts.
(212) 879-2717

A neighborhood fixture since 1928, offering a wide range of tasty sandwiches and salads.

THE PRINCIPALITY OF PICKLEDOM

Guss' Pickles
Lower East Side
85–87 Orchard Street, between Broome and Delancey Sts.
(516) 642-2634
Cash only

In the center of the Lower East Side, the neighborhood that was once a haven for Jewish immigrants, stands the ordinary storefront of a most extraordinary food producer. A recent move to Orchard Street, right near the LES Tenement Museum, has not changed the way that Guss' makes their pickles; they've been doing it in the same slow manner since 1910.

Guss' relies on their pickle-brokers to select the finest cucumbers from around the country, which the store then processes in a family recipe for brine that includes coriander, mustard seed, bay leaf, garlic, hot peppers, and sea salt (the exact recipe is a secret). The Full Sour pickles that Guss' peddles stand in the cold brine for no less than three months, Half-Sours for at least two weeks. Slowly, the cucumbers are preserved as the acid of the brine soaks in, preventing the growth of bacteria. No chemicals or preservatives are used in this traditional method, and heat is never introduced into the process.

In large commercial operations, by contrast, they cook the cucumbers, which softens the pickles, aging them so that the brine permeates the skin faster, and enabling a Full Sour to be achieved in two or three days. This kind of fermentation may be more rapid and economically "efficient," but the result is a textureless pickle that has lost most of its nutritional value—not to mention the intense variety of aromas and flavors that slow fermentation locks into the cucumbers.

Until the end of World War II, there were no fewer than five pickle-makers in a two-block radius of the neighborhood. Kosher dills, gherkins (cured in a sweet brine of sugar rather than salt) chopped into a mosaic of relish, sours, half-sours, and pickled tomatoes and peppers were a mainstay of an extraordinary culture. Today, Guss' stands alone, the last survivor of an increasingly gentrified neighborhood. They have received offers over the years from grocery chains for a buyout, offers that have been turned down; and though Guss' does supply restaurants, they are most content selling to the throngs of loyal customers who come from all walks of life. Sunday through Friday, long lines form down the block. One by one, gallons of pickles disappear as strangers discuss the merits of Full Sours and Half-Sours and watch chefs from nearby Chinatown make their purchases.

One beautiful spring day I was buying a quart of Half-Sours from the young man who presided over the huge plastic pickle barrels on the sidewalk in front of the store. Suddenly a boy on a school bus, probably on a class trip to the LES Tenement Museum, leaned out the window and shouted to us, "HEY! You make good pickles!" That kind of devotion is something you can't buy; it only comes from being the best at what you do, and from never compromising or cutting corners.

—*Allen Katz*

HAIL
Sunnyside, Queens
44–70 43rd Avenue, between 44th and 45th Sts.
(718) 937-7432

Korean ingredients and prepared foods.

Han Ah Reum
Garment District/Koreatown
24 West 32nd Street, between Fifth and Sixth Aves.
(212) 695-3283

Koreatown market carrying everything Asian, from *miso* pastes and pickled salads to dried noodles, frozen dumplings, and sweets. Plus a good selection of rice and *kimchi*.

Other Location
29-02 Union Street at 29th Ave., Flushing, Queens; (718) 445-5656

Hong Kong Supermarket
Flushing, Queens
37-11 Main Street, between 37th and 38th Aves.
(718) 539-6868

Large store featuring Chinese and pan-Asian foods.

Other Locations
109 East Broadway at Pike St., Manhattan; (212) 227-3388
6023 Eighth Ave. at 61st St., Brooklyn; (718) 438-2288
82-02 45th Avenue at Broadway, Queens; (718) 651-3838

Iman Food Market
Astoria, Queens
24–31 Steinway Street, between 25th Ave. and Astoria Blvd.

North African ingredients and specialty foods, including breads and cheeses.

Just Pickles
Theater District
569 Ninth Avenue at 41st St.
(212) 967-7205

Large selection of pickled vegetables and fruits in barrels and jars.

Kalustyan's
Gramercy Park/Flatiron District
123 Lexington Avenue, between 28th and 29th Sts.
(212) 685-3451

Spices for every cuisine, wonderful dried fruits, rices and lentils of all kinds, and Lebanese olive oil, notable for its fruitiness, at a great price.

Kam Man Market
Chinatown/Little Italy
200 Canal Street, between Mulberry and Mott Sts.
(212) 571-0330

One-stop shopping for Asian dry goods, and full of bargains, from dried delicacies to fermented sauces.

Katagiri
East Side
244 East 59th Street, between Second and Third Aves.
(212) 755-3566

In business since 1907, selling Japanese groceries of all kinds, including produce, *sashimi,* and prepared foods; dry, frozen, and pickled goods; and freshly baked Japanese-style breads and pastries.

Kitchen Market
Chelsea
218 Eighth Avenue at 21st St.
(212) 243-4433
Cash only

Mexican groceries and prepared foods.

La Risarolda Corp.
Jackson Heights, Queens
91-02 37th Avenue at 91st St.

Colombian and Peruvian food products.

Lien Hung Supermarket
Sunset Park, Brooklyn
5705 Eighth Avenue

Chinese and Malaysian foods and products.

Likitsakos Market
Upper East Side
1174 Lexington Avenue, between 80th and 81st Sts.
(212) 535-4300

Greek specialty and prepared foods and produce.

Massis
Sunnyside, Queens
42-20 43rd Avenue, between 42nd and 43rd Sts.
(718) 729-3749

Armenian, Lebanese, and Roumanian specialty foods and supplies.

May May Company Oriental Gourmet Shop
Chinatown/Little Italy
35 Pell Street at Mott St.
(212) 267-0733

May May makes more than a dozen kinds of *jung* (like a Chinese *tamale*), plus delicious frozen dumplings and other *dim sum*.

Matamoros Puebla Grocery Corp.
Williamsburg, Brooklyn
193 Bedford Avenue at North 6th St.
(718) 782-5044
Cash only

Dried herbs, chiles, and other items, plus great food made to order (see Mexican, p. 121).

Mexicano Lindo Grocery
East Harlem
2265 Second Avenue, between 116th and 117th Sts.
(212) 410-4728

Dried chiles and spices, plus other Mexican staples and specialties.

═A TASTE OF MOTHER RUSSIA IN BROOKLYN═

M&I International
Brighton Beach, Brooklyn
249 Brighton Beach Ave., between Beach First and Second Sts.
(718) 615-1011

In Brooklyn, Brighton Beach Avenue, running east from Ocean Avenue, bisects "Little Odessa," the home of thousands of immigrants from southern Russia. Advertisements and store signs are mostly in Cyrillic script. People speak Russian, not English. And the M&I International food market offers everything available in Odessa. Most people behind the counter (nearly all of them women) speak Russian, but you will be assisted by English-speaking persons. In fact, some of the best advice you'll get is from other customers, who chime in with their favorite selections.

Why shop at M&I International? How about the huge array of smoked fish, for starters. Not just deli lox and sable, but many varieties of sable and lox, both hot- and cold-smoked. There are always dozens of other smoked fish. Try my favorite: layers of chunked herring, beets, potatoes, and sour cream. This is practically the Russian national dish, and it's available at M&I in prepacked containers, or in bulk by the pound.

At the other side of the store, you'll find one of the largest selections of sausages and prepared meats available in New York. Not just sausage, but stuffed *dermas* with various fillings, whole boned chickens stuffed with crêpes and ground chicken stuffing. M&I also has a full selection of butcher meats, featuring pork products. If you want to witness true chaos, shop just before Christmas. Fight your way into the store and see whole suckling lambs and pigs being passed over the butcher counter to happy customers. I particularly recommend the chicken sausage (usually found on top of the counter), consisting of chunk dark-meat chicken with loads of garlic and spices, precooked for your delicious pleasure.

But wait—there's more! Russian cuisine features pickled vegetables, and you can select from 10 to 15 different types, all freshly pickled and delicious. Try the sauerkraut-stuffed peppers or cabbage. Another section of the store features dairy, with various cheeses (mostly feta) and cream cheeses with different seasonings and flavors. A long counter toward the rear has hot prepared foods, such as herring in onions, potato pancakes, cooked chicken, and other ready-to-eat items. Go upstairs to the bakery section and head right for the Russian items, such as small cookies, *rugalah*, or Russian coffee cake. Also upstairs is a huge selection of Russian canned goods, including terrific cherry jam.

—Howard Pfeffer

Myers of Keswick
West Village
634 Hudson St. between Horatio and Jane Sts.
(212) 691-4194

You can get mushy peas, Branston pickle, and three brands of yeast extract at this English specialty food shop, but the real draw is the smell wafting from the cast-iron oven in the back: sausage rolls, steak and kidney pie, and a "world-renowned" pork pie.

New Pakland Groceries & Halal Meat
Staten Island
320 Victory Boulevard
(718) 816-1096

After sampling the gaspingly hot Sri Lankan cuisine next door at New Asha (see Indian & Pakistani, p. 82), pass through a narrow door into New Pakland for a dozen varieties of *dal* (lentils) and all the spices and herbs needed to prepare the infamous "black curries" at home.

Nicola's
Midtown East
997 First Avenue, between 54th and 55th Sts.
(212) 753-9275

Founded in 1976 by Nicola Santilli, Nicola's is a neighborhood fixture, despite its tiny size. The shop has one excellent example of everything you need, from ingredients to prepared foods. The cheeses and meats, mostly from Europe, are particularly good. If Nicola is busy, his brother Freddie is there to help with advice or a funny joke.

Ninth Avenue International
Theater District
543 Ninth Avenue, between 40th and 41st Sts.
(212) 279-1000

Mediterranean and Greek specialties and prepared foods.

Oriental Pastry & Grocer
Brooklyn Heights, Brooklyn
170 Atlantic Avenue, between Clinton and Court Sts.
(718) 875-7687

Spices, grains, dried fruits, teas, sweets, and Middle Eastern supplies.

Pacific Supermarket
Elmhurst, Queens
75-01 Broadway at 75th St.
(718) 507-8181

Large supply of Asian ingredients.

Patel Brothers
Jackson Heights, Queens
37-27 74th Street at Roosevelt Ave.
(718) 898-3445

Patel Brothers offers a comprehensive lesson in the flavors and staples of Indian cooking. Fuzzy melon, banana flowers, and fresh gingerroot are just a few of the specialty items in the produce aisles. Rice, legumes, spices, chutneys, *ghee*, fresh cheeses, and breads are also sold here.

Other Locations
42-79C Main Street, between Blossom and Cherry Aves.,
   Flushing, Queens; (718) 321-9847
42-92 Main Street, between Blossom and Cherry Aves., Flushing,
   Queens; (718) 661-1112

Piemonte Ravioli Company
Chinatown/Little Italy
190 Grand Street at Mulberry St.
(212) 226-0475

Fresh filled pastas, including tortellini and ravioli.

Raffetto's
Greenwich Village
144 West Houston Street, between MacDougal and Sullivan Sts.
(212) 777-1261

Everything here—sausages, ravioli, pastas, sauces—is handmade with the freshest natural ingredients. It's been that way since the early 1900s.

Sahadi Importing Company
Downtown Brooklyn
187 Atlantic Avenue, between Court and Clinton Sts.
(718) 624-4550

Middle Eastern foods and supplies, such as homemade spreads, nuts, olives, dried fruit, legumes, rice, pickles, cheese, bread, and canned goods.

Damascus Bakery is just up the block, fragrant with fresh pitas, stuffed flatbreads, and phyllo pastries.

Sunrise Market
East Village
4 Stuyvesant Street, between Third Ave. and East 9th St.
(212) 598-3040

This second-floor Japanese grocery carries neatly tied bundles of arrow-straight noodles, sheets of *nori* seaweed, a small assortment of fresh vegetables, and sushi-quality octopus, tuna, and salmon.

Titan Foods
Astoria, Queens
25-56 31st Street, between Astoria Blvd. and 28th Ave.
(718) 626-7771

Greek supermarket that been called "the Zabar's of Astoria."

Todaro Bros.
Murray Hill
555 Second Avenue, between 30th and 31st Sts.
(212) 532-0633

Neighborhood shop with an excellent cheese and charcuterie selection, high-quality produce, and an extensive selection of specialty foods, from pasta to olive oil.

Trunzo Bros.
Bensonhurst, Brooklyn
6802 18th Avenue at 68th St.
(718) 331-2111

Italian specialty market with house-made sausages and breads.

Vegetable Garden
West Village
233 Bleecker Street at Carmine St.
(212) 929-7737

An old-fashioned green-grocer that provides locally grown fruits and vegetables whenever possible. The selection varies depending on what the farmers who supply the shop have available: for two weeks in the fall, fresh cranberry beans; in early spring, wild dandelion greens; in August, almost all of the outdoor bins are devoted to the best Jersey-grown tomatoes you'll find anywhere, and all at Greenmarket prices.

West African Market
Theater District
533 Ninth Avenue, near 40th St.
(212) 695-6215

Ingredients for West African cooking.

BUTCHERS & MEAT MARKETS

Belfiore Meats
Staten Island
2500 Victory Boulevard at Willowbrook Rd.
(718) 983-0440

Neighborhood store with meats and Italian prepared foods.

Corona Heights Pork Store
Corona, Queens
107-04 Corona Avenue at 108th St.
(718) 592-7350

Fabulous homemade sausages, mozzarella, prosciutto, and other high-quality products, plus some of the best hero sandwiches anywhere. Corona sells their sausage to some of the city's best pizzerias, including Grimaldi's and Nick's.

Dom's Fine Foods
Chinatown/Little Italy
202 Lafayette Street, between Broome and Kenmare Sts.
(212) 226-1963

Domenico Migliore is a fourth-generation butcher who came to New York from Naples to open up his shop. Dom and his brother Frank make *salsiccia di casa* and house-cured salami, *soppressata*, and, sometimes, black truffle sausage.

East Village Meat Market
East Village
139 Second Avenue, between 9th St. and St. Marks Pl.
(212) 228-5590

Polish and Ukrainian specialty goods and meats.

Emily's Pork Store
Williamsburg, Brooklyn
426 Graham Avenue, between Withers and Forest Sts.
(718) 383-7216

This well-known Italian meat store specializes in hot and sweet *soppressata*, which takes six to eight weeks to make depending on weather conditions. They also make a dried *salsiccia* (a thinner, more finely ground sausage) as well as their own fresh sausages: hot, sweet, fennel, and broccoli rabe.

Esposito's Pork Store
Carroll Gardens, Brooklyn
357 Court Street, between President and Union Sts.
(718) 875-6863

Open since 1922, sausages are the specialty, with many types available, including chicken and turkey. Try the *arancini*, deep-fried rice balls filled with meat or cheese.

Faicco's Pork Store
West Village
260 Bleecker Street, between Sixth and Seventh Aves.
(212) 243-1974

Family-owned for more than a century, Faicco sells its own selection of sausages (made in the Brooklyn facility), as well as Italian specialty and prepared foods.

Other Location
6511 11th Avenue, between 65th and 66th Sts., Bay Ridge,
   Brooklyn; (718) 236-0119

Florence Prime Meat Market
West Village
5 Jones Street at West 4th St.
(212) 242-6531
Closed Sunday–Monday

Sawdust on the floor, opera on the radio, and some of the best prime meat in the city. Florence is known for their "Newport Steak," a delicious and inexpensive sirloin cut that is a favorite with their loyal customers.

The French Butcher
Gramercy Park/Flatiron District
383 Second Avenue, between 22nd and 23rd Sts.
(212) 725-4165

Charcuterie and *saucisses* made on the premises are the specialty, as well as several kinds of pâté and a number of fresh and cured sausages, including *boudin noir* and *blanc.*

Grand Street Sausages
Chinatown/Little Italy
198 Grand Street, between Mott and Mulberry Sts.
(212) 966-3033

Chinese butcher specializing in fowls, sausages, and organ meats.

Kurowycky Meat Products Inc.
East Village
124 First Avenue at East 7th St.
(212) 477-0344
Cash only

This is a good old-fashioned Ukrainian butcher, but when it comes to traditional preserved and prepared meat products, they are extraordinary. Start with some of the best kielbasa and baked ham in New York, and then move on to the ham sausage, ham bologna, dried sausages, liverwurst, smoked shoulder, and smoked rib bacon.

La Granja Live Poultry Corp. #2
Harlem
1355 Amsterdam Avenue at 126th St.
(212) 662-6773; (212) 663-2193

Select a live chicken, which will be killed, cleaned, and defeathered as you wait. The meat of these birds is dense and flavorful. La Granja also sells turkeys, rabbits, and ducks, plus chicken, duck, and pigeon eggs. Spanish is chiefly spoken here; the scene (and smell) is not for everyone, but there's no fresher meat to be had in the city.

Lobel's Prime Meats
Upper East Side
1096 Madison Avenue, between 82nd and 83rd Sts.
(212) 737-1372

The grand tradition of the New York steak, perfectly preserved at $32.00 a pound. The prices at Lobel's are astonishing, but the aged beef is even more so.

========= AN OLD WORLD BUTCHER SHOP =========

Ottomanelli & Sons
West Village
285 Bleecker Street, between Jones St. and Seventh Ave. South
(212) 675-4217
Closed Sunday
Cash only

Frank Ottomanelli started working in his father's store when he was only nine years old, stopping by to visit on his way home from school in Greenwich Village, where he has lived his whole life. He "apprenticed" with his father, Salvatore, in the gradual, Old World manner: Frank got the "dirty jobs," helping to clean and eviscerate animals, and learned his knife-handling skills by scraping meat off bones with a butter knife.

Salvatore Ottomanelli was one of three brothers who emigrated from Italy and all of them worked as butchers and opened meat stores in the city. This is the reason why the Ottomanelli name is peppered all over the food map of New York; uptown, downtown, and in the Outer Boroughs; the other places are owned by cousins, but as Frank says of the Bleecker Street location, "We're the original Ottomanelli's."

All kinds of meat are expertly cut to order by the Ottamanelli brothers. The pork chops are extraordinarily flavorful; the calf's liver is divine; and the steaks and roasts are dry-aged to perfection, for 21 to 36 days. You can also order a wide variety of game meats, including rabbit, venison, and pheasant. Recently Ottomanelli's has started selling organic, free-range chickens that they buy from a supplier in Canada, and the demand has been incredible.

Frank and his brothers are already grooming the next (fourth) generation to take over the business someday. And though there are several such family-owned meat markets in the New York area, Ottomanelli's remains one of the best.

—*Ben Watson*

Pino Prime Meats
Soho
149 Sullivan Street, between Houston and Prince Sts.
(212) 475-8134

Italian butcher shop with excellent quality and service.

Plaza Meat Market
Long Island City, Queens
30-07 Broadway at 30th St.
(718) 728-4031

Greek specialty meats, including lamb and house-made pork sausage cooked in Greek spices.

Schaller & Weber
Upper East Side
1654 Second Avenue, between 85th and 86th Sts.
(212) 879-3047

German butcher that also sells specialty and prepared foods.

Sikorski Meat Market
Greenpoint, Brooklyn
603 Manhattan Avenue, between Nassau and Lorimer Sts.
(718) 389-6181

The oldest meat market in Greenpoint, Sikorski smokes their own kielbasa, pork loin, tenderloin, bacon, and ribs daily, and makes their own sauerkraut once a week.

Yorkville Meat Emporium
Upper East Side
1560 Second Avenue at 81st St.
(212) 628-5147

Hungarian butcher specializing in cured and smoked meats; also carries Eastern European specialty and prepared foods.

FISH & SEAFOOD MARKETS

Central Fish Company
Garment District
527 Ninth Avenue, between 39th and 40th Sts.
(212) 279-2317

Great fish at affordable prices and good service.

Hai Thanh Seafood Co.
Chinatown/Little Italy
17B Catherine Street, between East Broadway and Henry St.
(212) 964-9694
Cash only

Fresh fish and seafood at great prices.

Hong Kong Seafood and Meat Market
Chinatown/Little Italy
75 Mulberry Street, between Bayard and Canal Sts.
(212) 571-1445

Fish, meat, and produce.

Murray's Sturgeon
Upper East Side
2429 Broadway, between 89th and 90th Sts.
(212) 724-2650

Since 1946, a great place for smoked and cured fish of all sorts; expensive, but worth it.

Ocean Seafood
Chinatown/Little Italy
19-21 Henry Street at Catherine St.
(212) 227-3067
Cash only

Broad selection of fish and shellfish at good prices.

Park Slope Seafood
Park Slope, Brooklyn
215 Seventh Avenue, between 3rd and 4th Sts.
(718) 832-7638

Fish and seafood, plus Asian grocery products.

ELIZABETH LITTLES

THE TEMPLE OF SMOKED FISH

Russ & Daughters
Lower East Side
179 East Houston Street, between Allen and Orchard Sts.
(212) 475-4880

Little did Joe Russ know when he opened his quaint store for "Appetizers" in 1914 that nearly ninety years later it would be a New York institution. Known for one of the most comprehensive selections of smoked fish, patrons line up (early on the weekends) for lox, sable, and smoked salmon of every kind. Eventually, Joe Russ ran the store with his more-than-capable daughters, who passed the business on for future generations. In addition to the now-gentrified smoked fish, Russ & Daughters offers a variety of extraordinary traditional "Jewish Fare," including chopped liver, pickled herring, and a variety of homemade cream cheeses. Furthermore, the store window is loaded with a spectrum of beautiful dried fruits, from Argentine Jumbo Pitted Prunes to Turkish Apricots and Papaya Spears. Old traditions die hard in any institution, and the only downside for this otherwise marvelous store is their continuing promotion of Russian caviar at a time when Caspian sturgeon have been depleted in alarming numbers.

—Allen Katz

Sable's Smoked Fish
Lenox Hill
1489 Second Avenue, between 77th and 78th Sts.
(212) 249-6177

The name says it all: high-quality nova lox and sable.

Sea & Sea
Morningside Heights
60-62 West 116th Street, between Fifth and Sixth Aves.
(212) 828-0851

Large fish market with fresh, salted, and fried fish, plus takeout.

Sea Breeze
Theater District
541 Ninth Avenue at 40th St.
(212) 563-7537
Closed Sunday

This might be the city's oldest surviving retail fish market; great value.

FULTON FISH MARKET

Although the double-decker buses cruise past the tall ships in the South Street Seaport area every day, the Fulton Fish Market is not a top tourist destination. There are several explanations for this, not the least of which is the fact that market action wraps up in the wee hours of the morning. But there's more than meets the daytripper's eye—for history buffs (not to mention fish lovers), the story of the Fulton Fish Market is a fascinating voyage.

In 1821, the sundry markets scattered along the East River were combined into the Fulton Market. From the beginning, the most successful stands were those of the fishmongers, and they continued to flourish despite several setbacks. The Fulton Fish Market has survived numerous fires, the collapse of a building into the river, and the move of meat and produce wholesalers to the Bronx. After a decades-long clash between the seafood industry and the city, Fulton Fish dealers will leave their downtown home in 2004 to join the other wholesale markets in Hunts Point.

Until then, the market is open for business and insomniac wandering. The South Street Seaport Museum (212-748-8600) gives monthly tours of the Fish Market. Also of great value is Bruce Beck's hard-to-find book, *The Official Fulton Fish Market Cookbook,* which enthusiastically details the market's history.

—*Sara Firebaugh*

Other Location
8500 18th Avenue at 85th St., Bensonhurst, Brooklyn; (718) 259-9693

Wild Edibles
Midtown East
The Market at Grand Central Terminal
Lexington Avenue at 43rd St.
(212) 687-4255

Great selection of high-quality fish and shellfish (striped bass, sardines, soft-shell crabs in season, etc.).

Other Location
535 Third Avenue at 35th St.

GREENMARKETS

A HISTORY OF NEW YORK CITY'S GREENMARKET

It was 1974 in New York City.

It was a time of hard pink tomatoes, brown lettuce, and mealy apples. And in the Hudson River Valley and rural New Jersey and on Long Island's East End, relentless development and farm-unfriendly policies were threatening the disappearance of family farms.

An urban planner named Barry Benepe had a personal goal—a simple one, really—to buy a slurpy ripe peach in New York City in July. He and Bob Lewis, another planner, took a proposition to the then newly formed Council on the Environment of New York City. Their plan was to establish open-air markets where family farmers could sell and New Yorkers could buy good, fresh, healthy, seasonal, local produce.

After two years of planning and hard work, the first Greenmarket opened on 19 July 1976 in a lot at 59th Street and Second Avenue in Manhattan. Curious New Yorkers jostled for ears of sweet corn as they do for seats on rush-hour Number 4 Trains. By noon of that day, six intrepid farmers had nothing left in their trucks to sell.

People soon wanted more Greenmarkets, community organizations asked for more Greenmarkets, and as a result more Greenmarkets have sprouted throughout the city's five boroughs. There are big ones, such as Union Square in Manhattan and Grand Army Plaza in Brooklyn, and there are smaller ones, but they all deliver the best-quality farm produce, and they all are loved by their customers. Today, 25 peak-season and 9 year-round Greenmarkets offer more than the freshest fruits and vegetables. Folks can find eggs, poultry, meat, game, fish, bread, milk, cheese, jams, and wine—just about everything to fill a market basket.

The formula for success is simple: Offer folks crisp, pencil-thin asparagus and intoxicatingly scented strawberries in the spring; really ripe tomatoes and just-picked sweet corn in the summer; and more kinds of apples and squashes than you can count on your fingers and toes in the fall. Offer these things and they will come. And in coming, the Greenmarket's customers make it possible for farm families to continue doing what they love: farming. Greenmarket helps to keep some 8,000 acres, mostly in New York State, under cultivation. It's a wonderful idea, one that nurtures farmers and consumers, while maintaining our agricultural heritage and resources.

Greenmarket also provides 3,000 New York City kids with educational market tours each year; cosponsors the New Farmer Development Project, which helps recent immigrants who were farmers in their native countries become farmers again in this country; provides heirloom seed "scholarships" to farmers to help ensure biodiversity; donates thousands of pounds of food to City Harvest; and helps New Yorkers of all income levels buy fresh, healthy fruits and vegetables by accepting $750,000 in WIC coupons each year. In 2001, Greenmarket farmers made a commitment to refrain from selling genetically engineered produce.

So what keeps 250,000 customers coming to Greenmarket?

Well, for one thing they come for variety. Greenmarket farmers offer 70 different varieties of apples, including heirlooms such as the Newtown Pippin (first discovered on a Queens County farm two hundred years ago); 120 varieties of vine-ripened tomatoes, including occasionally ugly but always luscious heirloom varieties such as Aunt Ruby's German Green and Cherokee Purple; and more than 200 varieties of hot peppers, including the highly volatile Habañero Red Savina, which is rated at a mouth-scorching 557,000 Scoville heat units.

More than 100 New York City restaurants shop regularly at Greenmarket and among them are 22 of the top 50, as ranked by the Zagat Survey. They come to support dedicated producers who sell only what they grow or make themselves.

Folks come to enjoy the markets' seasonal colors and aromas, swap recipes, search for new ingredients, thump melons, sniff berries, and visit their friends, the farmers. Shopping at Greenmarket gives us urbanites a needed connection. No matter who we are or where we come from, one of our most important connections is food tradition.

To me, and for a quarter million other New Yorkers, our city would be a much poorer place without Greenmarket.

—Ed Yowell

GREENMARKET LISTINGS

All markets are open from 8:00 A.M. to 6:00 P.M. unless otherwise specified. (Updated September 2002.)

MANHATTAN

Bowling Green
Broadway & Battery Place
Year Round
Tuesday & Thursday 8:00 A.M.–5:00 P.M.

South Street Seaport
Fulton Street, between Water & Pearl Sts.
17 September–26 November
Tuesday 8:00 A.M.–5:00 P.M.

Tribeca
Greenwich Street, between Chambers & Duane Sts.
Year Round
Wednesday & Saturday 8 A.M.–3 P.M.

Tompkins Square
East 7th Street & Avenue A
Year Round
Sunday 10:00 A.M.–6:00 P.M.

St. Mark's Church
East 10th Street & Second Avenue
Year Round
Tuesday 8:00 A.M.–7:00 P.M.

Abingdon Square
West 12th Street & Hudson Street
Year Round
Saturday 8:00 A.M.–1:00 P.M.

Union Square
East 17th Street & Broadway
Year Round
Monday, Wednesday, Friday & Saturday

Dag Hammarskjold Plaza
East 47th Street & Second Avenue
Wednesday Year Round
Saturday May–November

Rockefeller Center
Rockefeller Place at 50th St.
11 October–16 November
Friday & Saturday

Balsley Park
West 57th Street & Ninth Avenue
Year Round
Wednesday & Saturday

77th Street—I.S. 44
West 77th Street & Columbus Avenue
Year Round
Sunday 10:00 A.M.–5:00 P.M.

All Souls' Church
Lexington & 80th Street
Year Round
Thursday

97th Street
West 97th Street, between Amsterdam & Columbus Aves.
Late May–Dec
Friday 8:00 A.M.–2:00 P.M.

Columbia
Broadway at 116th St.
Late May–December
Thursday

Harlem
Adam Clayton Powell Office Bldg.
125th Street & Adam Clayton Powell Boulevard
Year Round
Tuesday 8:00 A.M.–3:00 P.M.

175th Street
West 175th Street & Broadway
June–December
Thursday

BROOKLYN

Greenpoint—McCarren Park
Lorimer Street & Driggs Avenue
Year Round
Saturday 8:00 A.M.–3:00 P.M.

Williamsburg
Havemeyer Street & Broadway
July–October
Thursday 8:00 A.M.–5:00 P.M.

Bedford-Stuyvesant
Fulton Street, between Stuyvesant & Utica Aves.
July–November
Saturday 8:00 A.M.–3:00 P.M.

Borough Hall
Court & Remsen Streets
Year Round
Tuesday, Thursday & Saturday

Grand Army Plaza
NW entrance to Prospect Park
Year Round
Saturday 8:00 A.M.–4:00 P.M.

Windsor Terrace
Prospect Park West & 15th Street
April–November
Wednesday 8:00 A.M.–3:00 P.M.

Borough Park
14th Avenue between 49th & 50th Sts.
July 25–October
Thursday

Sunset Park
Fourth Avenue between 59th & 60th Sts.
July–November
Saturday 8:00 A.M.–3:00 P.M.

BRONX

Poe Park
Grand Concourse & 192nd Street
July–November
Tuesday 8:00 A.M.–2:00 P.M.

Lincoln Hospital
148th Street & Morris Avenue, south of hospital entrance
July–November
Tuesday & Friday 8:00 A.M.–3:00 P.M.

QUEENS

Jackson Heights–Travers Park
34th Avenue between 77th & 78th Sts.
May–November
Sunday 8:00 A.M.–5:00 P.M.

STATEN ISLAND

St. George
Borough Hall parking lot
St. Marks & Hyatt Streets
May–November
Saturday 8:00 A.M.–2:00 P.M.

ELIZABETH LITTLES

PASTRIES & BAKED GOODS

Buttercup Bake Shop
Midtown East
973 Second Avenue, between 51st and 52nd Sts.
(212) 350-4144

Walk into the Buttercup Bakery and you will find yourself in small-town America, circa 1955. It's cozy and small, with just enough tables and comfortable chairs to make you feel welcome. Brownies and cookies stand side by side in neat rows under the glass. Nice-sized cupcakes in every flavor await a quick swipe of frosting. Buttercup golden, red velvet, lemon, and devil dog are just a few of the choices. The cakes stand high above on pedestals: creamy coconut, milk chocolate, a delicious German chocolate loaded with pecans, and an almost perfect Lady Baltimore. Tender layers of delicate cake—vanilla-yellow or chocolate—combine with thick, creamy frostings. Dream up a combination for a Crowd Pleaser sheet cake to feed forty. By the time you're done, you'll be begging for a glass of milk.

Pies, coffeecakes, and mini-cheesecakes of many flavors round out the menu. If you can't find something here to satisfy your sweet tooth, then you might as well give up. My absolute favorite is the chilled 'Nilla pudding. Fresh custard made with real eggs and plenty of vanilla is then layered in a bowl with thin slices of banana and lots of crisp wafer cookies. It's cold and sweet—and one of the best things you will ever eat.

The coffee at Buttercup, both drip and espresso, is excellent, and the service is courteous and friendly. Order ahead for something special or just stop in for a treat.

The Doughnut Plant
Lower East Side
379 Grand Street, between Essex and Norfolk Sts.
(212) 505-3700
Cash only

In 1994, the Doughnut Plant was created by a wonder-boy baker named Mark Israel. Selling more than 1,000 every day, including wholesale, these fried cakes are well cooked through and through, then lightly browned and glazed with lots of different flavors. The all-natural chocolate glaze is made with delicious Valrhona cocoa, and real Tahitian vanilla beans are used in the vanilla frosting. The fruit glazes vary with the season and summer varieties include apricot, coconut, and blueberry. There is even a wonderful lime glaze that is very good with a cold glass of lemonade.

After making your purchase, it is very important to keep the doughnuts at a somewhat cool temperature, so they will retain their freshness. They are sold all over town at Dean & DeLuca and Oren's Daily Roast, but the Grand

Street location feels like a neighborhood shop, albeit with a commercial kitchen in full view. Stop by and peek in the window, and don't forget to try one of these beauties. Then you'll know what a real glazed doughnut is!

The Donut Pub
West Village
203 West 14th Street at Seventh Ave.
Open 24 hours

Imagine a world of cruller trees and honey-dipped bushes, where a chocolate, glazed sun rises over a steaming coffee lake. It exists on their T-shirts and in spirit at the Donut Pub, where you can fill your urge for a filled ring of dough any hour of the day. Family-owned since it opened in 1964, Donut Pub enjoys a devoted fan base, many of whom have been settling at the long, narrow counter for a coffee and cruller for decades. For regular customers, manager Bill Pappadimatos and the other sweet-slingers start bagging up their "usual" before they've even gotten all the way through the door. Which is good, because you wouldn't want to wait an extra second for these fresh, delicious doughnuts, made three times a day by the same people who pour your coffee. Every breakfast treat the Pub sells—muffins, cakes, cinnamon rolls, apple turnovers, biscuits—comes out of the small kitchen hidden behind one-way glass on the back wall. The jelly doughnut, dusted with powdered or granulated sugar or topped with vanilla frosting, is peerless; the Boston creme is a paragon of fried dough. And at $.65 each (a dozen will run you only $5.50), you'll never wait for the doors to unlock at Krispy Kreme again.

The Little Pie Company
Theater District
424 West 43rd Street, between Ninth and Tenth Aves.
(212) 736-4780

Often it's the simpler recipes, ones that are transcendently good in the home kitchen, that get screwed up when they try to go "commercial." Take the humble pie. At first blush there wouldn't seem to be much of a trick to it; one or two crusts and a filling, with maybe a lattice, meringue, or crumb top if you want to get fancy. But it's almost impossible to find a store-bought pie that measures up to your childhood memories. Maybe your ideal is that raspberry pie that Aunt Ellie made for the fireman's supper so many summers ago, or the homemade mincemeat or "shoo-fly" pie your grammie brought to Thanksgiving dinner. Those pies were made with absolutely fresh ingredients, as well as pride and love. That's a lot of expectation for a commercial piemaker to overcome.

The Little Pie Company sets the standard in New York for commercial pies, and, though they're store-bought, the quality is so good that any Thanksgiving table would be lucky to have one. In fact, they've become such a tradition that, if you want one around the holidays, you'll need to place your order at least two weeks in advance.

The fresh fruit pies are juicy and outstanding, but Little Pie Company offers a wide range of choices, everything from lemon meringue and key lime to coconut-banana cream and apple-sour cream-walnut, one of the store's most popular flavors. Pies are available in three sizes—5, 8, and 10 inches—and it's fun to buy several and host a pie-tasting party. Think of it as a citified version of the church social.

Other Locations
407 West 14th St., between Ninth and Tenth Aves.; (212) 414-2324
Dining (Lower) Concourse, Grand Central Terminal, 42nd Street
    at Vanderbilt Ave.

Poseidon Bakery
Theater District
629 Ninth Avenue, between 44th and 45th Sts.
(212) 757-6173
Closed Monday
Cash only

Demetrios Anagnostou was the Christopher Columbus of Greek bakers. In 1923, the story goes, he stepped off the boat from the old country at Pier 84, walked three blocks inland, and found the spot where he would start his bakery. He named it Poseidon, not only in honor of the sea-god, but because that was the name of his family's bakery on the island of Corfu.

Eighty years after Anagnostou planted his flag, so to speak, his own descendants are still running the business and making traditional Greek pastries. They make their own phyllo dough here, hand-stretching it in the time-honored fashion. Best of all, they sell the phyllo, which is prized by commercial pastry chefs and home bakers alike. Poseidon is the only place on the East Coast making and selling their house-made phyllo this way. That alone makes a trip there obligatory.

But Poseidon's sweet and savory pastries are the main attraction, from *baklava* that might induce sugar shock to delicious appetizer-size *spanakopita* (spinach and cheese tarts) and other offerings that may be less familiar to non-Greeks, such as *tiropita,* another kind of cheese pie that's seasoned with mint. The *finikia,* dense nut cookies that are flavored with orange oil, bergamot, and cardamom, are also special.

Many of the recipes Poseidon uses have been handed down directly from its founder. And from what we can see, they're definitely in capable hands.

Sweet Melissa Patisserie
Cobble Hill, Brooklyn
276 Court Street, between Butler and Douglass Sts.
(718) 855-3410
Subway: F, G to Bergen St.
Cash only

In the process of gentrification and community evolution, what used to be exclusively an old-school Italian bakery neighborhood fragrant with yeasty, blond loaves and sugary cookies by the pound has now opened up to more crusty, buttery, and sophisticated fare. Sweet Melissa Patisserie has a small and modest storefront, but upon entering the wood-paneled shop, the artfully arranged display of fragrant pastries, cakes, and breads on multitiered trays and baskets seduces the senses. The excellent sweet and savory muffins, whose seasonal flavorings vary by the day, round out a wide selection of croissants, cookies, scones, petits-fours, fruit tarts, and buttercream-frosted cakes large and small, and many other goodies.

Fill a box with an assortment of appetite-spoilers to go, or stay for breakfast or afternoon tea. In addition to the shop's pastries, the café menu includes homemade granola, seasonal fruit, and light sandwiches. Be prepared to linger since the service is slow, but the time will slip by pleasantly, especially if you choose to sit in the quiet rear garden in the warmer months, surrounded by blooming vines and blue sky.

Villabate Pasticceria & Bakery
Bensonhurst, Brooklyn
7117 18th Avenue, between 71st and 72nd Sts.
(718) 331-8430
Subway W to 71st St., N to 18th Ave.

A small town about ten minutes from Palermo in Sicily, Villabate is well known for its gelato. It is also Manny, the owner's, hometown. From the first visit to Villabate, simply taking in the sights and smells of the rows and rows of elaborate pastries, it's easy to see that Manny has done his town proud. Marzipan candies that look like miniature fruits and vegetables, mountains of chocolate-cream and chocolate-mousse-covered goodies, brioche filled with pastry cream, possibly the best cannoli in New York—and this barely scratches the surface. All the pastries are made

NEW YORK CHEESECAKE

The story of the New York cheesecake cannot be told without going back 4,000 years. Food historians first document the making of cheese as evidenced by cheese molds dating to 2000 B.C.E. Athletes at the first Olympic games were served a sweet cake made from cheese in 776 B.C.E., and a recipe was recorded soon thereafter.

Cheese-making spread across Europe following the Roman conquest, and was by then popular and widespread, with new techniques and local customs evolving, refining, and perfecting the process. When Europeans brought their families to America, they also brought along their treasured food traditions and recipes, and by the late nineteenth century cream cheese was born.

Some of the earliest American recipes for cheese desserts can be found in the 1824 book *The Virginia Housewife* by Mary Randolph. Almost a century later, Mr. Kraft brought Philadelphia brand cream cheese to every icebox, and cheesecake became an American citizen. Many early examples were a mixture of pot cheese and cream cheese made in the Eastern European style, while Italian home bakers always and only use ricotta and a bit of candied fruit. As far away as Michigan, Zingerman's Deli produces a lovely artisanal-quality cream cheese used in cakes that appear on select Slow-friendly dessert trays. Every imaginable variation on the basic plain cheesecake exists, and hundreds of recipes are available: with flavors such as pumpkin, amaretto, chocolate, and more, there is something to please everyone. Junior's, Eileen's, Lindy's, Bruno's, and Carousel are all famous New York cheesecake brands, available throughout the five boroughs.

The crust for a cheesecake is a straightforward preparation made with graham cracker crumbs, sponge cake, or simply butter and flour. The batter consists of cream cheese and sugar with eggs (for binding), a pinch of salt (for balance), and a drop of vanilla (for flavor). It is as simple as that. Bruce Zipes of Bruce's Long Island adds sour cream to his cake, while Junior's and Lindy's add citrus. A gentle hand is important in the preparation—lots of air, no overbeating! The cheesecake bakes in a hot oven for a short time, then continues baking "low and slow" until it is dry to the touch, a bit brown on top, and smells heavenly.

A slice of rich, smooth cheesecake is comfort food at its finest. It is the essence of the real New York—simple, sturdy, endearing, and enduring.

—Bernadette Kramer

fresh daily. As is the savory *sfuncioni,* a foccacia-like dough that is topped with breadcrumbs and cooked onions—a traditional Sicilian snack that definitely qualifies as Sicilian street food.

And then there's the gelato. With flavors like *fior di latte, zuppa Inglese, nocciola,* and pistachio, it's hard to select only one or two. All the flavors are made on the premises with the best ingredients and traditional flavorings flown in from Sicily. Many of the flavors change with the seasons and the availability of products. The most enjoyable way to consume this gelato is to ask for it *con brioche.* The person behind the counter will slice open a fresh brioche roll, stuff whatever flavors you select between the buttery halves, and—presto!—a Sicilian ice cream sandwich.

After careful observation and many sandwiches, I have determined it is best to treat the sandwich as you would an ice cream cone. You don't bite into the cone right away; you begin by licking the ice cream down to an appropriate level where you can then nibble on the cone without jeopardizing the structural integrity of the whole. Follow this advice and you may even get a nod of approval from one of the Sicilian natives who are often hanging about.

NOTE: Across the street from Villabate is Foccaceria. The inside looks like a large pizza joint, but what they're selling is far from your average pizza. Foccaceria produces Sicilian specialties such as *pane caí meusa* (spleen served with fresh ricotta and grated *cacio cavallo* on a small bun), *pane con panelle* (chickpea fritters served in the same fashion as above), massive *arancini* (fried rice balls filled with ground meat and peas), and many others.

NOTABLE

Black Hound
See Chocolate & Candy, p. 236.

Bruno Bakery and Pasticceria Bruno
Greenwich Village
506 La Guardia Place, between Bleecker and Houston Sts.
(212) 982-5854

Twin brothers Biaggio and Nino Settepani are as sweet as the baked goods they sell to their many loyal fans: wonderful little sandwiches, cookies, candies, and a dozen flavors of gelato. Table service is friendly and the coffee is very good.

Other Location
245 Bleecker St., between Sixth and Seventh Aves.; (212) 242-4959

Ceci-Cela
Chinatown/Little Italy
55 Spring Street, between Lafayette and Mulberry Sts.
(212) 274-9179

This little patisserie has about the best croissant and brioche this side of the Atlantic, not to mention tartes, financiers, and more. The croissants are guaranteed to explode in a flurry of crispy crust bits when chomped. There is a small seating area at the back for bowls of coffee and delectables. And did we mention the wonderful chocolate truffles?

City Bakery
See Brunch, p. 173.

Eileen's Special Cheesecake
Chinatown/Little Italy
17 Cleveland Place, between Centre and Kenmare Sts.
(212) 966-5585

At Eileen's, you'll be confronted with a dazzling array of cheesecake flavor choices: banana, pumpkin, cookies and cream, marble, cappuccino, and several fruit-topped ones as well. If you're having trouble deciding, get a box of nine assorted mini-cheesecakes and try them out. You can even get "low-fat" and sugar-free versions. Our favorite flavor? We have to admit, it's still the plain.

Hungarian Pastry Shop
Morningside Heights
1020 Amsterdam Avenue at 111th St.
(212) 866-4230

In the shadow of the glorious Cathedral of St. John the Divine, this little wonder has been in business for more than forty years with only two owners. Wendy and Peter Biniouris turn out delicious Eastern European treats for Columbia students and many other fans. The savory cheese puff they make here is terrific paired with a glass of Riesling.

Levain Bakery
West Side
167 West 74th Street, between Columbus and Amsterdam Aves.
(212) 874-6080
Cash only

Levain, as its name suggests, makes terrific breads, but cookies are their real claim to fame. They're huge and intensely chocolatey, dense and not too greasy. Eating one will make you feel like you've had a complete meal, which in terms of calories is probably not far off. But who's counting calories?

Magnolia Bakery
West Village
401 Bleecker Street at West 11th St.
(212) 462-2572

With its fantastically kitschy, candy-pink decor, and great old-fashioned cakes, this pastry shop has become one of the Village's neighborhood staples. Magnolia's perfectly luscious cupcakes draw crowds day and night (it's open late on weekends), and people gather outside to devour them.

Margot Patisserie
West Side
2109 Broadway at 74th St.
(212) 721-0076
Cash only

This warm and friendly bakery on the West Side has a new baby sister crosstown. The fruit tarts and little butter cookies are splendid, but do not miss the almond croissant, which is great with a cup of coffee. Margot's tuna sandwiches are delicious; you'd never see such an item in a patisserie in Paris—good thing we're in New York.

Other Location
1212 Lexington Ave, between 83rd and 84th Sts.; (212) 772-6064

Musette
Gramercy Park/Flatiron District
228 Third Avenue at 19th St.
(212) 477-3777

If you are pining for Paris or just a good light meal, stop by this small Gramercy bakery and takeout place and eat well for a fair price. In the morning enjoy a good coffee with a real butter croissant; at lunch try the mozzarella *panino* or the very popular turkey meatloaf, which you can finish off with a good cup of coffee and a mixed fresh fruit tart.

Payard Patisserie and Bistro
Lenox Hill
1032 Lexington Avenue, between 73rd and 74th Sts.
(212) 717-5252

Legendary *patissier* Francois Payard, who made his reputation at Restaurant Daniel, now supplies his pastries to many of the city's finest restaurants, but you can also enjoy a full spread of sweets and traditional French dishes at this bistro. Like medieval subtleties or *entremets*, Payard's creations are an artful marvel to behold—and to consume.

Rocco Pastry Shop
West Village
243 Bleecker Street, between Carmine and Leroy Sts.
(212) 242-6031
Cash only

The cannolis at Rocco are filled to order, and their Italian cheesecake is sublime. The biscotti are crisp, with a subtle anise flavor. The atmosphere is friendly and neighborly. This is the only place my grandmother would buy Italian pastries.

S&S Cheesecake
Riverdale, Bronx
222 West 238th Street, between Broadway and Bailey Ave.
(718) 549-3888
Subway: 1 to 238th St.
Open to 3:00 P.M. weekdays; closed Saturday–Sunday
Cash only

Great cheesecake is a matter of balance in texture, flavor, and sweetness. S&S clearly has it down to a science, and they do it by concentrating on what they do best—plain, unadulterated, crustless cheesecake. If you can't get up to the Bronx during business hours, you can find their cheesecake at Zabar's and a few other places in the city.

Soutine
West Side
104 West 70th Street at Columbus Aves.
(212) 496-1450

The place is tiny, but this might be exactly where you want to find yourself when ordering a cake for a special occasion. Baked goods are also delicious here, and the staff is just as sweet.

Wine and Roses
Midtown East
360 East 55th Street between First and Second Aves.
(212) 838-5411
Closed Sunday

No pastry section in any guide can go without a mention of Wine and Roses, a cute and sweet pastry store located in Midtown where you can find a delicious selection of beautiful cakes and scrumptious cookies. Everyone must taste a W&R brownie one day: happiness for the mouth! But don't stop at the brownie, because everything here is a huge temptation. They deliver, too.

Yi Mei Fung Bakery
Flushing, Queens
135-38 Roosevelt Avenue, between Main and Prince Sts.
(718) 886-6820
Subway: 7 to Flushing–Main St.
Cash only

Yi Mei Fung sells inexpensive buns stuffed with sweet or savory fillings, but try the Taiwanese moon cakes, which are filled with sweet bean paste. You can also buy some European-style pastries here in the heart of Queens' Chinatown.

Other Location
81-26 Broadway, between 81st and 82nd Sts., Elmhurst, Queens;
    (718) 898-8005

PATRICK MARTINS

STREET FOOD

Street food has age-old origins—from the market stands of ancient Greece to the muffin man and baked-potato vendor of nineteenth-century London. In New York, street food has always been emblematic of the city, commerce born of spontaneity, convenience, entertainment, and taste. What other American city has streets so ripe with the aroma, spectacle, and sheer diversity of fresh food being grilled, roasted, toasted, scooped, or poured to order?

And yet the full spectrum of street food experiences is not limited to food that is sold literally on the street: Many storefronts and shops sell primarily for takeout and immediate consumption, from pizza and sandwiches to ice cream and pastries. But sometimes the best eating comes from the serendipitous experience of detecting an aroma from down the street and then following your nose until you discover the stand and its vigilant purveyor, waiting to make good on the promise made to your nose by filling your belly with sweet or savory, dense or airy, crunchy or soft satisfaction.

Either way, we are a city of street eaters, our hands ready to cradle a snack without breaking our stride. Accordingly, the best street foods are usually designed for a hand-to-mouth delivery, from the built-in grip of a hot dog bun and the quintessential New York fold of a slice of pizza (lengthwise, down the middle, so the cheese doesn't slide off) to the paper cone sprouting Belgian *frites* and the corn-husk gift wrapping of a *tamale*.

In the early morning, street carts that have slept the night in garages on the periphery of the city are stocked with supplies and rolled onto trucks that transport them to marked territories—some prized for their tourist traffic, others for commuters and office workers, and still others for shoppers and neighborhood folk. These carts are perhaps the least diverse of all the street food to be found in New York, with just a few staple genres—doughnuts and coffee, hot dogs and pretzels, roasted nuts and ice cream—but there are moments when their proximity and ready service are all you could need or want, whether it's a snack while walking through Central Park or a tide-me-over before descending into the subway.

Some of the tastiest and most unique street foods take a little more effort to find, although sometimes they are right under your nose. Many are also based on the foods of other cultures that make legendary street food, from Mexican tamales to Greek *souvlaki*. Some places are natural offshoots in a neighborhood dominated by a particular ethnic community—or combination of such communities—while others are mavericks of good taste flying solo in a random location. Some of the most transcendent street food is oftentimes transient as well. A stand appears one day and then for no apparent reason is gone the next; local authorities will perpetuate periodic crackdowns on street vendors, supposedly in the name of cleanliness, seemliness, and bigger businesses. And some of the best places devote all their energies to making only one food, whether it's Belgian *frites,* cheese steak sandwiches, or soup. (Jerry Seinfeld's "Soup Nazi" legacy lives on at Al Yeganeh's Soup Kitchen International in Midtown.)

Either way, the idea is, when in Rome, do as the Romans do—or, in this case, as the Chinese, Mexicans, or Jews do. When in Harlem, look for fried chicken and other soul food classics on the West Side, and tacos on the East Side. In Chinatown, look for pork bun bakeries, *chow fun* noodle carts, and vendors of sweet little hot cakes, each the size of a quail egg. At Greenmarkets all over the city, you'll find ripe fruit and homemade baked goods; on the Lower East Side reside the last bastions of great kosher (and "kosher-style") appetizers, pastries, and snacks in Manhattan. And everywhere, from end to end of all five boroughs, pizza ovens churn out hot, crusty pies to be sliced up and gobbled down by anyone with a buck fifty and an appetite.

What follows are sketches of just a few major parts of the city that are particularly blessed with delicious and varied street fare, nearly all of them below 14th Street, where street foods seem to proliferate in a more ethnically diverse and jumbled downtown. (If the bias is Manhattan-heavy, it's only because we haven't yet discovered all the riches of the Outer Boroughs.) To go beyond these selections, though, is to discover for yourself the infinite variations of New York street food. and to acquire your own nose and intuition for hearty, flavorful, and instantly satisfying food of all kinds.

LOWER EAST SIDE

Many shops in this neighborhood close for the Jewish Sabbath, so on Fridays be sure to stop in by 2:00 or 3:00 P.M. at the latest, or be prepared to wait until Sunday.

Guss' Pickles

85-87 Orchard Street, between Broome and Delancey Sts.
(516) 642-2634

There's nothing like a new pickle (cucumber, tomato, pepper—take your pick) straight from the barrels of this LES institution to spark a sidewalk debate on the best New York pickle; Guss' has not only history but also taste, personality, and charm on its side.

Yonah Schimmel's Knishery

137 East Houston Street, between Forsyth and Eldridge Sts.
(212) 477-2858

Nearly a century's worth of memorabilia and clippings adorn the walls in this ramshackle shop; potato, kasha, and other vegetable- and nostalgia-

NEW YORK PRETZELS

You don't have to walk far to satisfy a soft-pretzel craving in New York City, but the history of this salt-encrusted, mustard-dipped twist of dough is more intimately tied to Philadelphia, where residents gobble more of the "world's oldest snack" per year than any other city. Numerous pretzel businesses are based in Pennsylvania, including Sturgis Pretzels, the oldest commercial pretzel bakery, and Martin's Pretzels, a New York Greenmarket favorite.

The pretzel's link to New York City may be due to its close association with the pushcart, an icon of the city's food history. Another suggested tie comes from Molly O'Neill's *New York Cookbook:* the dense, chewy pretzels are made from the same dough as bagels. At any rate, soft pretzels (and later, their hard, crunchy counterparts) have long been considered good luck charms, something everyone can use once in a while.

—*Sara Firebaugh*

filled knishes come up from the basement ovens in a dumbwaiter all day long, and customers snatch them up to eat warm on the spot or to take home.

Gertel's Bake Shop
53 Hester Street, between Ludlow and Essex Sts.
(212) 982-3250

Gertel's is a reliable standby for *rugelach, babka,* and other traditional kosher pastries.

Kossar's Bialys
367 Grand Street, between Essex and Norfolk Sts.
(212) 473-4810; (877-4-BIALYS)

A warm floury fragrance hits your nostrils when you pull open the door at Kossar's and kisses you good-bye when you leave with a (kosher) hot bialy, bagel, or onion disk in your hand, ready for munching as you go on your way.

The Doughnut Plant
379 Grand Street, between Essex and Norfolk Sts.
(212) 505-3700

What began as a labor of love for doughnut-maker Mark Israel, using a family recipe and his mountain bike to make his first deliveries, has found a cult following through sales both at the Grand Street store and in several shops around the city, including Zabar's, Dean & DeLuca, and Citarella. The yeast doughnuts are huge, airy, and barely sweet, and are flavored with fresh and seasonal fruit glazes—or something as simple and perfect as a vanilla bean glaze.

THE VILLAGE (EAST AND WEST)

Pommes Frites
123 Second Avenue, between 7th St. and St. Marks Pl.
(212) 674-1234

Twice-fried Belgian *frites* have cropped up in shops in various parts of the city over the past few years, but Pommes Frites did it first and still does it best. The mayonnaise-y *frites* sauce is the perfect dressing, made even better with a little ketchup swirled in.

Hero's
30 East 13th Street, between Broadway and Fourth Ave.
(646) 336-1685

Hero's is the only place on record to offer oddly compelling variations on the true sweet potato (yam), whether steamed, in a pita, or wrapped in rice.

Flor's Kitchen
149 First Avenue, between 9th and 10th Sts.
(212) 387-8949

Handcrafted Venezuelan cooking is the draw at Flor's, including perfect little savory pastries such as *cachapas, arepas,* and *empanadas*—just the right size to carry out a few, or to make a whole meal with a few more.

Panya
10 Stuyvesant Street, between Third Ave. and 9th St.
(212) 777-1930

Panya offers beguiling, fresh-made batches of that strange hybrid genre of Japanese pastries, modeled in some ways after French pastries, but with their own unique style. Lightly sweet, airy, and delicately frosted cakes sit side by side with savory fried or steamed buns, filled with curry or potato or red bean paste. Japanese students and club kids from the neighborhood satisfy their homesick cravings for crustless white bread sandwiches and a yogurt soft drink called Calpis.

THE NEW YORK HOT DOG

The history, the name, and the origin of the hot dog have all been widely debated, but one fact is clear: The hot dog has always held an honored place in the hearts of New Yorkers. In fact, simply eating a hot dog is an easy way to feel like a tried-and-true New Yorker. For a quick lunch on the run, grab a dog from a street vendor. Whether you're watching a game at Yankee Stadium or making a 4:00 A.M. pit stop at Gray's Papaya after a long night of partying, you'll feel like you have lived in New York for years. Eating a dog on the street makes you feel like you are part of the crowd. And the hot dog is the perfect food for either a tourist or native New Yorker on a budget because, let's face it, the Big Apple can be one of the most expensive cities in the world.

Typically made with Hebrew National Brand All-Beef Kosher franks, hot dogs are most commonly boiled and topped with mustard, ketchup, onion sauce, and/or sauerkraut. Yet eating at one of New York's famous grilled hot dog spots, such as Katz's Deli, will give you a different taste experience altogether. Katz's franks in their natural casing are grilled flat on a griddle and often dressed with sauerkraut and mustard.

Another alternative to eating dogs on the street is to take a trip to Coney Island for the World Hot Dog Eating Championship. If you want to earn the yellow belt here, you will have to consume more than 50 hot dogs in less than 12 minutes.

Hot dogs are frugal, convenient, practical, and even, dare I say—romantic? The story goes that actor Bruce Willis proposed to Demi Moore in front of a hot dog cart on the street. But however or wherever you pick up your hot dog, it's sure to provide a real New York moment.

—*Courtney Knapp*

Win49

205 Allen Street at East Houston St.
(212) 353-9494

Kushikatsu is traditionally breaded and fried pork on a skewer, but at Win49 you can also get this "homey Japanese food" as beef, chicken, shrimp, fish, or vegetable *kushikatsu*, à la carte or in a generous bento box with rice and scrambled egg. The tiny storefront also takes orders for party packs of *kushikatsu*—starting at 12 skewers and up.

BB Sandwich Bar
120 West 3rd Street at MacDougal St.
(212) 473-7500

Owner Gary Thompson gave up the life of a high-end chef for a more singular task: cheese steak sandwiches. It's not authentic Philly-style, but it may be the beginning of a truly respectable—and addictive— New York cheese steak, with thinly sliced, tender ribeye, American cheese, marinated grilled onions, chile peppers, and ketchup on a kaiser roll.

The Donut Pub
203 West 14th Street at Seventh Ave.

The Donut Pub is open 24 hours, so you can get your sugar fix at any time, day or night. Family-owned since 1964, the pub's delicious doughnuts emerge fresh from the small kitchen in back three times a day. Try the jelly doughnut, or the Boston creme, or grab a muffin, cinnamon roll, or one of the apple turnovers. A dozen doughnuts costs only $5.50 ($0.65 for singles), which has to be one of the city's best food deals.

Faicco's Pork Store
260 Bleecker Street, between Sixth and Seventh Aves.
(212) 243-1974
Closed Monday

Offering great sausages, cold cuts, chops, and other Italian specialties, this old-fashioned meat store is also one of the best spots to grab a traditional hero. The bread from Zito's (across the street) is always fresh, the meat juicy, and the fixings just right.

UNION SQUARE

Rainbow Falafel
26 East 17th Street, between Fifth Ave. and Broadway
(212) 691-8641

Being written up countless times hasn't changed how good the falafel is here—the long line down the block (which moves pretty quickly) will attest to this, not to mention the chunky, luscious *babaganoush* and other freshly made ingredients that blend perfectly with a dousing of tahini and hot sauce.

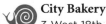

City Bakery
3 West 18th Street, between Fifth and Sixth Aves.
(212) 366-1414

Maury Rubin was probably the first guy downtown to charge more than
ten bucks a pound for his "salad bar" (which includes poached salmon
and fried chicken), but it's still the tastiest salad bar food around, not to
mention the multicultural soup bar (oatmeal, chicken soup, *congee* anyone?) and pyramids of seasonal pastries and confections.

Union Square Greenmarket
17th Street, between Broadway and Park Ave. South

Every Monday, Wednesday, Friday, and Saturday this flagship of the New
York City Greenmarket network sells whatever is in season, and fortunately some of the best prepared foods are in season—all the time! Bread
and pastries, pretzels, and fresh-squeezed cider, plus tastes of whatever is
on display make a stroll through the Greenmarket a delicious graze.

CHINATOWN

Few neighborhoods in New York inspire as visceral a reaction as
Chinatown does, for better or for worse, especially in the heat of summer.
But if you can get over the pungent aromas and sticky sidewalks,
Chinatown is the perfect place to get a snack, walking from one food vendor to the next, filling out all the elements of a multicourse nosh with just
a few dollars. Everyone has their own favorites, but as long as you follow
your nose and the savvy shopping crowds (not the tourists), you can't go
wrong. Your best bet is to walk on Canal Street between Lafayette and the
Bowery and on adjoining side streets; on Grand Street between Bowery
and East Broadway; and around the intersection of Division Street and
East Broadway. Here are some suggestions ranging from specific to general, meant to inspire adventure and steel the stomach.

Chow Fun Noodle Cart
Pike Street and East Broadway

This cart looks like all the others—quilted chrome and a blue tarp flap-
ping in the wind—but it's one of only a few that sell steamed *chow fun*
noodles (along with seafood stews and fried noodles). Ask for a $1 por-
tion, and the vendor will fish the long rolled noodles out of the steam
table, snip them in half and dress them with three different kinds of sweet
and spicy sauce, plus sesame seeds.

Fried Dumpling

99 Allen Street, between Broome and Delancey Sts.
(212) 941-9975

Five dumplings or four pork buns sell for the unbelievable price of $2 at this Chinatown fixture. For a full review, see Chinese, p. 42.

The Vietnamese Sandwich

Banh Mi Saigon—Under the Manhattan Bridge
108 Forsyth Street
(212) 941-1541

Viet-nam Banh-mi So 1 Inc.

369 Broome Street, between Elizabeth and Mott Sts.
(212) 219-8341

The *bahn mi,* or Vietnamese sandwich, made with shredded daikon and carrots, coriander, chile, roast pork sausage, and Sri Racha red chile sauce is one of the best and cheapest meals in town. Both of these places make them from the freshest ingredients. For a full review, see Southeast Asian, p. 141.

CHINESE PASTRIES AND BREADS

The best bakeries are always crammed with customers, but the service is quick, so you'll never wait long to choose from infinite variations on everything from fried and steamed buns filled with pork and other sweet or savory fillings, to sponge cakes layered with sweet cream and glazed fruit.

CHINESE MEATS AND POULTRY

Many Chinese noodle shops also double as prepared-meat counters, where the window dressing shows not *haute couture* but popular gluttony, with hanging slabs of barbecued pork ribs, sides of crisp-skinned roast pork, whole roast chickens, Peking ducks, and giant squid colored a lurid curry yellow. Everything is cut to order on massive circular butcher blocks by cleaver-wielding men in long aprons who can reduce a whole chunk of meat to bite-sized pieces with a few well-aimed thwacks, then nest the slices on a bed of white rice and—presto!—here's lunch.

TEAHOUSES

For a sweet finish, teahouses (as well as some bakeries) offer bubble tea, the ubiquitous tapioca pearl drink. Chinatown's answer to the frappuccino and smoothie comes in variations including sweetened iced tea and coffee, and tropical purées from avocado to lychee.

===== A TASTE OF CENTRAL AMERICA =====

Red Hook Playing Fields
Red Hook, Brooklyn
Bay and Clinton Sts.
Subway: F, G to Smith–9th Sts.

Local soccer and baseball teams gather for games at the Red Hook public playing fields on warm weather weekends, in beer-sponsor garb and surrounded by friends and family. Because the public facilities offer no official concessions—no watered-down beer, $5 hot dogs, or stale popcorn—the need to feed spectators has been answered by something so much tastier than Yankee Stadium could ever have dared to imagine: homegrown vendors selling sensational, handmade, and dirt-cheap Latin American foods of all kinds. It's a seasonal, transient, and Outer Borough niche, to be sure, but it only takes one visit to see the light and become a born-again *masa*-phile.

Vendors set up their stands on the paths ringing the fields, tenting blue tarps over barbecues and grills piled with *tacos, pupusas, huaraches, empanadas,* stuffed tortillas, deep-fried *flautitas,* grilled steak, fried chicken, and fried cassava and sweet plantains. Women and men stand behind the long grills, making many of these foods right in front of you: *pupusas* start as a ball of *masa* (corn-meal dough), which is stuffed with mashed red beans or shredded pork and grated cheese, flattened, grilled until crisp, and then garnished with *curtido* (pickled cabbage); *huaraches* are like an über-taco, also made of fresh *masa* but pressed into the shape of a big sandal sole and topped with sliced and grilled beef, refried beans, lettuce and tomato, salsa, chiles, crumbly *queso fresco* (fresh cheese), and a drizzle of *crema.*

Others sell roasted and deep-fried tamales dressed with *crema;* grilled corn on the cob smeared with crumbly *queso* and dusted with chile pepper; mangoes peeled to resemble a flower on a stick; sliced fresh coconut, cucumber, watermelon, pineapple, and cantaloupe to be dressed with lemon juice, salt, and chile pepper; not to mention the Jarritos fruit sodas that you find in *taquerias,* including tamarind, guava, lime, and tropical fruit.

Some stands are so casual that they look like private picnics, but nearly all will sell food to anyone who wants it—just ask and point. Bring a blanket or folding chair, because there is so much irresistible, delicious grub that you'll want to taste everything and then sleep off a food-coma on a nearby patch of grass.

—*Erika Lesser*

NEW YORK HOT DOGS

Nathan's
Coney Island, Brooklyn
1310 Surf Avenue at Stillwell Ave.
Subway: W to Coney Island/Stillwell Ave.
(718) 946-2202

The best and original Nathan's hot dogs are only to be had at the land-mark Coney Island shop, where the Brooklyn Cyclones (farm team of the Mets) play and the original Cyclone roller coaster resides in one of the oldest surviving amusement parks in the U.S.—an original "electric Eden," and a crumbling reminder of Coney Island's glory days as an elite resort destination.

Gray's Papaya
Greenwich Village
402 Sixth Avenue at 8th St.
(212) 260-3532

For a while, it seemed like the "recession special" at Gray's Papaya had become nothing more than a quaint reminder of leaner times, but there's never been a better time for this deal: $2.45 for two grilled hot dogs and a fruit drink. The dogs are crisp-skinned and nearly caramelized, the buns are toasted and crusty, and the kraut and onions are sassy—just like the service and the boisterous clientele who line up at all hours of the day and night. Come election year, Gray's Papaya proudly announces their candidate endorsement (Bill Bradley, customers learned, was our tallest presidential candidate since Abraham Lincoln), in addition to colorful quotes that always adorn the walls and windows, from critics' pronouncements of gastronomic bliss to testimonials on the nutritional benefits of papaya juice.

Other Locations
539 Eighth Avenue at 37th St.; (212) 904-1588
2090 Broadway at 72nd St.; (212) 799-0243

Hallo Berlin Pushcart
54th Street and Fifth Avenue

Hallo Berlin is not your average hot dog cart—in fact, they eschew the common frankfurter for the best of the wurst, including bratwurst, knockwurst, alpenwurst, currywurst, and Hungarian kielbasa, plus other German specialties such as red cabbage and potato pancakes.

Katz's Delicatessen
205 East Houston Street at Ludlow St.
(212) 254-2246

While the pastrami may take center stage at Katz's, the grilled, plump hot dogs are fantastic and more than worth the trek downtown. (Our suggestion: Go with a friend and split a sandwich so you have room for the dog.)

Sparky's American Food
See American p. 21.

WINE & BEER RETAILERS

Best Cellars
Upper East Side
1291 Lexington Avenue at 87th St.
(212) 426-4200
Closed Sunday

Revolutionary since it first opened in 1996, Best Cellars has become part of the fabric of the Upper East Side. The concept seems simple enough: great wines for everyday drinking. But the success with which the idea has taken hold and grown has contributed to the breaking down of the psychological barriers that have historically limited wine consumption among American consumers. Arranged neither by region nor by grape variety, the wines (about 100 selections, all priced under $15) are coolly categorized by delicious flavor profiles (Big, Luscious, Fizzy, etc.) to empower customers to choose wine in terms of more comfortable palate descriptors. Affordability aside, wines are selected from mostly small producers from around the world, many of which cannot be found at other retail locations. The sleek, award-winning interior is both efficient and engaging and the staff is well trained.

Best Cellars has surely contributed to a growing confidence and education among local wine drinkers and, most of all, has made the purchase and consumption of fermented fruit fun.

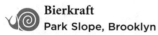 Bierkraft
Park Slope, Brooklyn
191 Fifth Avenue, between Union St. and Berkeley Pl.
(718) 230-7600
Subway: M, N, R to Union St.
Closed Monday

The ultimate beer store in the city, Bierkraft is dedicated to seeking out the highest-quality beers from around the world. Of the nearly 600 beers offered you won't find any "born on" dates, only fine craft beers, including 150 from Belgium alone, and an extraordinary selection of artisan beers from America's great microbreweries (including local brews from Long Island, Harlem, Staten Island, and, of course, Brooklyn!). In addition, the store offers regionally produced vintage American ciders, gourmet specialties, and a vast selection of award-winning cheeses. A mere block and a half from the subway, a visit to Bierkraft is convenient and worth the trip from any part of the city.

Chambers Street Wines
Tribeca
160 Chambers Street, between Greenwich and Hudson Sts.
(212) 227-1434
Closed Sunday

In Chambers Street Wines, one of the best new wine shops in Manhattan, Jamie Wolff and David Lillie have given oenophiles of Tribeca a store worth toasting. In an uncluttered, open space the co-owners place an emphasis on quality over quantity, offering a broad but focused selection of wines from around the world. Great care and attention have been paid to artisanal producers and wineries with small production that don't normally get mass recognition. In particular, a unique collection of French wines (especially from Loire, Rhône, and Beaujolais) stands out. Older vintage wines are also available at fair prices.

Italian Wine Merchants
Gramercy Park/Flatiron District
108 East 16th Street, between Union Sq. and Irving Pl.
(212) 473-2323
Closed Sunday

It is common to stroll into Italian Wine Merchants, with its long communal table and warm atmosphere, and peruse wines to the sounds of Miles Davis, Betty Carter, even Willie Nelson. A comprehensive selection of Italy's classic producers, as well as new wines from notable emerging estates, is offered in a simple yet elegant format. While single bottles remain on display for customers to study, the entire inventory is kept in a temperature-controlled cellar to ensure optimal storage until the wine is purchased. Individual orders are sent up from the cellar by dumbwaiter at a cool 55 degrees. Italian Wine Merchants carries wines from all over the country, but stands out in its Central and Northern selections, especially Piedmont, Tuscany, and Friuli-Venezia-Giulia (where co-owner, Joseph Bastianich, also owns a vineyard).

Interconnected by ownership with Babbo, Lupa, and Esca, the store also features many of the wines offered at these famed New York restaurants. A well-educated staff is available for consultation for single-bottle purchases or developing a personal wine collection featuring older vintages or rare finds. In the rear of the store, Studio del Gusto, a stylishly appointed tasting room equipped with a professional-style kitchen, provides a perfect environment for wine and food classes and cooking demonstrations.

Red, White & Bubbly
Park Slope, Brooklyn
211–213 Fifth Avenue at Sackett St.
(718) 636-WINE
Subway: M, N, R to Union St.
Closed Sunday

It's about time someone took some of the spotlight away from Manhattan! With a great name and refreshing attitude, Red, White & Bubbly is helping shine the light a little brighter across the East River in Brooklyn. Conceived by Darrin Siegfried, a Park Slope resident who is the former Education Director for the Sommelier Society of America, the store features a broad cross section of wines from both the Northern and Southern Hemispheres. Furthermore, a concerted effort has been made specifically to seek out distributors of small producers of both American and international wines. The wines are categorized by country of origin, and, with the aid of an eager and friendly staff, Siegfried offers a variety of specials such as a monthly four-pack and a best-buy two-pack at affordable prices, to encourage and develop an educated wine-drinking public. To that end, in-store classes are also held on the basics of wine.

Rosenthal Wine Merchant
Upper East Side
318 East 84th Street, between First and Second Aves.
(212) 249-6650
Closed Sunday–Monday

A unique merchant on the Upper East Side, Rosenthal offers the public a direct link to the producers carried by the company's founder, importer/distributor Neal Rosenthal. His wines are served at some of the finest restaurants in the city and available at other wine stores around the country. Yet rarely do we pay any attention to who distributes the wines we buy.

The real value of the store is the relationship the company has with each vintner it represents. Specializing in wine made in limited quantities using traditional production methods from French and Italian estates, members of the Rosenthal staff make annual visits to observe the current season and evaluate the vintages with the winemakers themselves. Back in New York, this information is readily shared with customers who are eager to have an in-depth understanding of the wines they are purchasing as well as thoughtful foresight into variations between different vintages.

Boutique in design, the modest storefront accommodates an expertly trained staff. The wine is all kept in storage pending its sale. If you can't buy wine from the producer himself, Rosenthal's is the next best thing.

Vino
Gramercy Park/Flatiron District
121 East 27th Street, between Lexington Ave. and Park Ave. South
(212) 725-6058
Closed Sunday

The name says it all! Featuring Italian wines exclusively, Vino is the sister store to the popular I Trulli Restaurant and Enoteca I Trulli just across 27th Street. Charles Scicolone, Wine Director for both the store and the restaurant, has carefully chosen wines that are representative of Italy's different winemaking styles, as well as outstanding wines from well-known producers in Italy's premier winemaking regions. It is useful that Charles tends to be either in the store or in the Enoteca and is easily accessible for questions or consultation. What's more, the entire staff at Vino is well versed in the world of Italian wine and is particularly adroit at pairing food with particular wines. The store is laid out by region, and certain whites and sparkling wines are available chilled. In particular, the store carries exemplary selections from the southern winemaking regions that are just now starting to come of age on an international stage, as well as an extensive selection of grappas. One block away, in the aptly named Vinoteca, frequent seminars and wine tastings are offered to the public.

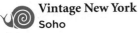

Vintage New York
Soho
482 Broome Street at Wooster St.
(212) 226-9463
Open Sunday

With the renaissance of winemaking in New York State continuing to emerge, Vintage New York has thrown open its doors to city consumers to promote the best of our truly local wines. Long Island, the Hudson Valley, and the Finger Lakes regions are well represented in a collection of more than 200 selections from 60 different wineries across the state. The flagship store has a wonderful Soho-meets-country atmosphere and, in addition to wine, features gourmet foods from some of New York's finest food artisans.

In an effort to create a greater awareness of the quality and diversity of New York State wines, the store has a tasting counter where wines are available for sample by the glass, and a vaulted cellar where frequent seminars are held for both wine tastings as well as wine and food degustations. The store is also a great resource for seeking out local winery tours and events. Perhaps the most notable feature of Vintage New York is that it is legally open on Sundays! Owned by a New York State winery, the store is considered a satellite to the agricultural endeavor and is thus exempt from local "blue laws."

Other Location
2492 Broadway at 93rd St.; (212) 721-9999

NOTABLE

(All closed Sunday unless noted.)

Acker, Merrall & Condit *(Wine)*
West Side
160 West 72nd Street, between Broadway & Columbus Ave.
(212) 787-1700

American Beer Distributing *(Beer)*
Cobble Hill, Brooklyn
256 Court Street, between Butler and Kane Sts.
(718) 875-0226

Burgundy Wine Company *(Wine)*
West Village
323 West 11th Street, between Greenwich and Washington Sts.
(212) 691-9092

Embassy Wines & Spirits *(Wine & Spirits)*
East Side
796 Lexington Avenue, between 61st and 62nd Sts.
(212) 838-6551

Garnet Wine & Liquors *(Wine & Spirits)*
Lenox Hill
929 Lexington Avenue, between 68th and 69th Sts.
(212) 772-3211

Morrell & Co. *(Wine)*
Theater District
1 Rockefeller Plaza , 49th St. between Fifth and Sixth Aves.
(212) 688-9370

═══ HIT YOUR NEIGHBORHOOD WINE SHOP ═══

Whether you're on your way home from work and need a great wine to have with dinner or are searching for a last-minute gift, local wine merchants are an integral asset to every neighborhood.

Is Wine (225 East 5th St.; 212-254-7800). A new storefront in the East Village specializing in great everyday wines from small producers around the world as well as New York wines, especially from the Finger Lakes, where one of the owners was a former winemaker himself.

Seventh Avenue in Brooklyn's Park Slope neighborhood is so packed with new shops and restaurants that it can handle three great neighborhood stores: **Prospect Wine Shop** (322 Seventh Ave., Brooklyn; 718-768-1232), **Big Nose, Full Body** (382 Seventh Ave., Brooklyn; 718-369-4030), and **Slope Cellars** (436 Seventh Ave., Brooklyn; 718-369-7307). This store conducts tastings on Saturday evenings. The staff is friendly and the prices are right.

Nancy's Wines for Food (313 Columbus Ave.; 212-877-4040). A stalwart on the Upper West Side, features a wonderful selection of reasonably priced wines and one of the best collections of Rieslings in the city.

Chelsea Wine Vault (Chelsea Market, 75 Ninth Ave.; 212-462-4244) has made a name for itself with a dedication to offering solid selections, and has become a valuable resource for wine storage for those who only have room to store wine under the couch.

Sea Grape Wine Shop (512 Hudson St.; 212-463-7688) in Greenwich Village carries many affordable wines from various regions in Europe.

Union Square Wines (33 Union Sq. West; 212-675-8100) has a great staff to guide customers through the vast selection of global wines. Regular free tastings and great offers on cases (as well as its proximity to the Union Square Greenmarket and subway) have become hallmarks of this neighborhood jewel.

Grand Wine & Liquor in Queens (30-05 31st St. at 30th Ave., Astoria, Queens; 718-728-2520) has one of the broadest selections of wine in the borough. It's conveniently located right near the Grand Street N station.

—Allen Katz

Mount Carmel Wine & Spirits   *(Wine)*
Belmont, Bronx
612 East 187th Street, between Arthur and Hughes Aves.
(718) 367-7833

Sherry-Lehmann   *(Wine)*
East Side
679 Madison Avenue, between 61st and 62nd Sts.
(212) 838-7500

Whole Foods Market   *(Beer)*
Chelsea
250 Seventh Avenue at 24th Street
(212) 924-5969
Open Sunday

RINALDO FRATTOLILLO

NEIGHBORHOOD INDEX

MANHATTAN

Chelsea

14th St. to 29th St. between Fifth Ave. and Hudson River

Chelsea Market, 267
Chelsea Wine Vault, 323
El Cid, 145–46
Garrison Confections Inc., 236–37
Kitchen Market, 277
L'Acajou, 65

La Luncheonette, 58–59
Le Zie, 89
Qasim, 84
Ronnybrook Farm Dairy, 254, 264
Sucelt Coffee Shop, 31–32
Whole Foods Market, 249, 269, 324

Chinatown/Little Italy

Madison St. to Houston St., between Lafayette St. and the Bowery; Canal St. to the Brooklyn Bridge, between Bowery and Essex St.; below East Broadway, east of Essex St.

Aji Ichiban, 270
Alleva Dairy, 251
Bangkok Center Market, 272
Bistrot Margot, 64
Ceci-Cela, 303
Chinatown Ice Cream Factory, 258
Chow Fun Noodle Cart, 313
DiPalo's Fine Foods, 252, 273
Dom's Fine Foods, 283
Double Happiness, 197–98
Dumpling House, 49
East Corner Wonton, 41–42
Eileen's Special Cheesecake, 303
Fong Inn Too Inc., 274
Funky Broome, 43
Ghenet, 6
Grand Street Sausages, 285
Hai Thanh Seafood Co., 287
Harmony Palace, 44
Hong Kong Seafood and Meat Market, 288
Jing Fong, 44–45
Joe's Shanghai, 45–46
Kam Man Market, 277
Le Jardin Bistro, 65

Lombardi's, 205–06
May May Company Oriental Gourmet Shop, 278
New York Noodle Town, 49
Nha Trang, 139–40
Nyonya, 115–16
Ocean Seafood, 288
Parisi Bakery, 234
Peasant, 96
Piemonte Ravioli Company, 281
Ping's Seafood, 46–47
Proton Saga, 118
Saint Alp's Tea House, 50
Sentosa, 116
Sweet-n-Tart Restaurant, 47–48
Ten Ren Tea and Ginseng Company, 249
Vegetarian Dim Sum House, 155
Viet-nam Banh-mi So 1 Inc., 141–42, 314
The Vietnamese Sandwich, 141–42, 314
Wong's Rice and Noodle, 50
XO Kitchen, 50
Yummy Noodles, 48

Clinton (Hell's Kitchen)

50th St. to 55th St. between Eighth Ave. and Hudson River; 56th St. to 59th St. between Fifth Ave. and Hudson River

Alain Ducasse, 59–60
Beacon, 19
Grand Sichuan International Midtown, 43–44
Hallo Berlin, 70–71
Hudson Bar at the Hudson Hotel, 169–70

Island Burgers and Shakes, 193–94
La Caravelle, 62–63
Molyvos, 75–76
Rinconcito Peruano, 114
San Domenico, 92
Town, 21
Uncle Vanya Café, 55

BRONX

Belmont (Arthur Avenue)

City Island

Concourse Village

Kingsbridge

Pelham Bay

Riverdale

BROOKLYN

Downtown Brooklyn

D.U.M.B.O.

Fort Greene

Greenpoint

Midwood

Park Slope

Prospect Heights

Red Hook

Sheepshead Bay

Sunset Park

Jackson Heights

Afghan Kebab House #4, 37
Arunee Thai, 138–39
Bello Mexico, 272
Grameen, 80–81
Inti Raymi, 111–12
La Risarolda Corp., 277

Malaysian Rasa Sayang, 118
Meson Asturias, 149
Patel Brothers, 281
Pearson's Texas Barbecue, 27–28
Tibetan Yak, 36–37

Jamaica

Carmichael's Diner, 135–36

Kew Gardens

Dani's House of Pizza, 208
Uzbekistan Community Center, 38

Uzbekistan Tandoori Bread, 232–33

Rego Park

Knish Nosh's Potato Knishes, 229

Salut, 36

Richmond Hill

Jahn's Ice Cream Parlor and Restaurant, 262

Sunnyside

Carniceria las Americas, 273
Cornel's Garden Restaurant, 55

HAIL, 276
Massis, 278

Woodside

La Flor Bakery and Café, 179
Sripraphai, 140

Warteg Fortuna, 118

STATEN ISLAND

Belfiore Meats, 283
Denino's Pizzeria & Tavern, 208
Eggers Ice Cream Parlor, 262
Killmeyer's Old Bavaria Inn, 73
New Asha, 82

New Pakland Groceries & Halal
  Meat, 280
Nunzio's, 210
Ralph's Famous Italian Ices, 264

ALPHABETICAL INDEX

CHELSEA GREEN

SUSTAINABLE LIVING has many facets. Chelsea Green's celebration of the sustainable arts has led us to publish trend-setting books about innovative building techniques, regenerative forestry, organic gardening and agriculture, solar electricity and renewable energy, local and bioregional democracy, and whole and *slow* foods.

For more information about Chelsea Green, publishing partner of Slow Food USA, visit our Web site at www.chelseagreen.com and find more than 300 *books for sustainable living.*

Select back issues of *Slow Magazine* are available through Chelsea Green. Please call (800) 639-4099.

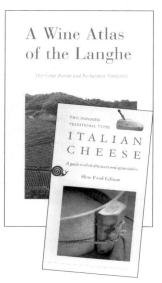